EX LIBRIS

DAILY
GUIDEPOSTS,
1984

GUIDEPOSTS

Carmel, New York 10512

Designed and illustrated by Elizabeth Woll.

Table of Contents

Introduction

Nearly two thousand years ago Jesus walked this earth with ordinary people like you and me, teaching, comforting and healing. Surely those years of our Lord were much the same as the year that awaits us—1984. There were family problems and financial worries, sickness and health. Emotions of love and hate, courage and fear, trust and doubt stirred the hearts and minds of God's children then, just as they do today.

So Jesus walked and talked with His friends, showing them the Way of overcoming their difficulties—the Way of our Father in Heaven. Often Jesus spoke in parables, homely little stories and anecdotes woven from the threads of true-life experiences of His hearers. These stories illuminated certain spiritual truths far more effectively than any sort of preaching, scolding or haranguing could.

"He who has ears to hear," said Jesus, "Let him hear."

This book, *Daily Guideposts, 1984,* was inspired by Jesus' parables. We asked twenty-four of today's finest Christian writers to walk through the year with you. Their little stories are much like parables, true experiences that illumine spiritual truths.

Walk with them. Listen for the voice of His Spirit in their words. Let 1984 bring you to a closer understanding of God's Word, a deeper appreciation of His Son's love and the guidance of the Holy Spirit in your daily life.

This eighth edition of *Daily Guideposts* has certain special features to enrich your devotional time throughout the year.

Prayer Poems by James McDermott introduce each month. Let them remind you of God's handiwork through the changing seasons of life—of His bounteous love for you and all His creation.

Praise Diaries at the end of each month are for you to record your daily concerns and your daily blessings.

Guidepeople, by *Guideposts* Magazine Editor, Van Varner, introduces you to some of the wonderful people whose stories lay the foundation of that amazing little magazine that is the foundation of the book you now hold in your hand.

Jesus, The Master Storyteller is a mid-month series of reflections on Jesus' parables by two of *Guideposts* master storytellers, Arthur Gordon and Fred Bauer.

Additional special treats await you: discover new lessons for holidays and holy days; fresh approaches to common daily difficulties, and spiritual fellowship on your walk with your *Daily Guideposts* friends.

Come. The year 1984 lies ahead. Let us enter it with positive hope and Christian courage. It is our prayer that with Jesus' leading, you will find comfort and healing as did His friends of old.

THE EDITORS

January

S	M	T	W	T	F	S
1	2	3	4	5	6	7
8	9	10	11	12	13	14
15	16	17	18	19	20	21
22	23	24	25	26	27	28
29	30	31				

Today, Lord, a snowflake
Fell on my glove
From the upper reaches
Of a gray sky.
First a formless water dot,
Then, refined by the trial of
A buffeted journey, it
Arrived to me:
Intricate,
Immaculate,
Individual,
Perfect.
Lord, do You mean to teach me
Something with this tiny gift?
Are You saying I too
Can see perfection through
Trials on my journey?
I think so.
I'm taking Your snowflake personally, Lord,
As a message to seek You
In the wintry days to come.

James McDermott

GUIDEPEOPLE: A Living Parable for January

1 SUNDAY

Now faith is the substance of things hoped for, the evidence of things not seen. —HEBREWS 11:1

Shortly after I came to *Guideposts* thirty years ago, our Editor Len LeSourd, sent me to East Stroudsburg, Pennsylvania, where a week before a flash flood had roared down from the Pocono Mountains.

"Don't forget," Len said to me, "a *Guideposts* story always offers the reader some kind of help." *But what, I wondered, could be helpful about the mud and destruction waiting in East Stroudsburg?* Well, help was there all right.

I found it through a group of three hundred men who'd come from a little Mennonite church two hours away. Farmers, lawyers and tradesmen, they brought their shovels and wheelbarrows and pitched in to dig the town out.

And help was there. One man had been away from home when the flood hit. His pregnant wife was forced to flee in waist-high water —a baby held over her head, another child clutching tightly to her neck. They reached safety, but it was two days before the frantic husband found them. Then the flood was over but the shock was not. Everything in their house was ruined, covered with thick mud.

"My house is mortgaged," he told me. "It's everything I own. But when I came back, I didn't want it any more. I just sat outside, paralyzed. I'd lost hope. Then the Mennonites started to work—on *my* place."

I saw then what those good Mennonites were actually contributing. It wasn't just friendship or labor: it was *hope.*

And for thirty years in the pages of *Guideposts* I've seen examples of what even the tiniest ray of hope can mean. Hope cuts a path through the darkness. Like faith, it is an intangible that makes life livable, and rich.

On this first day of 1984, and for the 365 days that will follow, let's all hold fast to *hope*. And, like those Mennonite shovelers, let's find opportunities to give it away to others.

Lord, let my work be more than tasks for myself. Let it be an example that gives hope to others. —VAN VARNER

---

2 MONDAY
...This is the gift of God. —ECCLESIASTES 5:19

As we were going through my father's things shortly after his death, we came across an old, and well-worn hard-backed ledger. As we studied the yellowing pages, we gained a brand-new insight into Dad's younger years. On page forty-nine, for instance, we read:

MY STANDING ON JANUARY 1, 1916

1 horse	2 cows
an automobile	7 swarms of bees
2 hogs	$47.00 due me
1 set of double harness	1 buggy
2 sets of buggy harness	25 bushels of corn
5 sacks of bran	1 ton of threshed hay
4 tons of granger hay	

As I start this new year, I wonder what I could write under the heading, "My Standing on January, 1984." How would I list my possessions? One typewriter, one car, one great kitchen range thirty-two years old. Would I list my home? Is it really mine—or the bank's?

I think that first and foremost I would list His love...the gift of His Son...His bounties of the earth. Then health...a precious family...dear friends. How would my ledger balance? It wouldn't, no matter how hard I tried. The assets just keep flowing in—faster than I could ever spend them—for the abundance of His gifts never ceases.

Dear Lord, the more I serve You, the wealthier I become.

—ZONA B. DAVIS

---

3 TUESDAY
And let us not be weary in well doing: for in due season we shall reap… —GALATIANS 6:9

One of my father's favorite verses was written many, many years ago by an ancestor of his. It goes like this:

> Life is mostly froth and bubble.
> Two things stand out like stone:
> Kindness in another's trouble,
> Courage in your own.

Kindness and courage. How those two qualities shone forth in the life of the Carpenter of Nazareth! From the beginning of His ministry to the end, the suffering and the sorrowing laid their troubles at His feet. Not once did He turn away. He treated each with kindness and compassion.

And when the time came for His own sacrifice, He did not flinch. He set his face to go to Jerusalem, where with quiet fortitude He endured the worst the world had to offer.

No wonder my father especially enjoyed that poem. It is one of my favorites too, for its truth has been revealed to us by the kindest and most courageous of all—our beloved Master.

Dear Jesus, may I follow in Your footsteps, with kindness toward all and courage in my times of trial. —ARTHUR GORDON

4

WEDNESDAY

Lay up for yourselves treasures in heaven, where neither moth nor rust doth corrupt, and where thieves do not break through nor steal. —MATTHEW 6:20

Once upon a time there was a miser who dug a deep hole in the ground and buried his gold in it. From that time on his greatest pleasure in life was strolling out to the spot where his fortune lay. There he would linger, happily gloating. One night, however, a servant who had been watching him, dug up the treasure and hurried away with it.

When the miser discovered what had happened, he screamed so loudly that he drew the attention of his neighbors, one of whom hastened to him.

"My gold!" the miser moaned, "Someone has stolen my gold."

"Be of good cheer," said the neighbor. "In a way you haven't lost a thing. After all, you weren't doing anything with the gold, but you still have the hole. Just put the dirt back and come back from time to time and pretend that your gold is still there."

That's a fable, of course, yet it does teach us, as Jesus did, about where and what our treasures should be. To this day, I never picture that miser standing over the empty hole in pathetic despair that I don't recall the words of the eminent English clergyman, John Henry Jowett: "The real measure of our wealth is how much we'd be worth if we lost all our money."

Dear Lord, let me be worthy of the real wealth You so generously bestow. —RUTH STAFFORD PEALE

5

THURSDAY

Now be ye not stiffnecked...but yield yourself unto the Lord... —II CHRONICLES 30:8

One day recently I was feeling somewhat overwhelmed by

11

the pressures of my job, family, various and sundry commitments....

Time for a flying lesson, I thought

Flying always helps me feel exhilarated and refreshed beyond measure. But on this day the air that had looked so clear from below proved to be turbulent, filled with thermal updrafts. My heart thudded with fear as the plane bounced around, and I held myself stiffly erect in the seat, clenching white-knuckled fists around the support strap.

"Don't fight it. Just relax and go with it," my instructor advised. "If you'll put your faith in flying this thing to a safe landing, you can sit back and enjoy the view."

I did as he suggested and my body automatically adjusted to the swaying plane. Soon I accepted the bumps as a part of the total experience and was able to give my attention to the beauty of the landscape below.

Maybe that's what we need to do in all parts of our lives. Relax and put our faith in a safe landing instead of wearing ourselves out resisting the pressures of life, and give our attention to all the beautiful people around us—in our family, in our job and in our outside commitments.

Father, You are the Master Pilot. I place myself in Your hands.

—MADGE HARRAH

---

6 FRIDAY

The Lord our God be with us...that he may incline our hearts unto him, to walk in all his ways, and to keep his commandments... —I KINGS 8:57-58

Ruth Bell Graham, in her captivating book *It's My Turn,* observes—somewhat tongue in cheek—that what with the popularity of obedience-training for dogs, many family pets may be better trained than the children. Do you know the main rules for obedience-training?

Mrs. Graham names four that are familiar to all dog trainers: 1) keep commands simple (one word and always the same word); 2) be consistent; 3) follow through (make sure that every command is obeyed); 4) praise for good behavior.

The Bible, it could be said, is an obedience-training book for the children of God. In it we find scores of stories recounting the blessings that came to those who obeyed God's commands. The list of people who trusted Him and went forth in faith includes Noah and Abraham and Isaac and Jacob and Sarah and Joseph and Moses and Samson and David and Samuel, to name only a few.

God's commands to us are simple too. Go, teach, feed, heal, comfort, serve, love, witness. But hearing His commands and obeying them are two different things. Those who obey, however, know the inner peace that comes from being in harmony with their Creator, and they can look forward to someday hearing these approving words: "Well done, good and faithful servant...enter thou into the joy of thy lord" (Matthew 25:23).

Give us ears to hear, Lord, and a heart that is eager to obey.
—FRED BAUER

7

SATURDAY

...Redeem me, and be merciful unto me.

—PSALM 26:11

It was one of those little skits put on by children. It lasted for only five minutes and I don't even remember what it was all about. I do remember, though, that my son wore a sign around his neck that read "Mr. Disagreeable."

All of the characters in the skit were impersonating certain human qualities. The lot of them paraded around — smirking, scowling, giggling — each trying his best to look his part.

The sight of my son with this sign hung around his neck made me pause and think. Do I label people with particular faults, tying the tags on them with double knots?

13

"You're so stubborn"…"You never listen to me"…"Why are you so careless all the time?"….

I had often said these things to my son. Suddenly now I saw my words as little signs, black-and-white yokes hung around his neck, bonding him to his weakness.

"Mama, untie the string." The skit was over and my son had backed up to me, wanting to be released from the sign. "You're free," I told him, slipping the string out of its knot. And I prayed that he would remain so.

The only sign that I will ever hang on him again is "Child of God."

O Father, help us to be sensitive to one another as You are to us.

—SUE MONK KIDD

8

SUNDAY

Study to be quiet, and to do your own business, and to work with your own hands, as we commanded you…

—I THESSALONIANS 4:11

I finished junior college during the Depression and was planning to go on to the university. Then Father suffered a stroke and was forced to retire. Worried, he urged me to drop out of school and go to work. But there were few jobs to be had in those days and most of them paid little. I was determined to finish school.

After a lengthy discussion, my father announced: "All right, we'll try a special combination."

"A special combination, Father?"

"Work and prayer. You work. Your mother and I will pray."

Somewhat puzzled, I agreed. A loan was arranged for tuition and fees, and with seventy-five dollars in my pocket, I set off by thumb to college a thousand miles away.

I arrived a week early and found a job waiting on tables. Later I fired furnaces, cut grass, washed dishes, served hotel banquets, surveyed at ten cents an hour, checked gym rolls and more. At graduation I had a hundred and fifty dollars in my carefully monitored bank account and splurged on a bus ride home.

My father greeted me, smiling. "Well, son, it worked, didn't it?"

"All I know, Father, is that *I* worked," I replied. "Seems like I did nothing but work—when I wasn't studying."

"I know, son," my father said softly. "That's what all our praying was about."

Thank You, Lord, for teaching me that prayer and action always go hand in hand. —SAM JUSTICE

---

9 MONDAY

In the beginning God created the heaven and the earth. And the earth was without form, and void; and darkness was upon the face of the deep.
—GENESIS 1:1-2

Monday morning.

I am surrounded by chaos. I wend my way around the piles of Sunday newspapers, through the weekend clutter of books and toys and toward the week's mountain of laundry. Last night's dinner dishes still sit in the kitchen sink.

Monday used to be the worst day of the week for me. Both home and office seemed to be overwhelming, filled as they were with the unfinished business of the previous week.

Then one evening I read Genesis again and made an exciting discovery. In the beginning the whole universe was full of chaos. And God said, "Let there be light. Let there be order. Let there be life." *It was from chaos that God brought forth creation!*

Now I approach Mondays—and any other chaotic situations in my life—with a real sense of excitement. Can this chaos, too, be turned into light, order and life? And, as I go about my work, I ask God to be my partner.

15

Sharing in creation. Can any partnership be more exciting—or rewarding?

Dear God, help me to create light, order and life from the chaos I encounter this day. —PATRICIA HOUCK SPRINKLE

---

10 TUESDAY

For God, who commanded the light to shine out of darkness, hath shined in our hearts...

—II CORINTHIANS 4:6

When I was a small boy, we would occasionally visit my Virginia grandmother. She lived in a gloomy Victorian mansion still lighted by gas jets that flickered and trembled inside frosted glass globes.

Those jets lighted my way upstairs at bedtime. That trek was a dreadful ordeal because ranged along the staircase walls were the heads of great antlered beasts: bison, moose and elk. In the gaslight their shadows wavered on the paneled walls. To make matters worse, some older cousins assured me solemnly that at least once every night these huge beasts jumped out of their skins and when they did, Heaven help any small boy found walking up the stairs!

Well, of course, nothing ever happened, but the memory of that walk of terror has lasted to this day. A light that doesn't waver makes a big difference—when you're young.

A faith that doesn't waver makes a big difference—when you're older.

Lord, let Your radiance shine steadily on my path today.

—ARTHUR GORDON

11 WEDNESDAY
Bear ye one another's burdens...

—*GALATIANS 6:2*

Sometimes I have migraine headaches. There! I've said it. And it took real courage to say it because it has always been difficult for me to admit to weakness. Often I tend to be stiff-necked and think that a Christian should be able to pray away his or her problems.

My prayer group prays for many people who have problems that are so much worse than any of mine. For this reason I felt that it would be selfish of me to ask the group for prayers, no matter the circumstances. Then a knock-down, drag-out headache struck me on a Thursday—our scheduled prayer-meeting day. Lying in bed, praying for relief and finding none, I swallowed my pride, reached for the bedside phone and called Verna.

"Please, will you put me on the prayer list today?" I asked her.

Almost as soon as I hung up, I felt a wave of relief from the throbbing, painful migraine. What a truly *freeing* sensation it was to let down the walls of false pride...to admit openly to another that I had a problem—yes, to *ask* for help.

And how much more relieved I was to realize that to seek prayers for myself doesn't at all mean that I'm self-centered—or a failing Christian. No, it means that I have enough confidence in others to place my weakness in their hands.

Do you have a stubborn problem? Why not ask the prayers of a fellow Christian or a prayer group today? They will feel blessed that you turn to them in your time of need.

Teach me to bow my head, Lord, and place my trust in others.

—MARILYN MORGAN HELLEBERG

12 THURSDAY
Unto thee, O Lord, do I lift up my soul.   —PSALM 25:1

Do you remember struggling over adverbs in school? "An adverb tells when, where and how." And how our teachers pounded home the rule! We learned to identify the slippery little words by the *ly* at the end of their root words.

Recently I was reminded of this because I've been thinking of the struggle that most of us face with prayer at some point in our lives. When I began really to consider the verb "pray," I asked myself the old questions: "When, where and how?" Eventually I came up with a list of what I call my "Pointers for Prayer." As you can see, not only is each one an *ly* word, but each starts with a *P*—for Prayer, of course!

Pleasantly: With a smile on my face and love in my heart.
Persistently: Morning, noon and night, "without ceasing."
Pleasingly: Praising God in all things.
Personally: I am talking to *my* God. His Son died for *me.*
Practically: "Give us this day…" He knows our needs.
Prudently: God has given us the words with which to approach Him.
Particularly: What are the needs of those close to us?
Patiently: God has His purpose for all things.
Proudly: I am proud to be one of God's children.
Presently: Without delay. Pray now!

I'm sure that with further thought the list could be extended almost indefinitely. Try it. What can *you* add?

Lord, teach us to pray.   —JUNE MASTERS BACHER

13 FRIDAY
A soft answer turneth away wrath: but grievous words stir up anger. —PROVERBS 15:1

Perhaps my greatest moment as a mother centers around a bucket of antique-white paint. My fourteen-year-old son decided to paint his room. He bought the paint himself and assembled all the needed materials. I had told him earlier that I would help him the next day. But Jeremy is like me. Impatient. Once an idea takes hold of him, he must take action.

Just as I reached the top of the stairs with an armful of laundry, I saw him. The open bucket of paint was turning upside down, seemingly in slow motion. For a brief instant our eyes met in horror. Then the paint flew everywhere—over my son, the hall carpet, the wallpaper. The only place it missed was the wall of Jeremy's room.

I didn't speak. I couldn't seem to form any words. I ran for wet towels. Jeremy did too. We started mopping up paint and flooding the carpet with water. Fortunately it was water-based paint.

Jeremy's eyes met mine frequently. At first his expression seemed to be: *Can you possibly consider forgiving me?* Then: *Surely you are going to scream at any minute now.* Finally: *Is there a chance that just this once you are going to understand that this was a horrible accident?* And as we got the last of the paint up, our eyes met once again and his clearly said: *You are the most wonderful mother in the world. I'll never forget this!*

I felt so good about having held my tongue and my temper. How I wish I had known how to react over spills when I was a younger mother.

Father, help me to hold my tongue over spilled milk.

—MARION BOND WEST

14 SATURDAY
I am one of them that are peaceable and faithful…
—II SAMUEL 20:19

When I was younger, I used to like to visit a friend for monopoly matches. Her folks had a really nice house, as I recall, except for the living room—we weren't allowed in there. It had something to do with how we might get it all dirty if we played in there. So the room was always spotless—and always vacant.

One afternoon my friend told me: "You know, Mom and I could probably be much better friends if she wasn't always worrying so much about a clean house." I don't remember where I learned the word *priority*, but I sure learned the concept that day. My friend's mother had set her priorities, and in her zeal with cleanliness, she had overlooked the comfort of the people who lived in that house.

Now that I have a home of my own and a wife and a job and a thousand and one demands on my time, I've discovered priorities too. And they begin with the important people in my life. That means that I set my wife Lynn right at the top of the list. If on occasion our place might seem slightly untidy (I'm not much for picking up sweaters and newspapers after I drop them, and Lynn, bless her heart, leaves her school books in the oddest places), I just smile. I have a wonderful wife and our relationship to each other as a family far supercedes any *things* in our house. Some call that a priority. Others call it a good stewardship of the time with which God has blessed us.

Me? I just say it's putting first things first—with love.

Lord, may our home always be a place of sanctuary for Your love—and ours.
—JEFF JAPINGA

15 SUNDAY
...And, lo, the heavens were opened unto him, and he saw the Spirit of God descending like a dove...
—*MATTHEW 3:16*

I can still hear his words: "I have a dream...."

I can still see him standing there on the steps of the Lincoln Memorial in Washington, D.C., a huge crowd gathered about to listen to him talk about his dream. It was a magnificent vision he had, one in which every single person on earth has an equal opportunity to achieve—regardless of race, religion or ethnic background—and to share the same rights and privileges with all. And, yes, the same responsibilities to each other, to our country and to our God.

When Jesus told the apostles to go forth and teach all nations, He did not preclude any people. He meant that they were to bring the Word to *everybody*. If we, in our Christian lives, exclude others from our hopes and prayers simply because of the circumstances of their birth or the manner in which they were raised, we dilute our hopes and diminish our prayers in the eyes of God.

On this day set aside in remembrance of Martin Luther King, Jr., let us share his dream and remember that we are all brothers, each to the other, in all ways and in all concerns. And I believe that this is more than just a dream for we who are Christians. It is how Jesus calls upon us to live, every day of our lives.

Father, help us to carry out the dreams of those who have died for You in the name of brotherhood for all men. —GLENN KITTLER

JESUS, THE MASTER STORYTELLER
Introducing the Parables

16 MONDAY

I've heard it said that a storyteller thinks in pictures, rather than words. I believe there's truth in this. A story consists of a series of scenes that the storyteller causes to flash across the mind of the hearer or reader. The scenes themselves are pictures and the more vivid the picture, the more effective the story.

Jesus was a genius at creating such pictures in the minds of His hearers, and He did it in various ways. Sometimes with a seemingly effortless phrase: "Consider the lilies... Solomon in all his glory was not arrayed like one of these." Instantly the imagination of the hearer conjures up the dazzling image of an Oriental monarch in splendid robes, sitting on a jeweled throne. At the same moment he is reminded that a beneficent God has made a simple flower of the field even *more* splendid.

Sometimes the scene evoked is tinged with humor: the camel struggling to go through the eye of a needle, the man with the beam in his eye. "Follow Me," Jesus says to James and John who are mending their nets, "and I will show you how to fish for men's souls." *With a net?* they must have asked themselves wonderingly. Well, yes, only in this case the net is the fine-meshed love of God that will not let the smallest soul slip through.

Sometimes Jesus forsakes the narrative technique for the single brilliant metaphor, as when He compares Himself to the vine and His disciples to the branches. God is the husbandman who owns the vineyard, but He—Jesus—is the only channel through which the sustaining life force flows from God to man. Without Him they can achieve nothing of value. In fact, without Him they *are* nothing.

If they ever forget this overwhelming fact—if any of us ever forget it—there is always the picture to remind us, the image of leaves

22

wilting and fruit dying because the connection to the life-giving vine has been severed or lost.

Is one picture really worth a thousand words, as the old saying goes? This picture may be worth far more than that, for it is one that is inestimable in value for the successful Christian.

Lord Jesus, thank You for Your life-giving parables. Let them remind us to depend on You—always.   —ARTHUR GORDON

---

17 TUESDAY
By love serve one another.   —GALATIONS 5:13

My kitchen sink and I had been waging a cold war ever since we met. It always seemed to me that the dishes I had just put away gleaming after the last meal turned right up again, their dirty faces staring up at me. And the very thought of preparing piles of vegetables left me wilted—as did the pots and pans, the tableware and the dishrags.

Then one afternoon I found my ten-year-old daughter setting up some experiments in the window right above the sink. Two avocado seeds suspended in water on toothpicks, the top of a carrot in a dish, beans perched on wads of wet cotton. And as she placed a piece of bread in a plastic container, she remarked, "There. That'll mold." Whereupon I muttered such unkind things that later, in penitence, I allowed the "garbage" to remain on the windowsill.

And then—you guessed it—I became absorbed by the events that took place over my sink! Heartily I cheered them on. The avocado greens split their shells, the carrot stub sprouted feathers, the beans uncurled their shoots and the bread spun cobwebs. Soon my sink chores were being accomplished effortlessly as I marveled at this miracle of life. That old sink took on a different light...like an altar, where our lives were being nourished every day...where our sustenance was prepared...a place of nurture and care in our home.

And, I thought, *how blessed I am to serve at this altar!* With that, I saw myself and my sink as privileged partners in the miracle of

23

unfolding life. At that moment I yielded my resentment in favor of loving service. That day the cold war ended.

Dear Lord, help me to serve my family with love in whatever circumstance You place me. —ELAINE ST. JOHNS

---

18 WEDNESDAY
Rejoice with them that do rejoice, and weep with them that weep. —ROMANS 12:15

When my wife Judy and I welcomed our long-awaited son David into our lives, it was with overwhelming reverence and gratitude, for we had fervently prayed for a child for seven long years. But our first week with David turned out to be an exhausting one. He was a very fussy baby. Then our good friend Jackie Medina, mother of three, arrived on the scene.

"First," Jackie said, "we're going to give David a bath."

She ignored the special nursery tub we had bought and instead filled up our kitchen sink—and not just with water. She had brought along a little yellow rubber duck that whistled. She tossed it in the sink and then added just about every small, colorful floating object that she could find. And what a bath it was! Jackie bounced David, she tickled him, she laughed, she formed a circle with her fingers and blew bubbles.

"Hey, this is fun!" Judy and I exclaimed.

"And so are babies!" Jackie smiled.

So ended the somber earnestness that had characterized Judy's and my care of our young charge. David's fussiness vanished overnight. And he and his proud parents have since enjoyed many a giggly bath and many a happy time after that first kitchen-sink bath.

How would we ever get along in this world without our wise and wonderful friends who rejoice *for* us as well as *with* us?

Gentle Jesus, teach me the art of being a true friend to others, as You are to me. —JAMES McDERMOTT

19 THURSDAY
Train up a child in the way he should go...

—PROVERBS 22:6

I earned my very first dollar from my grandmother. I was eight years old at the time and I will never forget the tough assignment she gave me: "Sam, if you learn the Ten Commandments by heart and recite them to me, I'll give you a dime for each one."

For two long weeks I struggled over the verses in Deuteronomy, pondering words such as *sanctify* and *graven image*, trying to get them all in order. I repeated those verses over and over, hour by hour, until I knew that I had the Commandments down by heart... and they have remained with me throughout the rest of my life. Although I have often struggled and stumbled in trying to obey them, just as I struggled and stumbled in trying to learn them, I've forever been grateful for their guidance.

It wasn't until later, though, that I realized the *other* essential lessons that Grandmother had taught me: first, the importance of providing an early framework of conduct to a young person, and second, the passing on to our children God's teachings so that their lives will rest on a firm foundation.

Do you know a child who would like to start earning dimes? It's not a bribe...it's a good investment.

Dear God, help me to pass along—by word and deed—Your teachings to a young person today.   —SAMANTHA McGARRITY

20 FRIDAY
Now the God of patience and consolation grant you to be like-minded one toward another...   —ROMANS 15:5

"The first snowdrops," my husband exclaimed, "and still January!" The tiny flowers were scattered all over the yard, nestled like pearls in the frosty grass.

We gazed at them in delight. Small, frail and silky, we put one of them in a bud vase. Gradually, it unfolded, lifting its little head—three shiny white petals framing a round white face.

"It looks like one of those French nuns—the ones who wear those pointy-petaled caps," I said.

For days my husband brought in delicate bunches of snowdrops to grace the breakfast table—and then snow began to fall. All the growing things stiffened and went tight, huddling close against the onslaught of cold. And the fragile snowdrops too were stiffened.

The next morning my husband brought one in to me.

"Kiss it and bring it back to life," he smiled.

So I touched it lightly with my lips. And within a few seconds, as it lay there in my hand, the miracle began to happen. Its petals began to stretch, its head lifted and it became a soft and tender little flower, warmed by the eternal wonder of love.

Dear Father, thank You for the little miracles of love that blossom in our midst when we least expect it.

—MARJORIE HOLMES

21 SATURDAY
Let us therefore follow after the things which make for peace, and things wherewith one may edify another.
—ROMANS 14:19

"How are things with you this evening?" Plaford amiably asked the obviously worn-out waitress while I studied the menu.

"Oh, I'm still here," she said with a little shrug.

"And you still have that great smile," he told her.

When she brought our order, her smile was broader and there was a fresh spring in her step. My husband has the most remarkable ability to say just the right word to encourage and light up a life. He doesn't even work at it; it's just there, within him.

"The youth choir sounded mighty good," he'll tell the director.

"I always feel comfortable when you're driving," he'll tell a friend.

"I like red," he tells my ninety-year-old mother. "It looks pretty with your snowy hair."

Turning the key in the ignition, he tells the repairman, "I have a lot of confidence in your work."

And he'll say, "Zona B., that lunch was just right," when I've served him a cold ham sandwich and warmed-over soup.

Sometimes I've teased him about this habit of his, but I'm wondering: *Couldn't we each make someone else's day a little happier or brighter simply by using a warm, friendly tone and manner?* As long as we're honest in what we say, it's really so easy to spread the joy of appreciation and to let other people know we think they're pretty nice. I know I like to hear that—don't you?

Today, Lord, let me find opportunities to brighten the lives of all those I meet.   —ZONA B. DAVIS

---

22 SUNDAY
For whom the Lord loveth he chasteneth...
—HEBREWS 12:6

When my brother and I were very young, we spent our summers with our grandparents in the little town of Lynchburg, Ohio. I will never forget one wild night when a tremendous storm came crashing around the house. In the flashes of lightning I could see the great maple tree in the front yard writhing and thrashing about. I pulled the covers over my head, convinced that the whole house was blowing away.

By morning all was serene. The sun shone. The big maple still stood, the ground around it littered with fallen branches. I asked my grandfather if the tree had been hurt by losing all those branches.

"No, son," he replied, "those are just dead branches, useless limbs that the tree didn't need any more. The wind is simply God's way of pruning a tree, making it healthier and stronger than ever, that's all."

27

I have often thought of my grandfather's words when trouble has entered my life or when I have seen it enter the lives of others. A tremendous storm may be God's way of removing the dead wood and debris that tend to clutter our souls and lives. And if we are firmly rooted in courage and faith when all is calm again, we will be stronger than ever, able to move forward refreshed, unburdened— and filled with gratitude for the wisdom of His ways!

I will seek out Your strength, Father, even as the storm passes.

—NORMAN VINCENT PEALE

---

23 MONDAY

Eye hath not seen, nor ear heard, neither have entered into the heart of man the things which God hath prepared for them that love him. —I CORINTHIANS 2:9

Our friend Jerry is a bachelor who has recently taken two teen-aged boys into his home.

The other day the thirteen-year-old—who can ask a lot of really tough questions—asked Jerry how long it took God to make the earth.

This time Jerry was ready for him. "Well, the Bible tells us it took Him exactly six days," he answered.

"Wow!" cried the boy. "Just think of how beautiful Heaven must be—He's had millions of years to get it ready for us!"

We chuckled when Jerry told us this little story. But when you stop and think about it, doesn't it voice all our expectations?

O my Father in Heaven, may my life today be worthy of eternal life with You. —DRUE DUKE

28

24

And because of all this we make a sure covenant, and write it . . .   —NEHEMIAH 9:38

One day in January our Bible-study teacher handed out blue stationery to the class.

"I want you to think carefully and then write an 'I will' sentence," she explained. "Think of some goal you believe God wants you to accomplish, or perhaps something He wants you to overcome."

I stared at the paper for a long while. All sorts of questions surfaced in my mind. *What are my priorities for this coming year? Where am I weak? What would God want me to overcome or accomplish?* Finally one thing became clear to me—it was an objective I knew God wanted me to reach for. So I scrawled it out, sealed my paper in the blue envelope, put my name on the outside and gave it back to the teacher.

As the days went by, I worked hard at my commitment, but soon the freshness and fervor faded. By March it was forgotten. Then one April morning there in the mailbox was my blue envelope, inside of it the paper with my "I will" sentence. *Isn't she a wise teacher?* I thought. She had never opened our envelopes but had saved them for the moment when a commitment is apt to need its second wind. With that extra push, I was at last able to accomplish my goal.

If—like me—you need an extra portion of encouragement, why not place your spiritual resolution in a sealed, self-addressed envelope and hand it to a friend with a note that says, "Please mail this to me in April"?

Dear Father, help me to honor all my commitments to You.

—SUE MONK KIDD

25 WEDNESDAY

And thou shalt rejoice in every good thing which the Lord thy God hath given thee, and unto thy house.

—*DEUTERONOMY 26:11*

The drive down California's legendary Highway One from San Francisco to San Simeon is said to be one of the most beautiful in all the world.

That's why Lynn and I were so disappointed when the day dawned cloudy. By the time we reached Monterey it was rainy, foggy and travelers' advisories warned of gusty winds, treacherous roads and rock slides. And yet we went on. We had come too far—3,000 miles across the country—to miss it.

Eventually nineteen miles of highway would be closed—covered with enormous boulders or simply washed away by rampaging rivers of mud. We dodged the first of those washouts and gingerly inched our way around hairpin curves.

And yet we saw the most beautiful stretch of road we had ever driven. Anywhere. Any time. Even in the midst of the storm, the rugged beauty of the cliffs and the storm-swept ocean was revealed as clearly as though the sun were shining.

That day will stand out in my memory for the rest of my life—not for the scenery, but for the lesson it brought me. Now instead of concentrating on the rocks that are tossed in my way, on the places where storms have washed away my chosen path, I just slow down and look at the blessings with which God has surrounded me, all those blessings of family and friends and love.

O Father, bless my loved ones, who are always there.

—JEFF JAPINGA

26 THURSDAY
And all that believed were together... —*ACTS 2:44*

I can remember helping one of our children with a geography assignment years ago. It was then that I realized I would never meet people from faraway places such as California and New York. It was a sad thought because some of those people I would never meet might have become my dearest friends. On the map I let my finger touch the state of Washington and then slide down to a western state. From there I traced the route to New York and then back to California.

"What are you doing, Mama?" Julie asked.

"Oh, just thinking of how there are so many dear people in all those places across the country and I'm never going to meet them. Some of them are probably a lot like me and we could be such good friends. But I'm going to live my life out right here in Georgia."

Only recently have I understood that God has given me a way in which I can make contact with strangers far away. Through my writing, people in distant places have reached out to me. We have become friends through countless letters, sharing our joys, disappointments and prayers. I have pictures of my faraway friends, their children and grandchildren—and their dogs and cats too!

Yes, it's as I suspected. There are many dear people out there in the world, just waiting to be friends.

Father, thank You for the wonderful chain of friendship You have given us. Help us to circle Your world with it.

—MARION BOND WEST

27 FRIDAY
So God created man in his own image, in the image of God created he him... —GENESIS 1:27

The ringing of the telephone roused me out of bed at four o'clock in the morning. Normally it would have been cause for alarm, but not this time. My wife Shirley and I were expecting the call.

"It's a girl!" exclaimed our daughter Laraine, speaking from her hospital bed two hundred miles away. She had just delivered her first child—our first grandchild—and before falling asleep she wanted us to hear the good news.

Back in bed, I was reminded of the thrill I felt at Laraine's birth twenty-eight years earlier. I was in the army, hundreds of miles away from home. But when the news arrived that I was a father, I set out just as soon as leave could be arranged in the middle of the night. I couldn't wait to see my first child.

Part of the trip took me through Cincinnati at daybreak on a bus. I was the only passenger. "Where are you heading, soldier?" the gray-haired driver asked.

"Home to see a new baby girl," I answered proudly.

"Congratulations!" he exclaimed. He was the father of three children, he told me, and for the rest of the trip, he talked about the joys of being a parent. He wasn't wrong.

There's nothing quite like the birth of a new baby to bring life into focus, to remind one of the greatest gift of all God's creation: life.

Father, thank You for the precious gift of life—now and eternal.

—FRED BAUER

28 SATURDAY

...When thou prayest, enter into thy closet, and when thou hast shut thy door, pray to thy Father which is in secret... —MATTHEW 6:6

Some months ago I read about a tribe in Uganda that has the sacred custom of allotting to each adult member a tiny patch of land just outside the village. Each clearing has its own private path and is used as a place of prayer and meditation by its designated owner. Should a tribesman become quarrelsome or overstep himself, he is reminded by others that grass is growing on the unused path to his prayer place.

Suddenly I felt a kinship with those faraway people who not only realize the importance of private contact with God but, by setting aside a special place in their midst, go one step further and prepare the way so that each might pray alone with the Lord.

Whenever you find yourself becoming cross or out of sorts, remember that distant Uganda tribe and their wise recognition of the soothing power of prayer and meditation. If you can't manage to get to church at the time, go into your room, close the door and kneel to your Lord. Don't let grass grow on *your pathway* to prayer!

Help me to keep my prayer path smooth, Father, so that I may come to you quickly and quietly. —DORIS HAASE

29 SUNDAY

I will extol thee, my God, O king; and I will bless thy name for ever and ever. —PSALM 145:1

The gift that my friend handed me was an exquisite little gilt frame. The gold leaf bore a soft patina and the velvet backing was gently faded.

"It's a *mathom*," she told me.

33

When I looked puzzled, she explained that in Tolkien's *Fellowship of the Ring*, the elflike hobbits never throw away anything that they have been given.

"*Mathoms*, they call them," she said. "Their favorite *mathoms* are passed along as gifts to others."

I was really touched. And later I began to wonder if I might have a *mathom* stored away to share with others. It would have to be something old but durable, something I treasured, a meaningful gift to another.

And then I realized that the finest *mathom* I have is the Good News! It meets all the requirements.

Today, it's time to pass it on. Will you?

Help me spread Your Good News today, Father—for it's the best news of all.   —MADGE HARRAH

---

30 MONDAY
Heal me, O Lord, and I shall be healed...for thou art my praise.   —JEREMIAH 17:14

How do you say goodbye to such a good friend?

Trooper had been with me for fourteen years, since he was a puppy with glazed newborn eyes. Now his eyes were glazed again, but with oncoming blindness. He had been deaf for a time, too, and his hind legs were stiff with arthritis.

Two years earlier I had almost lost him to a liver ailment. The rest of my world was falling apart then, too, and I knew I couldn't handle such a loss. But Trooper recovered, much to the astonishment of the veterinarians. And sadly I knew that one day I would have to let Trooper have his rest.

Finally the day came when it was time to let him go. His sense of smell was gone. He could no longer identify those he knew, and every approaching footstep was a threat to him. I couldn't allow my dignified, loving friend to be destroyed by fear and confusion.

The doctor was compassionate. I stayed with Trooper until the end, which was gentle.

How do you say goodbye to such a friend? You don't. You weep, and you let God share your tears. And you thank Him for the love that came into your life—because you know now that that part of your friend will be with you forever.

I need time to grieve, Lord. Let me walk with You a little while in silence until my heart is ready to speak again.

—PHYLLIS HOBE

---

31 TUESDAY
If I ascend up into heaven, thou art there: if I make my bed in hell, behold, thou art there. —PSALM 139:8

During a routine physical examination, I queried my doctor about the beeping heart-monitor machine that was attached to my body.

"Why doesn't the screen show a straight line instead of those peaks and valleys?" I asked him.

The doctor replied, "If that line was straight, it would mean that you were dead. Those ups and downs show me that you're healthy and alive."

I suppose that in a similar manner our Great Physician allows us to have "ups and downs" in our spiritual lives, so that we might be strengthened in our faith and made healthy in our attitudes. Perhaps the "downs"—the disappointments, failures and stumblings common to all of us—only serve to deepen our understanding of one another's problems and to heighten our sharing of one another's joys.

One thing is for certain: Without the lowly valleys we travel through, we would never reach the highest peaks.

Help me to use the "ups and downs" in my life, Father, to grow in understanding, wisdom and compassion. —ISABEL CHAMP

35

Praise Diary for January

1

2

3

4

5

6

7

8

9

10

11

12

13

14

15

16

17

18

19

20

21

22

23

24

25

26

27

28

29

30

31

February

S	M	T	W	T	F	S
			1	2	3	4
5	6	7	8	9	10	11
12	13	14	15	16	17	18
19	20	21	22	23	24	25
26	27	28	29			

Ice…the pond in my neighbor's field is black with it,
A great onyx glaring heedlessly at uncolored skies.
But, as I pass the pond,
It gives a hollow croak that draws me to it.
Down through that dark window
A minnow wiggles and a sleek dark muskrat surges,
Leaving trails of bubbles that dance white
Against their dark roof.
Back at roadside I barely hear a busy hum
Pulsing beneath iced-over wires,
Then scarcely see buds bulging
Under winter-crackled wraps.
I understand, Lord.
February is not a deathly, silent month,
But rather Your quiet time,
That seeks my most discerning eye,
My most attentive ear.

James McDermott

GUIDEPEOPLE: A Living Parable for February

1 WEDNESDAY

...As he thinketh in his heart, so is he. —PROVERBS 23:7

On my first meeting with Dr. Norman Vincent Peale, he gave me a sample of his famous positive thinking. Although I didn't quite recognize it at the time.

I had gone to his office on upper Fifth Avenue for the last of a series of interviews that would determine whether I was to be hired as a *Guideposts* assistant editor. We talked about my educational background, which seemed sufficient, and my publishing experience, which was limited, and the interview seemed to be going pretty well until Dr. Peale asked, "Tell me, are you a happy man?"

The question caught me off guard. I thought for a moment. "Well, yes," I replied, "I guess I'd have to say that I am."

This news seemed to please him. "Good," he said. "Of course, we all have two choices, don't we? We can choose to be happy or we can choose to be unhappy." For a moment I just stared at him.

"Yes," I said, but my reply didn't ooze with conviction. Frankly, I wasn't altogether sure what the good Doctor was getting at. You either have reason to be happy, or you don't. Then the telephone rang and we never got back to the subject.

I did get the job though. And now, thirty years later, I know exactly what the good Doctor was saying. Our conscious decision to be happy, Dr. Peale was meaning, creates a climate where happiness can take root and grow, for attitudes shape the direction of our lives.

Most of us have a longer list of reasons for happiness than we are inclined to admit. We have people to love, and people who love us. We have our own precious integrity. We live in a great and caring country. And just in case those assets are not enough for starters, we have the breath of life and a God Who loves us.

Tell me, have *you* chosen to be happy?

Help me, Lord, choose happiness each day this month.

—VAN VARNER

2 THURSDAY

For the world is mine, and the fulness thereof.

—PSALM 50:12

The puppy was only seven weeks old and there wasn't much to her. When I picked her up, she felt like little more than a handful of fluff. She had never been out of the kennel where she was born, and I was worried as I drove her home. *I don't like change either,* I told her. *I like to hold on to the familiar things too.* She nestled close to me and I kept one hand on her, giving her small, reassuring pats.

When we arrived home, I lifted her out of the car. She was frightened by her new world and I could feel her trembling. I stood there for a moment, cuddling her. Then she raised her head and began to sniff the air with her little wet nose. Gently I lowered her to the grass. I doubt that she had ever seen grass before, but obviously she liked the way it smelled and the feeling under her feet. She took a few steps and then, as a moth flew by, she swatted at it playfully.

I smiled with relief. Yes, the world was still a brand-new experience for my puppy, but she was discovering that there are some very good things in it.

Isn't that the way it is with most of us? We're reluctant to leave the familiar and to move beyond the past. But we are *supposed* to change—to grow, to deepen our spiritual awareness, to become better Christians. And when we do finally dare to let go... to greet a stranger... to travel to an unfamiliar place... to gain a new insight into a Bible verse... to question our old ways... we too discover a brand-new world, with some very good things in it!

Father, every day I will seek Your marvelous works.

—PHYLLIS HOBE

3

FRIDAY

Now mine eyes shall be open, and mine ears attent unto the prayer that is made in this place.

—*II CHRONICLES 7:15*

The Wycliffe Bible translators travel to the far corners of the world, and because of their work, countless people in remote places of the earth can today read the Good News in their own language.

But Helen and Bill Elliot, who were sent to Guatemala in 1953 to translate the spoken language of the Ixil tribesmen into the written word, ran into difficulties. The natives refused contact with the Elliots and their three children for nearly two years. Then two young Indian boys were severely burned in an accident. Although not a nurse, Helen went to their aid. When she arrived, she found that someone in an effort to help had covered their burns with motor oil and ashes!

Helen washed away the oil and dirt, wrapped their wounds in sterilized cloth and administered some antibiotics. Then she left them in the care of their families, promising to return later. When she came back, she was confronted by a witch doctor. He had removed the bandages from the boys and covered their burns with pepper! "The white devil" would kill the boys, he declared. Then Helen demanded that the parents choose between her and the witch doctor. They chose her.

The denouement of the story is that the boys did recover and the Elliots won acceptance by the tribesmen. The first word they translated was *shum*. That word, they learned, means to give without expecting anything in return—or, in our language, *love*. And isn't that really what spreading the Gospel is all about?

Father, help me to find a way to spread Your Word today.

—FRED BAUER

4 SATURDAY
*For where your treasure is, there will your heart
be also.* —LUKE 12:34

The carpeting in our bedroom and hallway had become so worn that there were actually holes in it. I wanted to replace it but my husband said that our budget didn't allow for it. Disappointed, I felt somewhat rebellious and pretty soon I was complaining constantly that our house was "falling apart."

Then while sitting at the kitchen table one day, I happened to read a news story about a family whose house and possessions were completely destroyed in a fierce storm. When a reporter asked the young son how he felt about losing his home, the boy replied:

"Oh, we haven't lost our home. We just need a house to put it in."

Startled, I stopped reading and looked around. The copper kettle bubbled away on the stove. My larder was well-stocked. The basket on the table was filled with bright yellow marigolds. No, our house was far from falling apart. Sure it needed some repairs... but not as many as my relationship with my husband.

I resolved then and there to stop nagging about the worn carpet, the faded wallpaper, the rust spots in the sink, and to tune in to the beauty that surrounded me. *Why the most beautiful thing in all my home was the love my husband and I shared!* With such a blessed treasure, my house could fall down around my ears, but my home?

Never!

Should I forget, Father, remind me that wheresoever two hearts dwell together in Your love, the place is holy.

—MADGE HARRAH

5 SUNDAY
Remember the sabbath day, to keep it holy.

—EXODUS 20:8

It seems that Sundays are becoming just another hectic day in which to shop, work, do household chores and seek entertainment. Whatever happened to the Sabbath?

Last year some of us in our church began to ask that question and to wonder: *What does it mean to "remember" the Sabbath?* We made a study of Jesus' actions on the Sabbath and concluded that He used the day for restoring *Shalom*—that marvelous Hebrew word for peace, wholeness, health. That gave us several ideas for how we might best make our Sabbath more meaningful, and here are some of them to share with you:

...Take time to read a book that you have been wanting to read, especially one that will deepen your relationship with God;

...Spend a longer time at prayer, or for journaling;

...Use the day to deepen family relationships through special occasions for relaxation and fun;

...Give thought to restoring broken relationships or to mending broken hearts—and then write a letter, make a phone call or pay a visit.

Jesus declared that "The sabbath was made for man..." (Mark 2:27). What a wonderful gift from God! One day out of every seven for increasing *Shalom* in our lives and on the earth. Let's make the most of it!

Thank You, Father, for Your holy gift of the Sabbath. Help me to use it in holy ways. —PATRICIA HOUCK SPRINKLE

44

6 MONDAY
The words of the wise are as goads...
—*ECCLESIASTES 12:11*

I've had a history of problems with my back. All kinds of medical attention has failed to produce anything more than temporary relief. Finally I joined a health club, thinking that swimming and other exercise might help.

One day while luxuriating in the sauna, I recognized my doctor. When he asked about my back, I replied that exercise seemed to be helping a little.

"Good," he said. "But stand up straight. You slouch too much."

Slouch! I was already annoyed by his professional failure as far as my back was concerned...and now this criticism cut like a knife. But I must admit that I instinctively straightened up. And every time after that when I thought of his words, I automatically stood tall. And the taller I stood, the better I felt.

Then it occurred to me that I should be grateful to that outspoken man. A few incisive words—all free—had accomplished what several thousands of dollars' worth of treatments and long hours spent in doctors' offices had failed to do.

I guess that sometimes we just need to be pushed hard for our own good—and then be big enough to bless the person who cares enough to do it and humble enough to take the advice.

Father, teach my reluctant heart to listen when You speak to me through another.   —SAM JUSTICE

7 TUESDAY

Say not unto thy neighbor, Go, and come again, and tomorrow I will give; when thou hast it by thee.

—PROVERBS 3:28

Like most people, my husband and I enjoy an open fire. Cozy, inviting, a fire warms the heart and house. But to get the big logs burning, kindling is needed, and for this reason we have made it a habit to gather this kindling, or "starters," whenever we walk about the gardens. Little fallen branches, pieces of shed bark or scraps of wood lying around—useless, dead, going to waste.

But put them on the grate and touch a match to them, and lo, they come to life again! Leaping and dancing, flinging up their golden arms. Their flames embracing and licking at the logs, crackling into the air. The big heavy logs will burn for hours. Yet they too would have lain dead and useless except for that match to those little sticks.

How much life itself is like a fire in the fireplace. Every accomplishment, every invention, depends on something smaller to start it, warm it, feed it. The greatest plane or rocketship can only sit helpless, unable to get off the ground, until somebody fuels it and turns the switch. Without thousands of humble, nameless "starters," man would never have crossed the ocean, let alone landed on the moon!

Each of us is necessary in God's wonderful plan. However humble our job, however small our contribution may seem, we are useful, we are needed. Words of encouragement, a helping hand, a gift or a loan—these can serve as the "starters" that get another person's plans and projects going.

Dear Lord, help me to be a humble "starter," for when I fuel another's fire, then I too burst into new light and life.

—MARJORIE HOLMES

8

WEDNESDAY
Charity never faileth...   —*I CORINTHIANS 13:8*

As a small group of us were praying, I was taken by surprise to see that my twenty-two-year-old daughter was crying softly.

Then someone asked, "What are your needs?" She hesitated. "I—I—have to be perfect. I've always done just what was expected of me. I don't dare make any mistakes, *ever*. I can't fail. I'm so afraid of failing at something... at anything."

Memories of this nearly perfect child flashed through my mind. Homework always done way ahead of time. Clothes laid out the night before for school. Straight A's. Leadership roles in school and church. Always responsible and dependable. She had never in her life even been late. The oldest child, I had often put her in charge of the other children. She had never once let me down.

And now she sat crying in despair over the pressure of having to always measure up. I put my arms around her quivering shoulders and prayed, "Lord, forgive me for my part in this. Now in the name of Jesus I release this child from any pressures I have put her under. Please, in Your gentle, loving way, show my daughter what You can do with failures given to You. Let her fail in something."

I *almost* added, "Successfully"—but I didn't.

Father, help me to free those dear to me by loving them enough to relinquish claim.   —MARION BOND WEST

9

THURSDAY
...Yes, Lord...   —*MARK 7:28*

At a church supper the other night, the pastor handed out pencils and paper and challenged a group of us to write a one-word prayer. There was much furrowing of brows and chewing of erasers. Some people wrote down the word "love"; some wrote "praise";

others wrote "alleluia." I wrote the word "Yes." "Yes, Lord, You are always there." "Yes, I am sure of it." "Yes, I believe I can talk to You." "Yes, I believe that You *will* answer."

I have to confess that the idea was not mine. I borrowed it from Dag Hammarskjöld, the remarkable Christian who was Secretary General of the United Nations for many years. There is an entry in his diary that reads as follows:

> "I don't know Who—or What—put the question. I don't know when it was put. I don't even remember answering. But at some moment I did answer Yes to Someone—or Something—and from that hour I was certain that existence is meaningful and that therefore my life, in self-surrender, had a goal."

When we answer "yes," isn't that the shortest and sweetest prayer of all?

Yes, Lord.

—ARTHUR GORDON

---

10 FRIDAY

Let all bitterness, and wrath, and anger, and clamour, and evil speaking, be put away from you, with all malice...
—EPHESIANS 4:31

A fellow member of the school committee had, I thought, been unduly aggressive at our last meeting, and I was hurt. I wrote him an angry letter. Then I remembered a story that I had once heard about Abraham Lincoln and his Secretary of War, Stanton.

Stanton was incensed by a major-general who had spoken to him abusively. Lincoln encouraged Stanton to write the major-general a sharp letter in reply. But just as Stanton was about to mail the letter, Lincoln stopped him, saying, "Now that you have the anger out of your system, burn the letter."

I reread my letter. Why, I was being even ruder to the committee member than he had been to me! I tore up that letter, and the next time our committee met, we worked out an amiable compromise.

Wrath is such a futile and destructive emotion — it harms the giver as well as the recipient. Perhaps that is why the Bible, in all its wisdom, warns us against it so often.

Father, teach me to overcome anger and to deal peaceably with my neighbors. —MADGE HARRAH

---

11 SATURDAY
...Therefore choose life, that both thou and thy seed may live... —DEUTERONOMY 30:19

Yesterday my husband and I attended the funeral of a dear ninety-four-year-old lady named Ollie Anderson. When we saw her son later, he told us that on the day after his mother died, the mailman delivered a package of garden seeds that she had ordered for spring planting.

What a beautiful expression of faith! I thought. It made me ashamed of myself. Here I had been grumbling along and nursing a bad case of the mid-winter blahs while this lovely woman, who had scant assurance of ever seeing another spring, was making a truly soaring gesture of hope.

I decided that the next time I become bogged down in February dreariness, I'm going to deliberately plant some seeds of anticipation in my mind. I'll start to plan next summer's vacation...or arrange for a big family reunion...or visualize an answer to a long-standing prayer—or imagine myself completing a satisfying piece of work. Maybe I'll even order some garden seeds!

I've no doubt that Ollie Anderson's pathway into Heaven was strewn with hyacinths and daisies.

Oh, Lord, help me to keep on choosing life. All my life.
—MARILYN MORGAN HELLEBERG

49

12

SUNDAY

Thy word have I hid in mine heart...   —PSALM 119:11

Not long ago I visited Knob Creek in Kentucky, where a great American President spent his early boyhood years. I walked across the little plot of history, recalling the words of poet Carl Sandburg: "Welcomed into a world of battle and blood, of whispering dreams and wistful dust, a new child, a boy..." That boy, of course, was Abraham Lincoln. I had often wondered how that awkward, simple lad had risen up from an obscure, backwoods poverty to set a people free.

Now my mind was seeking an answer among the old shadows and stories of the place. I paused beneath a tree and saw how the Nashville-Louisville road had once run past the Lincoln cabin, where young Abe had first glimpsed slave dealers on horseback, driving their slaves down the road with whips. Hundreds of other people had witnessed similar sights. Why had they burned so fiercely in Abraham?

I walked back to the tiny one-room cabin, the old Lincoln homestead. I stepped inside on the crude dirt floor. My gaze embraced the simple fireplace, the hearth, a chair—next to it a Bible. Then a forgotten piece of history returned to me: young Abraham leaning at his mother's side, watching her face as she read the Bible to him. Perhaps such passages as "You shall know the truth and the truth shall make you free," or "Stand then as free people," or "If the Son makes you free, you will be free indeed."

I had found my answer.

What treasures there are in the Word of God to shape young souls and the destinies of nations! I resolved to go home and read the Bible — to my children and to myself — every day.

Father, help me to mine the treasures in Your Word and to follow Your calling for me in my world. Amen.   —SUE MONK KIDD

13 MONDAY
The secret things belong unto the Lord Our God…
—DEUTERONOMY 29:29

Tomorrow is St. Valentine's Day. I expect that I'll receive a lovely card from my son. And there will be the usual little love note beneath my plate at breakfast, signed "Guess Who?"—and that man in my life will take me out to dinner. My mother will remember, just as she did when I was a child. And maybe I'll hear from a few friends.

But none of these will have the strange, hard-to-explain meaning of the simple greeting that reached me in today's mail. Surrounded by forget-me-nots, the caption, "To a Special Friend," appeared across the front. Inside, there was a friendly greeting and then a handwritten note: "Just another chance to tell you in secret what you have meant in my life." And the card was unsigned!

I have no idea of the identity of the sender—or what I could possibly have done to merit such words of appreciation. But I do know that that person did a lot more for me than just send a card. She inspired me to resolve to do more and better things for our Lord—secretly, quietly, thoughtfully.

You might want to try it today—for a special friend!

Thank You, Father, for keeping my secrets. I know they're safe.
—JUNE MASTERS BACHER

14 TUESDAY
That thou mayest love the Lord thy God…and that thou mayest cleave unto him: for he is thy life…
—DEUTERONOMY 30:20

Although my daughter lives in a city far from mine, we talk often by telephone. And never does a conversation end without

51

her saying, "I love you, Mom." Of course I know she loves me, but it always makes me feel so good to hear her *say* it.

Just a little while ago I had a talk with God. I praised Him...and I thanked Him...and I confessed to Him...and I petitioned Him... and I said, "Amen." Then I sat quietly for a moment, deep in thought of my Heavenly Father. How precious He is to me! I bowed my head, closed my eyes and added, "I love You, God."

How long is it since you gladdened the heart of God by telling Him—*saying* it right out loud—that you love Him?

Again—I love You, God. I love You.   —DRUE DUKE

JESUS, THE MASTER STORYTELLER
Parable of the Lost Sheep —LUKE 15:3-7

15   WEDNESDAY

When I was a young boy of ten or eleven, I frequently was called upon to sing solos at my church in Montpelier, Ohio. One of my favorite numbers was "The Ninety and Nine," the music for which was written by Dwight L. Moody's evangelistic partner, Ira D. Sankey. Many years later I was fascinated to learn that George Beverly Shea had played on the old organ that Sankey had used to introduce that hymn in Scotland in 1873.

The inspiration for that famous, much-loved hymn came, of course, from Christ's Parable of the Lost Sheep. What a marvelous analogy between God's love for each of us and the love of a shepherd for his flock—a love so deep that he would leave "the ninety and nine that safely lay in the shelter of the fold" to go in search for one lost lamb:

> Away on the mountains wild and bare,
> Away from the tender shepherd's care.

That beautiful story made a great impact on me as a youngster and the years have done nothing to lessen the significance of Christ's parable, as indelibly graphic as a painting. How reassuring to know that we serve such a personal, caring God, Who celebrates each time one of His straying children is recovered and returned to the fold.

"Rejoice with me," Christ said, "for I have found my sheep which was lost." Let us rejoice today for the tender care of us by One so loving and gentle as our Saviour .

We glory in the knowledge that You care for each of us, Lord— individually, personally, continually.   —FRED BAUER

---

16 THURSDAY

And if a kingdom be divided against itself, that kingdom cannot stand.   —MARK 3:24

During the Revolutionary War, George Washington received especially warm friendship and help from the members of the Jewish congregation in Newport, Rhode Island. Later, when Washington became President, the leaders of the congregation wrote to him, congratulating him and offering their continuing support.

In his reply Washington said that he well remembered the help the people of Newport had given him as well as the hardships that the Jewish people had endured throughout the world for so many centuries. Washington pledged to do all he could to build the new country into a land that would "give to bigotry no sanction, to persecution no assistance."

This week we celebrate Brotherhood Week. It seems fitting to me that the man who won our freedom from the tyranny of state should also give us our freedom from the tyranny of bigotry.

Today let us re-dedicate ourselves to the finest in our heritage and double our efforts to bring peace and love to the hearts of all men everywhere. We may think that "all for one and one for all" is a worn

53

and over-used phrase, but think about it! Isn't that what Washington meant?

Isn't that what brotherhood is all about?

Almighty God—Father of us all—help Your children to dwell together in mutual love and support. —GLENN KITTLER

---

17 FRIDAY

…I will lead them in paths that they have not known: I will make darkness light before them, and crooked things straight. —ISAIAH 42:16

A sign on a certain road in Australia reads, "Choose your rut well. You'll be in it for the next twenty miles."

It's a funny thing about ruts. They don't have to be *miles* long. They can be *months* long. Maybe even *years* long. And ruts don't have to be rough either. They can be smooth, simply because they have been traveled in for so long.

Lately I've realized that I'm quite familiar with ruts and that I've been traveling in lots of them for a long, long time. For example:

—I favor familiar hymns with lines that rhyme.
—I'm suspicious of people whose attire is different.
—I'm defensive with those of unfamiliar denominations.
—I withdraw from people whose customs are foreign to me.
—I sit in the same seat every Sunday at church; I mingle with the same friends all year long; I quote and requote the same Bible verses.

Yes, staying in a rut is comfortable. But eventually stagnation sets in, and then we face the really tough job of pulling ourselves *out* of our rut.

Take a few minutes today to look at the road you're traveling. Do you see any old, well-worn ruts? Do they restrict your journey to the narrow lanes, where you can't see the scenery?

Free me from the bondage of habit, Father, and refresh my soul.
—ISABEL CHAMP

---

18 SATURDAY

Why art thou cast down, O my soul? and why art thou disquieted within me? hope thou in God...
—PSALM 42:11

When I left for college in my late teens, I left home, left friends and—most traumatically—left a young lady for whom I had a very special regard. We had vowed that distance would not change our relationship. But of course it did. We were each growing up—growing apart, not together—and somehow the same feelings were just never there again.

Thoroughly depressed about it, I got into my car one night and drove aimlessly through the dark streets of town. I wondered if changes in my life would always hurt this much. The radio was playing a popular song, and the words floated out into the air: "A *new day is dawning... people are changing....*" I'm sure that if I smiled at all, it was ruefully.

Well, to make a long story short, we never did get together again, she and I. But today all the painful adolescent sadness is gone... and I realize now that happiness and growth come not by clinging to the past, but by looking to the future.

It seems that with the passage of time, my inner roots keep reaching out in ever-spreading directions through experiences that continually change and enrich my life. Although I no longer remember the title of that song, I do remember the words that taught me of God's great truths: "A *new day is dawning... people are changing....*"

The next time you feel frightened by the changes in your life, why

55

don't you think of those words too... and welcome the new day with the blessed assurance that change is simply God's purpose at work in your life?

Father, for Your wisdom in change, we praise You; for Your strength during its pain, we thank You. —JEFF JAPINGA

---

19 SUNDAY

And Jesus said unto them, I am the bread of life: he that cometh to me shall never hunger; and he that believeth on me shall never thirst. —JOHN 6:35

Katie has baked homemade bread for communion, a fragrant, golden loaf. We pass it around the table and each breaks off a piece before handing the loaf to her neighbor. But when it has been around, there is so much left! I am hungry and find myself wishing I had dared to take a larger piece. Why didn't I? Was I afraid there wouldn't be enough for everyone? Was I wanting only an amount I could easily chew? Did I think it would be bad manners to take more than a token piece?

As I gaze at that lovely bread lying unclaimed by those for whom it was intended, I meditate on how often I take small tokens too of the One Whom the bread represents. I remember tentative, small prayers... when I hungered to pray big ones. I remember taking minor risks in His name... when I hungered to dare great ones. I remember expecting little miracles... while I hungered for life-changing ones. And I wonder how my own choice of small pieces of the Bread of Life has limited His ability to feed me.

Abandoning traditional manners, I reach again for the loaf. I am still hungry, and there is so much bread left. Come, won't you join me? There's an abundance of the Bread of Life—enough to satisfy all our hungers.

Dear Jesus, today I dare to bring all my hungers to You—for You are the Bread of my life. —PATRICIA HOUCK SPRINKLE

20 MONDAY
A good man out of the good treasure of his heart bringeth forth that which is good... —LUKE 6:45

"They say my new boss is really hard to get along with," I lamented to my friend Peggy. "Maybe I should start to look for another job. You know how I don't like working under pressure."

"Wait and give him a chance," Peggy urged. "My students thought I was difficult when I first began teaching. They didn't know that I was only scared. All it took was a few kind words to turn me around."

"Turn you around...?"

"Yes," she explained. "The father of one of my pupils really saved me. He said, 'Your explanation about *ten* being the building block for larger numbers made quite an impression on my son. Now David is already piling them up! You're a great teacher and I thank you.'"

"How nice of him," I said. "And then...?"

"I positively glowed. My self-confidence returned and I was no longer 'difficult.'" Peggy smiled. "Maybe all your new boss needs is a boost like that. Try it and see what happens."

I took her advice. I greeted my new supervisor with warmth and words of welcome and, like good seed sown in good ground, in due time those words bore the fruit of respect and friendship.

Frequently the opportunity arises in our lives when we are called upon to turn a potentially unpleasant situation around—and all it might take is a smile and a single word of kindness.

Dear Father, teach me to anticipate the best in others... and to bring it out. —DORIS HAASE

57

21 TUESDAY
For I am the Lord that healeth thee. —EXODUS 15:26

"Ugh!"

That was all I could say when the real-estate agent let me into the cottage. Paint peeled from the walls, the floors were water-stained where windows had been left open, the woodwork was nicked and scarred from countless collisions with furniture. Could it ever be made livable?

"Of course the owner will fix it up," the agent assured me. "He really loves this place."

Well, I needed a house in a hurry and I agreed to rent it. But I had my doubts.

When I returned a month later, ready to move in, I was astonished. Perched on its little grassy knoll, the house fairly gleamed with pride. And with good reason. The owner had gone over it from top to bottom, sanding the floors, scraping the walls before he repainted them, filling in all the scars in the woodwork. His loving care was evident in every room.

As I stood there marveling at the transformation, I realized how much damage a loving person can undo. And I thought that this is how our Heavenly Father works in our life every day. Patiently, with great care, He repairs the neglect and hurt we may have suffered ... and makes us whole again.

Thank You, Father, for undoing my hurt and repairing my spirit. I will pass it on today. —PHYLLIS HOBE

22 WEDNESDAY
*But he that is greatest among you shall be your
servant.* —*MATTHEW 23:11*

It was during the Revolutionary War that a man in civilian clothes came upon a corporal who was arrogantly ordering his men to hoist a heavy beam. The soldiers were pushing and straining under the load, obviously in danger of losing their footing.

"Why don't you help them?" the man asked the officer.

The indignant answer was, "Sir, I am a corporal!"

Whereupon the stranger removed his coat and assisted the men in lifting and placing the beam.

When the task was finished, the stranger said: "Mr. Corporal, whenever you haven't enough men to do a job, call on your Commander-in-Chief. I'll be glad to help."

With that, George Washington put on his coat and left.

Christ set the supreme example of service when He washed His disciples' feet. George Washington strove to live up to it.

Today—President's Day—let us remember that we who would be great must first be willing to serve.

Dear Jesus, teach me to live each day with humility in my heart.
—ZONA B. DAVIS

23 THURSDAY
I will fear no evil: for thou art with me… —*PSALM 23:4*

When I was a small child, I was afraid of the dark. We lived way out in the country and had no neighbors, unless you counted the Rollins, who lived a mile and a half up the road. With so few people around, the rustling noises in the quiet rural nights could seem mighty spooky.

By the age of eleven I felt babyish about being afraid and I decided to try to overcome my fears. I set myself the challenge of walking the perimeter of our place at night all by myself...sort of like taking a walk through the valley of the shadow of death. After all, who knew *what* might be lurking about out there in the woods?

So one evening I did just that. I left the flashlight behind, begged God to come with me, took a deep breath and set out.

I had been hiking for close to half an hour when I realized that my eyes had adjusted so well to the dark that I could see quite clearly. I also realized that no one was lurking behind the bushes, waiting to snatch me away. There were only the two of us—God and me—moving along the path. As I finally walked back up to our house, I knew then that I would never again be afraid of the dark. Since that time I have walked in the dark many times, driven in the dark, even camped out in the dark.

Now whenever I begin to feel afraid of anything, I remember that walk through the night with God, and my fears dissolve in the assurance that God will be with me no matter the time, the place or the situation.

Dear Father, help me to remember that there is nothing to fear because You are always right here beside me.

—SAMANTHA McGARRITY

---

24 FRIDAY
...Be likeminded one toward another according to Christ Jesus. —ROMANS 15:5

While going through some old photographs the other day, I came upon a batch of pictures from my sports-writing and sports-announcing days. One of them showed me interviewing Paul (Bear) Bryant, who before his recent death set an all-time record for victories achieved by a college football coach.

But the Alabama coach never once mentioned "his" victories. He spoke only of his team's victories. "If anything goes bad," the Bear said, "then *I* did it. If anything goes semi-good, then *we* did it. If anything goes real good, then *you* did it."

Bear Bryant knew well that winning teams and winning relationships depend on teamwork. When the goals are set high and everyone pitches in together, great results can be won. As a wise soul once wrote, "It's simply amazing how much can be accomplished when no one cares who gets the credit."

We Christians, working together on His team, have always known this truth—for He has given us the supreme example of humility. And since we're each a member of God's team, each of us determined to win for Jesus, aren't we united in spirit as one?

Then as one, let's join hands today and really pitch in!

Dear Father, teach me humility so that I may be a good member of Your team. —FRED BAUER

---

25 SATURDAY
Hear, O Lord, when I cry with my voice…and answer me. —PSALM 27:7

Hurriedly I opened the desk drawer where I keep my address book. And then I remembered—I had loaned it to a friend who wanted to update her phone list.

I felt a sense of panic. The little book contained my list of prayer warriors and I urgently needed to talk with someone who understood and loved me. Someone who really cared. I knew several of the numbers by memory but when I dialed, one line gave a busy signal and there was no answer to the others.

I must talk to someone, I thought, near tears.

As I stared at the telephone, my eyes fell on my Bible there on the table. Very gently the suggestion came: *Why not talk to Me about the problem? I understand you. I love you. I really care.*

I picked up God's Word and we had a long conversation. He gave me His undivided attention and the answer I so sorely needed. Later

I was glad that my address book had been out on loan—for I learned that I need never again wonder Who to call in my need.

Thank You, Father, for being my true Prayer Warrior and Comforter—all the time. —MARION BOND WEST

---

26 SUNDAY
Into thine hand I commit my spirit... —PSALM 31:5

When I was little girl, my father and I would sometimes play a special game—a secret shared by just the two of us—in which we would send a message back and forth to each other. It consisted of three little hand squeezes. Very simply, they meant "I—love—you."

I could hardly keep from giggling out loud when I would sit beside him on the church pew and reach for his big, warm hand and give it three secret squeezes, all the while keeping my gaze on the preacher as though nothing delightful and magical was going on. But every now and then I would steal a side glance at Daddy as I delivered the message. And of course he would be looking straight ahead so as not to give anything away, but the corners of his mouth would twitch with a tiny smile, and I could see a flickering of happiness light up his eyes. Oh, how I loved to send my father secret messages when no one else was looking!

Today when I sit in church, all grown up now with a daughter of my own, I often recall those moments. And then I am reminded that *everything* I do sends a message to my Heavenly Father. It makes me wonder. What secret message do I send my Father when no one else is looking? Does it make His eyes light up with happiness? Does it say "I—love—you"?

Father, may everything I do today send a message of love to You.

—SUE MONK KIDD

27 MONDAY

This is the Lord's doing; it is marvellous in our eyes.
—*PSALM 118:23*

When I first arrived in New York City, fresh from a small Midwestern town, I was appalled. The city seemed to loom over me, enormous and impersonal, too noisy, too dirty, completely depressing. And three years of walking from the train station to the midtown offices of *Guideposts* did little to dispell that first impression.

Then last summer some friends from Switzerland came to visit. "What a beautiful city this is!" one exclaimed, studying a graceful old stone building nestled between two towering skyscrapers. "How splendidly the old and the new are mingled!"

"I walk this street almost every day," I said, somewhat startled, "but I've never before noticed that building."

"Ah-ha!" replied my friend. "But when you visited us in Switzerland, you pointed out many beautiful things to us that *we* had simply taken for granted and hadn't even bothered to look at."

Today I don't walk to the office nearly as fast as I used to. Now I raise my head and look around—for I don't want to ever again miss any of the magnificent beauty that God so generously strews on our way. For if we're alert and pay close attention to His loving gifts, we truly walk in beauty.

Walk with me, Lord, so I may be continually aware of the beauty of Your world. —JEFF JAPINGA

28 TUESDAY

Turn thou us unto thee, O Lord, and we shall be turned; renew our days as of old. —*LAMENTATIONS 5:21*

When my daughter was working in a supermarket, she rescued a discarded fern from the trash basket. The plant was

63

scraggly, brown and brittle, but since Karen had discovered about half an inch of green growth on one of the stems, she placed the fern on her windowsill, where she watered it, fertilized it, talked to it and loved it back to life. Today the plant is tall and full and richly green, thriving on Karen's dedicated care.

There is a relationship in my life that has been gradually withering. Petty resentments have stifled the happy relationship my friend and I once shared. It would be easy for me just to discard the friendship, the way the supermarket manager discarded the fern. Yet I wonder? Could there be a spot of green still clinging to life near the roots? There is something unspeakably sorrowful about a living thing left to die of neglect.

I think I will call my old friend tomorrow and invite her to meet me for lunch. And while we're together, I am going to try—really try—to find a surviving patch of green growth to nourish into bloom again.

Is there a neglected relationship in your life that is now withered? I'll bet that there's a patch of living green there yet, just waiting to be nourished back to health with love and care!

Jesus, teach me how to cultivate love afresh!

—MARILYN MORGAN HELLEBERG

---

29 WEDNESDAY
Behold, now is the day of salvation.

—II CORINTHIANS 6:2

In a friend's house not long ago I noticed a framed sampler on the kitchen wall. Its precise little stitches read:

Bless our home, Father,
That we may cherish the bread before there is none,
Discover each other before we leave,
And enjoy each other for what we are while we have time.

While we have time! To me, those are the most important words in the prayer. None of us knows how much—or how little—time we may have in which to carry out our good intentions, achieve those worthwhile ambitions or simply turn our everyday dreams into realities.

I once had an easy-going cousin whose favorite phrase was "one of these days." One of these days, he would predict, he would take that back-pack trip in the Rockies with the youngsters; one of these days he would learn to play the guitar; one of these days he would take his wife on the church retreat for married couples. Then, on one of those days, he had a sudden heart attack—and there were no more days.

"This is the day," the Psalmist sang. Not tomorrow, or the day after, or the day after that. *This* is the day for us to rejoice and be glad in it.

I have no days to waste, Father. Each one belongs to You.

—ARTHUR GORDON

Praise Diary for February

1

2

3

4

5

6

7

8

9

10

11

12

13

14

15

16

17

18

19

20

21

22

23

24

25

26

27

28

29

March

S	M	T	W	T	F	S
				1	2	3
4	5	6	7	8	9	10
11	12	13	14	15	16	17
18	19	20	21	22	23	24
25	26	27	28	29	30	31

Today, Lord, walking along
A hardscrabble county road,
I glimpsed a heifer calf
Frolicking in a cowyard.
Brown as chocolate,
White as milk
Her nose as pink as a baby.
Fresh and clean, a brand new life…
But already wise enough to
Sniff hints of change
In the moist March air
And be Spring's first celebrant.
Now she snuffles under her mother's neck,
Now she wings and bucks and trots,
Setting her haunches in a jumbly rhumba,
Dancing to a subtle music
I've not yet heard.
Because, of course, I haven't listened,
Nor sniffed the air
With the ageless wisdom of that calf.
Time now, then, to sight the robin
And those first blades of green green grass,
To catch that first sweet whiff
Of new beginnings!

James McDermott

GUIDEPEOPLE: A Living Parable for March

1 THURSDAY

Commit thy way unto the Lord, trust also in him; and he shall bring it to pass. —PSALM 37:5

Catherine Marshall was a woman of luminous faith. She was a member of the *Guideposts* family for almost three decades during which time she helped readers—and those of us on the staff—to learn more about the limitless variety of prayer, about finding divine guidance in the day-to-day, about the robust and joy-filled Jesus Whom she knew.

For all of her deep spirituality, Catherine was a practical Christian who wrote from her own experience. And the foundation of her faith, the touchstone she always kept at hand, was the soul-deep change she underwent many years before she had published a single word.

Catherine was a young wife and mother—married to the much-admired pastor, Peter Marshall—when she fell ill with what she always described as "a wide-spread lung infection." She never used the word "tuberculosis." She languished in bed for months, and the months turned into years. As her body grew thinner, so did her spirit. Then came a day of decision. Catherine stopped struggling. She stopped beseeching God to do as *she* asked and let Him do as *He* desired.

"I gave him a blank check," she told me once. Catherine surrendered her vanity, her willfulness, her sins, her worries, her happiness and, yes, her life. From that point on, she began to recover.

"The crisis of self-surrender"—that's what the great philosopher William James called it long before Catherine discovered it for herself. James described it as the vital turning point of religious life. It was, for Catherine Marshall, the surest step toward God that a human being can take.

Lord, help me to know the victory of surrender this month.

—VAN VARNER

2 FRIDAY
Use hospitality one to another... —*I PETER 4:9*

You know how it is when you live in a big apartment building—you recognize your neighbors by sight, you greet one another with a smile or a nod and then you keep going. For many years I lived in a high-rise building, I didn't even know the name of my nearest neighbor.

Then one morning an elderly woman fell and broke her ankle right in front of the entrance to my building just as I was leaving for work. I didn't realize until after I had called an ambulance and accompanied her to the hospital that she lived only two doors down the hall from me. Her name was Beth Miller. Beth was a widow whose children lived away and, like me, she was alone.

When Beth was discharged from the hospital, she was quite helpless. So every day I delivered her breakfast and dinner, and every night I tucked her into bed. And I mustered the courage to knock on another neighbor's door and ask her if she would fix Beth's lunch.

That was how I came to meet some of the best friends I have today—through Beth Miller's broken ankle. Not only do we keep in touch with one another, but once a year we have a reunion... with Beth as our guest of honor. And on those occasions I am always pleasantly reminded of the need to keep my eyes open and my heart attuned to those around me—even strangers. Maybe *especially* strangers. For the lovely gift of friendship may lie hidden in every new encounter.

If I can be of help today, Father, lead me to my neighbor's door. —PHYLLIS HOBE

3

SATURDAY

A man's pride shall bring him low: but honour shall uphold the humble in spirit. —PROVERBS 29:23

As a small child I used to leap and twirl around in the front yard by the hour pretending I was an accomplished dancer on stage. Oh, such glory!

Then when I reached the age of ten, I took tap-dancing lessons. One of the students in my class was a boy of thirteen, a football player who hoped that tap dancing would help him to score more touchdowns on the field.

He was awkward and ungraceful, but he doggedly practiced all the steps to the routine our teacher assigned us. I knew that I could dance circles around him and generally ignored him during our lessons.

Then came the day of the recital. My knees turned to jelly and my feet might as well have been two bricks.

As I stood there confused and embarrassed, my dancing football partner whispered into my ear, "I'll give you the calls. Just follow what I say. You're going to do okay." And he got us through.

I have never felt so humbled in all my life, and that tap-dancing athlete will always be a hero to me.

Dear Heavenly Father, thank You for lessons in humility.

—SAMANTHA McGARRITY

4

SUNDAY

He hath made every thing beautiful in his time…
—ECCLESIASTES 3:11

A few weeks ago a newcomer joined our Sunday-school class. Reluctantly I had to admit that I found her personality unpleasant and abrasive, and I was all set to ignore her when I suddenly remembered how my former art teacher once rescued a painting I had discarded. She placed it on something called a "finder"—two ninety-degree angles cut from mat board. By moving those pieces of framing about so they enclosed different portions of the painting, she finally located a section that held together as a lovely composition. Then she cut the section out, framed it and hung it on the wall.

"There is beauty in almost every painting," she told me, "but sometimes you have to block out the rough spots to find it."

With that in mind, I began to study the personality of my new classmate with a mental "finder," enclosing one quality at a time. And I made some remarkable discoveries! Courage. Honesty. Openness. All fine qualities that led to respect and eventually to friendship.

I've since used that "finder" on others, including members of my own family, and especially during times of disagreement! It's amazing how my negative attitudes change when I block out the troublesome areas and "frame" the beautiful aspect of the other person.

Today, Father, help me find the beauty in each person I meet.
—MADGE HARRAH

---

5 MONDAY
...I will put my laws into their mind, and write them in their hearts... —HEBREWS 8:10

Last winter my wife and I were privileged to be aboard the great Cunard liner *Queen Elizabeth II* as she made her majestic way through the Panama Canal.

The locks of the canal are exactly 110 feet wide. The *Queen Elizabeth II* has a beam of 105.2 feet. That meant a clearance of less than thirty-six inches on either side. Little electric locomotives running alongside the lock held the huge ship with taut wire cables and steadily eased her through.

"It's a tight fit," one of the young officers told the spectators on deck, "but don't worry. Those little 'mules', as we call them, will keep us in the straight and narrow."

"Sort of like the Ten Commandments," someone behind me murmured.

"Well, yes," the young man replied, "but notice that nothing happens until contact is made and kept. We have to throw out lines to the crews that manage the 'mules'. The 'mules' are useless to us until we reach for them and take advantage of their strength and stability."

That's not a bad mini-sermon, I thought to myself. We need to reach out, and keep contact with the strength and ability God offers through His Word, if we want to wend our way ahead—on course—until we safely dock in home port.

Lord, remind us to reach out every day to the guidelines You have given us. —ARTHUR GORDON

---

6 TUESDAY

Better is an handful with quietness, than both the hands full with travail and vexation of spirit.

—*ECCLESIASTES 4:6*

The verse above brings the story of Mary and Martha to mind.

Martha, you recall, was the one who complained to Jesus that her sister should be helping her in the kitchen. Maybe Martha even banged the pots and pans together to make her point. Her desire to prepare a lavish meal for their guests was admirable, but a feast was not what He most needed.

Jesus was aware that it would not be long before he would face his greatest trial. Surely He preferred quiet and understanding fellowship with His close friends during such a time of stress.

Frequently my husband and I have as our houseguests missionaries who are on furlough. When we ask, "What would you like to do while you're here?" invariably they reply, "Just walk in your woods and sit beside your stream." And we understand.

Even if you don't live by the woods with a stream, your home can be a gentle sanctuary for a friend who seeks quiet and rest from the turbulence of life and its problems. If you are like Mary, you will be quick to recognize the need, and then say simply, "Come in."

Father, help me to provide a sanctuary in my heart and in my home to those who seek the spirit of peace. —ISABEL CHAMP

---

7 WEDNESDAY
If any man serve me, let him follow me; and where I am, there shall also my servant be... —JOHN 12:26

Recently I reread the passages from Matthew 4:18-22 wherein Jesus calls upon Peter and Andrew, James and John to become His disciples. First Jesus comes upon Peter and Andrew as they cast their nets into the sea.

"Follow me," Jesus tells them, "and I will make you fishers of men." The Scripture states that "...They straightaway left their nets and followed him."

Then Jesus makes the same promise to James and John as they mend nets in a ship with their father. Matthew reports that "they immediately left the ship and their father, and followed him."

Note that Jesus offered His disciples neither wages, pension plans nor paid vacations. No, they responded to His call because they were drawn by His great cause, because they believed whole-heartedly in the Man and His mission. In a word, they were not afraid of the risk.

Suddenly I was struck by the sheer routine of my life—the ordinariness of my days—as I realized anew that Jesus calls to us now just as He called to His disciples. I began to wonder. Am I willing to drop whatever I am doing, eager to place my future in His hands? For a Christian there can be only one answer to that question: *Oh, yes, Lord, I'm right behind You. Lead me.*

No matter where!

Lord, even if the way is steep, I will follow You.

—FRED BAUER

8   THURSDAY
He that hath ears to hear, let him hear.   *—MATTHEW 11:15*

"You must listen to what they're *not* saying," the hospital administrator told the volunteers one day.

"Sometimes we may *seem* to listen to the patients," he went on, "but we aren't really tuned in to their message. As a result, this little mini-course is being given to help you better evaluate what is actually being said. Pay close attention to the patient's facial expression. Be alert to feelings, for often they're the principal message. Non-verbal language—a shrug, a smile, a nervous laugh, gestures and body positions—they all speak volumes. It takes real concentration and undivided attention to truly observe and *hear*."

Do you suppose that's what Jesus meant? No matter who we're with—dear family members, close friends or total strangers—listening with undivided love and concern is the only way really to get the message they're sending us.

Yes—I get the message, Lord.

From now on, Father, I will try to listen—really listen—with all my heart and soul.
—ZONA B. DAVIS

9 FRIDAY
O Lord... all the earth is full of thy riches.

—PSALM 104:24

Although it started out as a child's game, it continues in our house to this day—despite the fact that the children are grown now and have left the roost.

When our son was very small, he and his preschool friends liked to count their pennies and dream of what they would buy. One rainy day, to my surprise, I overheard Bryce say, "But all my pennies can't buy rain!"

"Or snow," another giggled.

"Not sky either—"

After that Bryce and I made a little game of listing the things that money would not purchase. It was a fun way for him to master his ABC's. But far more than that came from it—for both of us. Now when we gather as a family of adults, we rejoice in the ABC's of our blessings.

"Take the letter *h*," someone will say. "Can you name three things starting with *h* that money can't buy?"

"Well, yes," someone else will reply. "There's health, hope and happiness!"

Then there's *a*ppreciation, *b*eauty, *c*omfort....

Yes, our God-given world—from A to Z—is just brimming over with His wonders that no amount of money can ever buy!

Thank You for Your wondrous gifts, Lord, all freely given.

—JUNE MASTERS BACHER

10 SATURDAY
...She turned herself back, and saw Jesus...

—*JOHN 20:14*

It is seven o'clock on a Saturday morning. I stretch luxuriously, taking pleasure in every bone and muscle. From my bed I can see a vivid blue sky partially hidden by a cobweb of winter branches.

A brand new day, I think, and my mind begins to expand with the many things I plan to do, until soon all the nooks and crannies are filled.

Now it is noontime. I rush about, busily fulfilling those early morning plans. And then—so soon?—it is five o'clock. So little time is left. *If I hurry, I can still get to the cleaners before it closes, and the market stays open until nine.*

Ten o'clock! The day has ended. *But I'm not ready*, I protest. *There's more I should do.* I bathe and climb into bed, strangely dissatisfied. In the now-black, star-studded sky, a single shimmering beacon of light catches my attention—and I remember.

Long ago a star led three Wise Men to the manger in Bethlehem. Tonight a star leads the thoughts of this one unwise woman back to Jesus, and as I ponder, I realize what is missing. I left no time in my busy day for the One Who gave it to me. Quietly I fold my hands. No, it *isn't* too late. There is still time to do the most important thing of all.

Dear Jesus, my day is not complete without You.

—DORIS HAASE

11 SUNDAY
And be ye kind one to another... —*EPHESIANS 4:32*

Eyes glued to the floor, nervous fingers running through her hair, a woman in our prayer group poured out her heart. While

78

she was out of town, her teenager had tried to end his life with sleeping pills.

"He's going to be all right," she said, "but I felt so *guilty*. I thought, if only I had stayed home he might not have tried it. I was convinced that I was a total failure as a mother. I actually hated myself. Then my husband handed me a note that had arrived in the mail on that very day. It read, 'Your solo last Sunday was such a blessing. There is so much joy and gladness in your voice. Thank you, blessed child of God. Love, Carolmae.'"

Carolmae had had no idea when she wrote that note that our prayer-group member would be experiencing such heartbreaking problems on the day it reached her—but God surely knew.

How often I feel a nudge to write a letter that might carry a touch of brightness, a word of hope, into another's day. And how sorry I am later if I forego the opportunity. Could it be God who nudges us to reach out to one of His children with some loving and caring words, God who prompts us to act on His behalf?

Lord, help me to heed Your least nudge and send that note or card today. —MARILYN MORGAN HELLEBERG

---

12 MONDAY
Behold, what manner of love the Father hath bestowed upon us... —I JOHN 3:1

I once shared a two-day speaking engagement with Louis Nizer. He was a man who arrived in the United States as a little boy with his penniless immigrant mother, yet became one of our country's most famous lawyers and the author of many important books.

So vital, cordial, sincerely interested in other people, he had an electric quality, bright eyes, and a strong handclasp. And his wife—a dear, gracious lady—told me: "He is always like that, an absolute joy to live with. He wakes up every morning acting as though it's his birthday!"

And then it came to me—of course that's the secret. Every day *is* his birthday, and he knows it. He realizes, as we all should, that each time we emerge from sleep, we are new. The day stretches before us and we can claim life for our very own.

God wants us to celebrate our existence and to embrace the gifts we too often take for granted. Freedom and opportunity. Sunshine and air and food and friends. The ability to speak and see and hear and love.

People like Louis Nizer make me realize anew that we are each a guest of God upon this incredible earth. And if we're truly grateful for His hospitality, every day is certainly cause for celebration.

Thank You, Lord, for the precious gift of life, wherein we are born anew with the dawning of each day. —MARJORIE HOLMES

---

13 TUESDAY
Open rebuke is better than secret love. —PROVERBS 27:5

My friend Barbara was angry with me and I knew the reason why. She had asked me to address her creative writing class and I had said that I'd be glad to. But when I checked my schedule, I found that I had a conflicting appointment, and when I told Barbara this, she couldn't understand why I didn't change it.

She had a point, but so did I. To my way of thinking, an appointment is an appointment, and I stood firm on my viewpoint. Barbara wasn't willing to discuss our difference in the matter and she began to avoid me.

Then one day I ran into her—literally—at the supermarket. I turned into an aisle and my cart collided with hers. We both laughed.

"Barbara, I want to talk to you," I said.

"Not now," she replied, beginning to turn away.

"Yes, *now*," I insisted.

So right there, surrounded by soaps and fabric softeners, I told her that I loved her and prized our friendship. Further, I said, she had hurt my feelings by withholding her friendship, just as I had hurt hers by taking such a stubborn attitude.

Finally she smiled and said gently, "You know something? I've missed you."

"I've missed you too," I replied, "and if we ever become angry with each other again, let's bring it out in the open and"—I looked around at all the laundry aids and laughed—"and then let's just wash it away!"

Teach me to bring my anger into the open, Father, and free me to love. —PHYLLIS HOBE

---

14 WEDNESDAY
By love serve one another. —GALATIANS 5:13

The couple who recently moved in across the street turned out to be newlyweds—and of course they reminded me of my own early days of marriage. After all, I had been married for twenty-five years.

One day I was picking up the evening paper when I saw the young husband drive into their carport. He had hardly parked the car before his wife came running out of the house and flung open the door, throwing herself into his arms. They embraced for quite a while. I hurried on back inside with the evening news.

I didn't read the paper, but the "evening news" seemed to be: You need to show your husband that you love him. *Of course he knows I love him!* I thought...but...but maybe some extra expression of care, some unexpected demonstration of affection that would be appreciated?

When he drove up the driveway, it was dusk. I watched him get out of the car with his briefcase. He looked a little tired. Before he opened the front door, I popped out and hugged him, giving him a great big kiss. He was obviously delighted and the rest of that evening took on a little special aura of its own.

Whether we've been married one year, twenty-five or fifty—showing love and care to our spouse should never be "old hat."

Father, help me to remember that everyone needs to know he is loved—especially those closest and dearest to us.

—MARION BOND WEST

JESUS, THE MASTER STORYTELLER
Parable of the Dishonest Steward
—LUKE 16:1-13

15 THURSDAY

There was a rich man who had a dishonest manager and planned to fire him. The manager, trying to curry favor with the rich man's debtors, allows them to tear up the notes and contracts they have with the rich man and to write new ones for smaller amounts. The manager figures that when he is dismissed, these people will be so pleased with him they will take care of him.

The story goes on to say that the rich man was impressed with the manager's shrewdness, dishonest though it was. Perhaps he had grown rich by using sharp practices himself.

And Jesus says: "Make to yourselves *friends* of the mammon of unrighteousness; that, when ye fail, they may receive you into everlasting habitations."

Is Jesus condoning dishonest practices? Put a scornful emphasis on "they" and the sarcasm comes through in the notion that fellow conspirators can offer a dishonest manager "everlasting" shelter.

Jesus ends his story with the warning that those who are dishonest in small things will be dishonest in large ones. It's something to ponder whenever we're tempted to pad an expense account, or run personal mail through the company's postage meter, or fudge a little bit on income taxes. Nothing subtle or ambiguous here. Just the straightforward reminder that partial honesty isn't enough. Under the steady gaze of Jesus Christ, only total honesty will do.

Lord, help me to choose rightly in all situations—especially when one of the choices is You. —ARTHUR GORDON

---

16 FRIDAY

Thou shalt not bear false witness against thy neighbour. —EXODUS 20:16

My daughter Kris got her first car—a small station wagon she named *Georgie Girl*—when her own daughter was a baby. Ten years and three children later needing a larger car, *Georgie Girl* was advertised for sale. Since the money would be used to offset the cost of a new car, Kris prayed earnestly and was inspired to stand on the Ninth Commandment.

"That car has been a blessing to us," she said, recalling joy-filled family outings, church and school excursions. "It should be a blessing to the new owner too. But we know that it needs repairs and it won't be a blessing to anyone unless we're honest about it."

So Kris made a list of necessary repairs and set a fair price. Potential buyers came, studied the list, then either fled or tried to bargain. Kris stood firm. Finally when the ad had run its course, a college student, a former member of Kris' church youth group, arrived with her uncle.

"Why, it's *Georgie Girl!*" she cried. "Oh, *that's* my car!"

Kris offered her list, they drove around the block, the uncle approved. "It's a good deal," he said. "I'm a mechanic. I know."

"So you see," Kris reported gleefully, "if we keep God's law, what blesses one blesses all."

Father, keep me alert, actively practicing Your precepts lest unknowingly I harm another. —ELAINE ST. JOHNS

83

17 SATURDAY

*Wherefore take unto you the whole armour of God,
that ye may be able to withstand in the evil day, and
having done all, to stand.* —EPHESIANS 6:13

St. Patrick of Ireland left many legacies to the world but none so lovely as his "Lorica" or "Breastplate Song" which he urged believers to sing upon arising in the morning. Based on Paul's instruction to daily put on the "whole armour of God" including "the breastplate of righteousness" this song is still an appropriate way for Christians to begin their day. It reads in part:

I arise today
in the Might of God   for my piloting;
Power of God   for my upholding;
Wisdom of God   for my guidance;
Eye of God   for my foresight;
Ear of God   for my hearing;
Word of God   for my utterance;
Hand of God   for my deliverance;
Path of God   for my direction;
Shield of God   for my protection.

The Lord is Saviour, Christ is Saviour,
Saviour, Lord, always be with us. Amen.

Dear Lord, I ask you to be my armor for this day ahead.

—PATRICIA HOUCK SPRINKLE

18 SUNDAY

*But now in Christ Jesus ye who sometimes were far
off are made nigh…* —EPHESIANS 2:13

My friend Margaret asked me to visit her church one Sunday. As we walked through the door, I signed the guest register.

Later the pastor read aloud the visitors' names and introduced each stranger to the congregation. At the close of the service a number of people crowded around and shook my hand in welcome.

"What a fine practice!" I later exclaimed to Margaret. "If people were always that friendly, there would never be any strangers in church."

Margaret smiled. "If people were always that friendly," she said, "there would never be any strangers *anywhere*." Then she looked at me thoughtfully and said, "You're right, it is a fine practice. Why don't we try to greet at least three strangers every day? Starting tomorrow."

Enthusiastically I agreed.

The next morning when I went downstairs to pick up my mail, I met the new mailman.

"Hi," I greeted him. "Welcome to our neighborhood!"

"Why, thank you," he answered, and his friendly grin told me that I had made my first "stranger-friend." Now—every day—I look for others to greet, and Margaret is doing the same.

Won't you join us?

Welcome, Friend Jesus.   —DORIS HAASE

---

19 MONDAY
He that doeth good is of God...   —III JOHN 11

One freezing night during the last week of basic training, my buddy Jack Daniels and I tried in vain to hammer our tent pegs into the crusty ground. The trouble was that we had been issued wooden pegs instead of the usual metal ones.

"Jack," I said, "it's going to be a long, cold night if we don't get this tent up." He nodded in agreement and we struggled on, managing only to break another wooden peg.

Then someone said over my shoulder, "You guys look like you could use a little help."

He was a tall man, a little older than Jack and me, and dressed in the same army-issue clothing. He had a small sledge hammer and six brand new metal tent pegs. It took him no more than a minute to set up our tent. We stammered our thanks as he moved off to help another struggling pair.

"I was praying for help," Jack muttered, "but I never expected an angel."

I've thought about the incident many times since, and I now believe the tent-peg man *was* an angel. We never saw him again, and no one was ever able to account for his presence that night. Long after that army experience a situation arose wherein I was able to do someone an anonymous favor. It was a small thing, really, and accomplished easily, but I believe the deed was rather significant to the person it helped.

Why am I telling you all this? Well, just in case you have been a little skeptical about angels, I'm reminding you to stay alert. You might have been helped by one. And you might be called upon to be one.

Keep me alert to Your promptings, Holy Spirit, so that I may act at Your least call.

—JAMES McDERMOTT

20 TUESDAY

I said, I will take heed to my ways... —PSALM 39:1

"Well, did you have a good day?" my husband asked at the dinner table last night.

"Oh, pretty good. I got quite a bit done," was my vague reply.

"Mom!" our daughter Karen exclaimed. "Is *that* how you decide whether or not you've had a good day—by how much you got done?"

It was as though she had held up a mirror before me. I suddenly realized that yes, for most of the time, "getting things done" *is* my yardstick—and that it's a pretty poor measure of a day. Maybe if I had chosen *joy* as my gauge, I would have gone for a praise-walk to soak up God's masterpiece of glorious fall colors. If the standard of my day had been *love*, I might have visited Anna, who has been sick...or played a game with my son John...or spent extra time with God in prayer.

Surely I need to be more conscious of my daily measure. I wonder what would happen if every morning I would check my "To-Do-Today" list against two very simple questions: first, "What are my three top values in life?"...and, second..."Does my plan for the day truly reflect those priorities?"

Tomorrow if anyone asks me, "Did you have a good day?" I might just reply, "It's been a wonderful day! I didn't get much done, but...."

Dear Father, remind me that it's not how much I do, but what I do that matters. —MARILYN MORGAN HELLEBERG

---

21 WEDNESDAY
Let your light so shine before men... —MATTHEW 5:16

One day my small daughter painted her very own "stained-glass" picture—a plastic sign that spelled the word "joy." She filled in the panes with translucent purples, blues and reds. I propped it in the kitchen window, where it caught the sun's rays and reflected a rainbow of light into the room. It was almost like looking at joy itself. Every morning when I arrived in the kitchen, there it was—joy streaming in through the window.

But one morning I walked into the kitchen in a dark mood. The joy sign made such a contrast to my feelings that impulsively I reached up and pulled the curtain across it. *Like snuffing out a candle*, I thought. All the colorful brightness it had smiled into the room disappeared.

Later as I crossed the back yard to empty the trash, I glanced up at the window, expecting to see the sign shining as gaily as it had from the other side. But a curious thing had happened. The word "joy," usually so brilliant, leaned against the sill dark and dull. The sun

87

was still beaming down into the little piece...but why were the once-vibrant colors so downcast? Then I saw it. The curtain I had drawn now served as a backdrop that prevented the light from filtering through. Shining *in* was not enough to light it; the sun had to shine *through.*

People are like stained glass, I thought. *We're not meant to let God's light simply shine in on us—we must let it shine through us. Otherwise joy will darken and fade away.* As I returned inside, the kitchen curtain was not the only thing I had resolved to open wide. It occurred to me that there were a few curtains of my own, drawn between myself and others, that needed opening as well.

Dear Lord, please let Your light shine through *me...and* onto *others.* —SUE MONK KIDD

---

22 THURSDAY
A man of understanding shall attain unto wise counsels... —PROVERBS 1:5

Her name was Miss Hutton and she taught American History in my high-school years. Her reputation was one of toughness. She gave spot quizzes, lots of homework, and high grades were hard to come by. Assigned to one of her classes, I began the semester filled with apprehension.

But I grew to like Miss Hutton. Sure she was tough and the class difficult, but that was because she loved her subject, and she could bring her students around to loving it too.

The next term I was again assigned to Miss Hutton, but the class was overloaded with students and some of us would have to be transferred to another teacher. The class advisor came into the room and announced that there were vacancies in a class across the hall. We all knew the teacher of that class. She did little teaching. There were no tests. No homework. Most of the time she merely showed movies to the students.

When the advisor asked who among us wanted to be assigned to this teacher, dozens of hands shot up. I noticed the fallen expression on Miss Hutton's face...I even wondered if there were a few tears about to spill. So I decided to remain with her class. It was hard work, but I thanked my lucky stars for the opportunity.

They call it "tough love," don't they? And for that privilege, I'll be tough-skinned any day.

Father, I'm listening. Be firm with me.   —GLENN KITTLER

---

23 FRIDAY
Behold, I have graven thee upon the palms of my hands...   —ISAIAH 49:16

When I first read that God has graven us on the palms of His hands, I thought it quite a strange idea.

Then one day I met a doctor who had inked several names and phone numbers on one of his hands. "Why have you done that?" I asked him curiously.

"Oh," he replied, "these are special people whom I absolutely must not forget today."

Ah, I thought to myself, *now I understand.*

How special are we to God? We're so special that He has counted the hairs of our heads. We're so special that He has known us from our mothers' wombs. We're so special that He has our names written on the palms of His hands. Yes, we can be certain that we are those whom God will not forget today!

So wherever you are, whatever you are doing—will you be sure to remember that?

Thank You, Lord, for Your attention to me—today and always.
     —PATRICIA HOUCK SPRINKLE

24 SATURDAY
Forgive, and ye shall be forgiven...   —LUKE 6:37

I was wrong...and I knew it. It had happened in an emotional moment and now I regretted it.

"Phil," I said, "I'm sorry I flew off the handle during the game—and sorry for what I said."

"Okay," Phil said. "Forget it."

But I couldn't, and I couldn't believe that Phil had either. So when I met him in the dinner line that night, I apologized again... and later that evening, again.

That's when he pulled me aside. "You don't have to keep apologizing, Jeff. Really, I've forgiven you. But I don't think you've forgiven yourself."

I guess I hadn't—it all seemed too easy, getting rid of a wrong so quickly, so painlessly. And so I'd made myself feel guilty and then tried to satisfy that guilt—to pay the price, so to speak. But it hadn't worked. I was still paying when Phil put an end to my charade and made me really look at the meaning of forgiveness.

A few years have gone by since that day, and yet sometimes I still have to convince myself that I'm worthy to receive the merciful forgiveness the Bible tells us God has promised: "Man, thy sins are forgiven thee" (Luke 5:20).

It's true! It's real! And yes, Jeff, it really is that simple!

Thank You, O Father, for the forgiveness that reaches beyond our grasp... and then for helping us to grasp it.   —JEFF JAPINGA

25 SUNDAY
Be not forgetful to entertain strangers...

—HEBREWS 13:2

I recently read of a man who was traveling through the South on a Sunday morning many years ago. He was alone, a stranger far from home, and he decided to stop at a small village church for the morning worship service. The members of the congregation greeted him warmly, and their ready acceptance of him soon dispelled the deep loneliness he had been carrying.

Although his later travels never took him to that locale again, he always remembered the special welcome and the friendly people. When he died in New Jersey at the age of ninety, his attorney informed the church's pastor that the old man had bequeathed his large fortune to the little church.

"One Sunday when he was sad and lonely, he stopped in your church," the attorney wrote. "You took him in with no thought that he was a stranger nor with any regard for his position. He never forgot the kindness and warmth you showed him."

The story made me pause and wonder. Is there a stranger in my church? Or in the place where I work? A newcomer in my neighborhood? If so, perhaps he too is lonely and in need of a friend.

To be remembered in someone's will for a kindness once shown is truly rewarding, but how much more rewarding is the blessed assurance that we have obeyed our Saviour when we reach out to the lonely stranger with warmth and welcome in our hearts.

Lord, I will be alert for that someone You would have me befriend today. —DRUE DUKE

---

26 MONDAY

Let us hold fast...our faith without wavering; (for he is faithful that promised;)... —HEBREWS 10:23

My five-year-old cat Jessica was terrified of the vacuum cleaner from the time she was a kitten. Often the vacuum and I would surprise her by entering a room where she was sleeping. Instantly her eyes would flash open, her ears flatten in fear and she would dart out of the room in panic.

One day as I took out the vacuum, I spoke to her in my most gentle, reassuring voice: "It's all right, Jess. Trust me. You're okay.

Stay put, kitty." The usual terror filled her eyes, and her ears flattened back, but she remained curled up on the bed as I vacuumed around it. This happened again...and then again. Finally the day came when she would open one sleepy eye, glance at the vacuum in ho-hum fashion and continue her nap.

I learned something from Jessica. You can't outrun fear. Sometimes you just have to stand your ground. Jessica ran for five long years but now she can claim victory over her mortal enemy, the vacuum cleaner. Like Jessica, I'm learning to heed that Voice that comes to reassure me when something frightening looms on the horizon of my life and I am tempted to flee in panic. Standing fast is difficult at times, but when the victory comes—as it surely will— what joy and peace we have won!

If there is something in your life that you find frightening, try to remember the courage of Jessica—who conquered fear only when she let herself be reassured.

Father, with Your loving support, I stand fast today.

—MARION BOND WEST

---

27 TUESDAY

But we have this treasure in earthen vessels, that the excellency of the power may be of God, and not of us.
—II CORINTHIANS 4:7

Several weeks ago my wife Shirley began to tap our maple trees for sap as part of a local school project. And this morning I have been the beneficiary of some mighty tasting syrup spread lavishly over hot, buttery pancakes.

Of course one doesn't just plug a tree, collect the sap and pour it over pancakes. No, indeed. Shirley boiled gallons upon gallons of the woody liquid for hours on end—until I feared the wallpaper would fall right off our kitchen walls! I learned, to my amazement, that it takes about forty gallons of sap to make one gallon of syrup. No wonder pure maple syrup is so costly.

Observing a pan of sap steaming on the stove the other day, I was struck by a parallel in human relationships. At first impression some people we meet seem to be less than attractive, less than interesting, less than appealing. Like the pallid liquid that comes from the maple trees, there is little hint of a hidden dimension. But as time goes on, with the addition of a little care and concern—with "distillation", shall we say?—we find that inside of every individual there is always some heavenly sweetness—placed there by the very same One who hides the sweetness in the maple trees.

Father, let me always remember that each of my brothers is Your child, fashioned with Your love. —FRED BAUER

---

28 WEDNESDAY
...Call upon me in the day of trouble: I will deliver thee... —PSALM 50:15

Years ago I worked in a television studio, where I was experienced in operating the television control board with its myriad of monitors, meters and buttons.

One day my boss said, "You'll have to handle the next program alone. Call me if you need me."

"Oh, I can handle it," I assured him.

Shortly after he departed, a piece of film broke and although the program itself continued without interruption, I was frantically pulling —by hand—2,160 feet of film into the room, where it coiled and spiraled itself into billowing black bubbles.

Now I'll stop here for a moment to ask—have you ever seen the disorganized and messy squiggles that a small child makes with a pencil on paper? Well, that's the way the control room looked when my boss returned.

He was aghast. Weakly I said, "I did my best."

With great control, he quietly answered, "Doing your best should have meant that you sent for me."

Looking around at the mountains of loose film, I knew he was right. Do you suppose that's really what our Heavenly Father wants to tell us when He sees us making a mess of things and trying to correct them on our own?

Teach me, Father, not to be too proud to call on You when I need help.
—ISABEL CHAMP

---

29 THURSDAY
Thou wilt shew me the path of life: in thy presence is fulness of joy; at thy right hand there are pleasures for evermore. —PSALM 16:11

My friend Mary Ann sometimes mentions what she calls a "Sam-ism" of mine: "Life has to be fun—or I refuse to participate." I said those words in recollection of a chilly November night when there was no hot water in my apartment house.

My cousin Diane was spending the night with me, and I felt it my duty as a hostess to provide her with a hot bath. Embarrassed by the inconvenience, I heated water on the stove. When it was boiling, I poured it into the tub, causing billowing clouds of steam to rise up in an engulfing blanket. Then I ran a little cold water in the tub so that Diane wouldn't be burned.

"What a great bath!" I heard her call out a few minutes later. "With all this steam, it's like being in a sauna. What fun!"

I had never thought of those stove-heated baths as being special in any way, and certainly I hadn't thought of them as *fun.* I decided then and there that I would henceforth regard them as joyous experiences until the boiler was repaired. I could pretend that I was a pioneer taking a sauna, or a traveler in some faraway exotic place, anything to put some humor into the situation.

Is there an annoyance or inconvenience grating on your mind

today? Why not try to use your spirit of adventure to conquer it? That's why the Lord gave us laughter and fun, to help us overcome.

Father, thank You for the gift of laughter that helps us over the rough spots. —SAMANTHA McGARRITY

---

30 FRIDAY
...And all the members of that one body, being many, are one body... —I CORINTHIANS 12:12

For three years we have needed a prayer meeting in our church. You could ask anybody—we all agreed that *somebody* should start one.

Then last Sunday two young men stood up. "We're going to meet for an hour of prayer each Wednesday night," they announced. "You are all welcome to join us." Members of the congregation were elated.

Why didn't this happen sooner? I wondered. Because we were waiting for *somebody* to do it—and *somebody* was really on an extended vacation.

Now some of us are talking about a few other things we've been wanting *somebody* to do around here: initiate a Bible-study project, begin a ministry to our Spanish-speaking neighbors, start a program for the young adults. Perhaps this wishful thinking might actually be a hint that it's time for us to rise up and *be somebody*. Could God be calling *my* name?

I'm coming, Father.

When You speak, Lord, Your servant answers.
—PATRICIA HOUCK SPRINKLE

31 SATURDAY
Lay not up for yourself treasures upon earth...
—*MATTHEW 6:19*

A grand happening took place recently at our house: The penny bank overflowed! After years of docilely accepting casual pennies, the big jar reached full capacity and would take no more. Not one additional cent could we squeeze into it.

So we emptied it out onto a towel—a huge mound of copper, some pennies new and gleaming, some green with age, here and there a dingy dime that had crept in by mistake.

Everyone watched, fascinated, including some of the neighborhood children. Someone recalled that sixty-eight pounds of pennies equal a hundred dollars. Did we have sixty-eight pounds? Not quite, but almost. Such excitement! Even after tithing, we'd all be rich!

"And the best part," I said, "is that we never even missed the pennies all the while we were dropping them in the jar."

"Yes," said the precocious little nine-year-old from next door. "It's like good deeds, isn't it? Or kind words. You drop them here and there without hardly noticing. But when the time finally comes to add them all up, you have a treasure in heaven."

A treasure in heaven! Well-spoken, little Katherine. And now let's see what each of us can do to add to that treasure in the course of this new, shining day that lies ahead—as we set out to replenish our coinage of good deeds and kind words.

Today, Lord, let me be generous with the small coins of kindness.
—ARTHUR GORDON

Praise Diary for March

1

2

3

4

5

6

7

8

9

10

11

12

13

14

15

16

17

18

19

20

21

22

23

24

25

26

27

28

29

30

31

April

S	M	T	W	T	F	S
1	2	3	4	5	6	7
8	9	10	11	12	13	14
15	16	17	18	19	20	21
22	23	24	25	26	27	28
29	30					

The last thing I remember
Before I went to sleep,
Was the whisper of a warm April rain
Softening the windswept March landscape.
And now, pulling the curtain back
On this bright new day,
I gasp.
A magnolia that hours ago
Was just a barren clutch of limbs
Is now an extravagance of pink blooms.
I can smell, even from my upstairs window,
The womanly scent of rich brown earth
Just now released from frost's
    faltering grasp.
The sight…the smell…the feel of
April's moistness against my cheek
And curling in my nostrils…
"Oh, God," I call,
Your name bursts from my lips
Without my mind summoning it.
"Oh, mighty God, how great a gift it is
To have my senses quicken to
The first fine day of Spring!"

James McDermott

GUIDEPEOPLE: A Living Parable for April

1 SUNDAY

Thy faith hath made thee whole. —MATTHEW 9:22

The late Grace Oursler was one of *Guideposts'* early editors and a profound force in shaping its spiritual quality. When I met the widow of the famed writer-editor Fulton Oursler, she was engaged in a long war with ill health. And what a glorious battle that was, for Grace was a courageous fighter.

"I've often wondered," she said once, "why my prayers for others get such prompt attention, while personal requests seem to go begging." She was not complaining; just making an observation, for then she added, "I've concluded God has some special use for my illness."

I think she knew what that use was, for on another occasion she talked about the Catholic shrine at Lourdes in France where so many remarkable healings had been recorded.

"When patients arrive there," she told me, "they don't just lie around. They're expected to work." Then Grace explained how the sick are required to tend to the needs of their fellow sufferers and to pray for both the sick *and* the well.

"The strange phenomenon of Lourdes," Grace said, "is how quickly the sick forget about themselves. When that happens, their prayers are like dynamite! That's when many of the healings happen."

Grace knew that God answers prayer and that the beautiful mystery is that He does it in His own way. For Grace Oursler was surely healed, not physically, but spiritually. By serving people she was made spiritually whole.

And that is the greatest healing of all.

Only through You, Lord, am I made whole. —VAN VARNER

2 MONDAY
Ponder the path of thy feet, and let all thy ways be established. —PROVERBS 4:26

Recently I made a long trip through mid-Africa, principally by car. From the very first day I noticed that every few miles along the road there stood some sign of religious significance. It might be a simple cross made of reeds or a small shrine, complete with a clay figure of Jesus and bedecked with flowers.

I commented to my missionary companion: "You must have a lot of pious people around here. I've never seen so many shrines."

"Those aren't shrines," he said. "They're bus stops."

"Bus stops?"

"Yes," he replied. "In Africa we don't have definite bus schedules and sometimes people have to wait many hours for a bus, or even a couple of days."

"But why..." I asked.

"Well," he answered with a chuckle, "when you're hanging around for a long time with nothing else to do, you might as well pray."

I thought then of the many hours I had spent in waiting for a bus or a train, my impatience growing steadily. How much wiser I would have been had I spent that time in prayer. How about you?

Lord, may my path be filled with "bus stops"—small moments of quiet pauses for prayer to You. —GLENN KITTLER

3 TUESDAY
Thou shalt not take the name of the Lord thy God in vain... —EXODUS 20:7

Although my Aunt Bessie was a regular church-goer, she had fallen into the habit of invoking God's name in every other sentence.

If Aunt Bessie heard bad news, her reflex reaction was to exclaim, "Oh, my God!" If someone called and asked her to go shopping, her reaction might be, "Oh, God, I'm not dressed yet." She was quite taken aback when it was pointed out to her that such use of God's name constituted a violation of the Third Commandment.

For a time after that she was very careful. Then one day she became upset over a mislaid bank statement. "Oh, God, I had it in my hands only ten minutes ago! Now where is it?"

"Aunt Bessie," I said, "there you go again—profaning God's name. We're supposed to hallow and reverence His name—if we are His children."

She drew herself up stiffly. "Well, I am certainly one of His children...." She paused and then shook her head with determination. "I know you're right," she agreed. "From now on I'll reverence His name. You'll see."

And she did—for several weeks—until one night at dinner she tipped over the gravy bowl on a white linen tablecloth. Instinctively it came out: "Oh, Go-o—" The word stuck and Aunt Bessie froze. She sucked in her breath and peered covertly around the table. We waited. And then came "—d, thank You for good gravy!" With that, her head came up proudly, a triumphant smile on her face!

And a hearty round of laughter and applause filled the room.

Teach us to use Your Name, God, only in love and reverence.

—SAM JUSTICE

---

4 WEDNESDAY
Behold, the Lord's hand is not shortened, that it cannot save; neither his ear heavy, that it cannot hear...
—ISAIAH 59:1

As I stood at my kitchen sink one day, my thoughts were nearly paralyzed by a problem that I couldn't seem to solve. The problem was too big...I was too small. Surely God wouldn't have any interest in it. Engulfed in self-pity and doubt, I decided not to even approach my Father.

I leaned forward and stared out the window, tense and miserable. Then a slight movement caught my eye. Scratching around there in the dry leaves on the ground was a young brown wood thrush, determined to unearth a tasty morsel. He refused to abandon his busy efforts even though he obviously wasn't finding any food. Not even one tiny bug. *Scratch, scratch, scratch,* the tiny sounds continued.

"Oh!" I cried softly. Just as I had heard the little thrush's attempts to fulfill his needs, why wouldn't my Father hear my pleas too? I ran outside with a bag of birdseed and filled the empty feeder. Back in the house and once more at the window, I watched the tiny bird light on the feeder and begin to feast hungrily. Still watching him, my small, scratchy prayer began—

Father, O Father...   —MARION BOND WEST

---

5 THURSDAY
But be ye doers of the word, and not hearers only...
—JAMES 1:22

Have you ever been in Joppa? In Scripture, Joppa was a port of departure for two men—two men who heard a word from God and reacted in opposite ways.

Jonah sailed from Joppa when God ordered him to Nineveh, a big, bustling city that frightened him. Yes, Jonah ran away from God.

Peter too left Joppa. God ordered him to go visit Cornelius, the Roman centurian—a Gentile, and unclean. Peter was reluctant upon first hearing the word from God, but he didn't flee as Jonah did. Instead, he obeyed.

I stand in Joppa more than I like to admit—when I read a word in Scripture that puts me in a dilemma and I would rather not obey... when I encounter someone who makes demands on me that I would rather ignore... when I am wearied by my children and long for respite from them... when I meet someone who is different from me and I am hesitant to share the Gospel with him.

There I stand on the shores of Joppa. I look first at the stern of Jonah's retreating boat and then to Peter's obedient steps. I must follow one of them. Which will it be?

Strengthen me today, Lord, and help me to obey Your every command.
                                            —PATRICIA HOUCK SPRINKLE

---

6 FRIDAY
...Comfort one another...   —I THESSALONIANS 4:18

"The doctor will be with you shortly," the receptionist assured me with a pleasant smile.

"Shortly" could be roughly translated into half an hour (if I were lucky), experience told me. Resigned, I sat down in the waiting room. Then I noticed a little book: *What To Do Until the Doctor Comes.* Curious, I picked it up.

"To make the waiting seem less long," the author advised, "take your mind off the reason for your visit by doing something constructive. Write a note to a friend—bring your address book up to date—list those who would appreciate a call. *Seek out someone near you to comfort at this moment.*"

Seated next to me was a woman crippled with arthritis. Slumped in a chair across the room was a frightened-looking child. And I was there for nothing more than an annual check-up!

My name was called all too quickly—because suddenly I was having a wonderful time, as were the woman and the little girl. We three were just chatting away, somehow comforting one another with friendly words, smiles and gentle expressions of reassurance. That day I learned that time is not measured only by minutes—but also by the way we use it to help one another!

Lord Jesus, let me bring comfort to others today, in Your service.
                                            —JUNE MASTERS BACHER

7 SATURDAY
*Come in, thou blessed of the Lord; wherefore standest
thou without?* —GENESIS 24:31

I spend my weekends with my brother John, who is mentally ill. Because I was afraid that he might become restless and cause a disturbance in church or that the long service might be a strain on him, we've made it a habit to spend Sundays hiking in the mountains and then sharing a quiet Bible reading and prayer there in the woods.

But on one recent weekend we were in New York City, where we leisurely meandered up Fifth Avenue for a change of scenery. It was a lovely sunny day and we were enjoying the bustling crowds and having a good time window-shopping. But when we reached Saint Patrick's Cathedral, we stopped. Although it was a Saturday, there was a service in progress, and so we entered and stole quietly into a back pew. John sat very still and kept his head bowed throughout the service.

That evening when I asked him what part of the day he had particularly enjoyed, he answered, "Going into church."

It was then I realized that despite my good intentions, I had probably been denying my brother a portion of the spiritual comfort he needed—that of actually being in church and experiencing the fellowship of other Christians, worshiping as part of the Body of Christ.

Now I'm planning to reorganize our weekends—not only because I've recognized John's need to visit God's house—but my own too.

Heavenly Father, we accept Your invitation.

—SAMANTHA McGARRITY

8

SUNDAY
Love worketh no ill to his neighbour... —ROMANS 13:10

Years ago in Syracuse, New York, I was the young pastor of a church whose congregation included many professors from the university. Because I wanted to impress these learned men and women with my own great mental prowess, my first sermons were filled with big words and lofty abstractions.

After several weeks of this, one of the professors dropped by "just to say hello"—or so he said. A little later he observed rather casually, "You must meet the new minister up the street. Has a refreshing simplicity. Gives them the real stuff. Just tells them about Jesus Christ." Then he mentioned another minister, no longer in town, who tried so hard to impress the university faculty that few people ever got the point he was trying to make.

Well, *I* got the point! From that time on, I started bringing my sermons down to earth.

This Syracuse friend knew the art of constructive criticism. He was able to help without causing anger or resentment. Jesus Christ had the same kind of tact and compassion and He showed it often, especially in the incident with the woman taken in adultery. Jewish law required that the woman be stoned to death, but were Jesus to ask her accusers to show her mercy, He would be breaking the law. "He that is without sin among you," Jesus said, "let him first cast a stone at her" (John 8:7). Jesus let the would-be stone-throwers do the deciding.

That's the positive way to criticize! It's an art we all should try to master.

Lord, let me love with my heart—and my head.

—NORMAN VINCENT PEALE

9 MONDAY
Beloved, let us love one another…   *—I JOHN 4:7*

I received a birthday card last week from a friend with whom I had spent many hours praying, via long-distance phone, over a period of many months. Enclosed with the card was a generous gift certificate to be used at the local Christian store. My first reaction was: "No! I can't accept this. I prayed with him and for him because I wanted to, because I care about him. Praying for him was a joy." Then another friend, Anita, caught me up short. "You say that praying for Bob was a joy because you care about him. Would you deny him the joy of showing that he cares about you? The trouble with you, Marilyn, is that you need to learn to let yourself be loved."

Those two words, *be loved*, lingered in my mind for a moment and then they merged to form one word—*beloved*! Anita was right. To be beloved, one must allow oneself to be loved. Sometimes pride makes it easier for us to give love than to accept it.

Today I visited the Christian store and with Bob's gift certificate I bought a lovely cross on a gold chain—a symbol of a very special friendship and a reminder that the admonition to "love one another" calls upon me to let myself be loved also.

Lord, grant me the humility to accept expressions of love from others with grace and joy.   *—MARILYN MORGAN HELLEBERG*

10 TUESDAY
…Render therefore unto Caesar the things which be Caesar's…   *—LUKE 20:25*

Oh, the misery of income-tax time! It's not so much paying out the money to Uncle Sam (although that's bad enough), it's the agony of doing all the arithmetic, scouting around for misplaced receipts and fumbling through umpteen canceled checks.

But the worst part (and this *always* happens to me) is when you've added everything up, made all the calculations and completed your return, you recheck it once more only to find that your totals don't match. You have to do your whole return again!

The other night, trying to find where I had gone wrong in a column of figures that I'd added three times with three different results, I remembered something that C.S. Lewis once wrote about the nature of sin. He said that it wasn't enough to admit your sins and be sorry. He said that you have to go back, make restitution and set things to rights exactly at the point where they went wrong in the first place. He likened it to a mistake in arithmetic, explaining that you'll never come up with the right answer until you retrace your steps, locate the original error—and correct it!

I know all too well that that's true when I've made a mistake in addition. And I'm willing to wager it's just as true when I've made a mistake in life!

Lord, give us the honesty to admit past mistakes and the courage to go back and correct them. —ARTHUR GORDON

---

11 WEDNESDAY
I will arise and go to my father... —LUKE 15:18

One bright April morning a teenager named Alice left home to return a library book. She didn't come back. Three days later a note from a distant city arrived, saying, "Don't worry about me. I just had to get away." Then in mid-December there was a Christmas card, but no return address.

For over a year I watched the anguish etch its marks on the mother's face, the torment slow the father's steps. I dug deep for new words of comfort and we became daily prayer partners on their daughter's behalf. Then came the July-morning phone call and the heartfelt cries of a jubilant mother.

"Alice called! She's coming home tomorrow!"

"Praise the Lord!" I said happily. "Where has she been all this time?"

"I didn't ask." The woman's voice rang with joy and relief. "I don't care where she's been or what she's done. She's *my child*, and she's coming home!"

When we hung up, I said a quiet prayer of thanksgiving before taking out my Bible to reread the parable of the prodigal son. Then I noticed that a strange thing was happening—I was substituting *my* name for Alice's name as I read the story. I suddenly realized that a huge portion of the treasure of my God-given days had been wasted in frivolity, that I had squandered His blessings, that I had brought pain upon myself, and that the regrets I carried in my heart were of my own doing.

But, I knew, far greater than all my errancy was my Father's love for me, and His forgiveness. All I had to do was to go back to Him. I put the Bible aside and took the first step toward Him—on my knees.

Receive me again, dear Lord. —DRUE DUKE

---

12 THURSDAY

And Jesus came and spake unto them, saying, All power is given unto me in heaven and in earth.
—MATTHEW 28:18

I needed to get away—from the phone, from appointments, from work and pressure. So I rented a little house in Vermont. It was really isolated. I couldn't see another house and there wasn't a church within miles. Then I realized that I had completely overlooked the fact that I would be there over Easter—and alone.

Back home I had always attended sunrise services on Easter morning. *Well, this year I will just have to miss it,* I thought. But wait—why not make do with what I had? Surely I could receive

Christ's message anew...surely the sun would still rise...and, yes, I would surely be there to witness it!

Arising before dawn, I heard the steady sound of rain. *There goes my sunrise,* I thought, saddened. I put on my poncho and trudged outside, flashlight in hand, and headed through the woods. Coming across a small hill, I sat down to await the coming of day.

Then—slowly, steadily—the world grew light. Long streaks of illumination reached through the mists and pushed back the darkness. I couldn't see the sun, but I knew it was there. And I knew that Christ was there and, more, I knew once again that He is *always* present, just as so long ago He promised.

Greeting Easter there alone in the early morning mists, I knew there was no place in the world where I could ever be alone.

No matter how dark my days, Lord, You always come to light the way. —PHYLLIS HOBE

JESUS, THE MASTER STORYTELLER
Parable of the Lamp
Under a Bushel —LUKE 8:16

13 FRIDAY

A wrong turn on the trail had cost us nearly an hour, and by the time we reached our campsite the last vestiges of light had vanished. Hikers in our group struggled to set up tents in the half-light of hand-held flashlights and gas lanterns. Then someone got the idea that that we could improve our vision if we hung the lanterns on the branches of overhanging trees. There, raised from the ground, the lanterns increased our visibility many-fold and we completed our setup in record time.

The incident reminded me of Christ's parable about witnessing to our faith by sharing God's truths. Matthew, Mark and Luke all record Jesus' admonition not to hide our "light" under a bushel (or a bed or a vessel), but it is Luke who spells it out most fully.

"A city that is set on a hill, cannot be hid," he quotes Christ. "Neither do men light a candle and put it under a bushel, but on a candlestick; and it giveth light unto all that are in the house. Let your light so shine before men, that they may see your good works, and glorify your Father, which is in heaven."

When Christians team up, they increase their wattage and together dispel great swaths of darkness. Like the campers pooling their lanterns, we need to cooperatively raise our lights in order to glorify the Light of the World.

Make us reflectors of Your saving Light, not only absorbers of it.
—FRED BAUER

CELEBRATING HOLY WEEK:
Spiritual Windows into the Life of Christ with Sue Monk Kidd

14 **SATURDAY BEFORE PALM SUNDAY**
He that saith he abideth in him ought himself so to walk, even as he walked. —I JOHN 2:6

One day recently at the approach of Holy Week, I walked through my church and looked at the beautiful stained-glass windows, each one depicting an event from the life of Christ. Of course I'd seen them many times before, but somehow I'd viewed them only as decoration. This time they seemed to draw me beyond the art, beckoning me right into His life itself. *Like spiritual windows to His time*, I mused. *I'm surrounded by the unfolding of Christ's life.*

And I wondered. Could it be possible for me to experience anew —and with greater understanding—Christ's journey through life on earth by imaginatively entering the scenes of these lovely windows?

111

Could I view the events that crowded in upon Him not as dusty old happenings of the past, but as fresh and living realities that might touch my life today? Were there any long-lost messages hidden in those window scenes that could help me to find new meaning in Easter?

In this Holy Week I'm going to take a unique spiritual journey. I hope you'll join me in this venture of the imagination and step into the past by entering a different stained-glass window each day. It is my further hope that the scenes will come to life around us, enabling us to actually partake in His days as they might have been.

Come. Draw close. Let us together relive the life of our Saviour as we follow the holy paths upon which He trod.

Lord Jesus, make me a faithful follower of Thee.

—SUE MONK KIDD

15

PALM SUNDAY
For God so loved the world, that he gave his only begotten Son, that whosoever believeth in him should not perish, but have everlasting life. —JOHN 3:16

It's the second window on the left-hand side of the church, the one with Mary, Joseph and the Baby Jesus in the stable. As I sit here before it, studying its fractured light, I wonder: *What can the Nativity possibly say to me at the beginning of Easter week?* Hoping to discover the answer, I set forth upon a journey that takes me deep into the window itself.

Entering the little dwelling, I look about, recalling it as the place lent to Him by an innkeeper of Bethlehem. In the corner of the stable stands a donkey—the stalwart little beast that has brought Him here with His mother. And suddenly my mind leaps ahead, past thirty-three years, to another place that, oddly enough, would also be lent to Him—a tomb. I recall His last days, especially the

112

Palm Sunday ride. Twice it was a lowly donkey that carried Him toward His destiny.

Turning, I see Easter mirrored in the baby, too. This One—Who emptied Himself to lie on straw in all humility and love—would die emptying Himself upon a cross in humility and love. *Truly*, I think to myself, *His beginning foreshadows His end.* Standing here at the manger, I am overpowered by the sense of where the course of events is leading. I feel the joy of it...I savor a veiled hint of something to come. Even the angel over Bethlehem who brings the Good News leads my thoughts to the angel who will later stand watch in an empty sepulchre.

And now I know that I have found the hidden message I seek: *In every life—yours and mine—wherever Christ is born, God plants the signs of a resurrection to come!* Yes, Easter is foreshadowed in *our* lives just as surely as it was foretold in His life here in the manger at Bethlehem.

I leave the little stable, stirred by this new realization: if we but look for the promise of resurrection, we can surely find it. In the springtime...in church windows everywhere...in the Bethlehem manger...in our heart...where Christ is born and reborn.

What better way to enter Holy Week than to make one's heart a manger in which to welcome our Lord?

Dear Jesus, come. My humble heart awaits you.

—SUE MONK KIDD

---

16 **MONDAY**

And when they found him not, they turned back again to Jerusalem, seeking him...after three days they found him in the temple, sitting in the midst of the doctors... —LUKE 2:45-46

Today a peacefulness pervades the church. It is in sharp contrast to the atmosphere in the Jerusalem temple on the day that

Jesus attacked the money-changers by overthrowing their tables and driving them out. Here the air is as quiet as a whisper. I gaze at the stained-glass window depicting another episode in Christ's life— "The Boy Jesus in the Temple"—and allow the scene to come to life in my mind's eye.

Only twelve years old, Jesus stands among gray-bearded doctors of law, listening intently and astonishing them with His understanding. But I remember that an intense search is going on out beyond the temple walls. For three whole days Jesus has been missing. His parents are scouring the streets of Jerusalem, looking for Him.

The mother in me shakes her head at this little boy. I recall the time that my own son was lost for thirty minutes in a shopping mall and the clammy fear that gripped me until I found him. *Poor Mary*, I whisper. As I stand close to this child Who is the Christ but still so young and tender, my heart goes out to His mother. But then suddenly two breathless figures burst upon the scene. Mary rushes past Joseph to her son, reaching out for Him. Young Jesus' face fills with love as He embraces her.

As I watch this loving reunion, it strikes me that this is a far different Jesus than the One Who will upset this same temple twenty-one years later. This is the youthful Jesus, the dutiful son, and yet the Son whose words even now foretell His mission as he asks his relieved parents, "Didn't you know that I would be here, taking care of my Father's business?"

While I sigh in gratitude that Mary and Joseph's search is over, I know that deep in my own soul the search goes on—the search that will bring me to Jesus today, and every day. And I must search not only for the tender Jesus Who welcomes me with an embrace, but for the mature Jesus as well, the Jesus Who speaks to me with the authority of His Father's Word. . . the Jesus Who comes to overthrow the complacencies that lodge within my own heart.

Lord Jesus, may I serve as a temple for Your Father's business.

—SUE MONK KIDD

17 TUESDAY

...Jesus came from Nazareth of Galilee, and was baptized of John in Jordan. —MARK 1:9

Today our window depicts the baptism of Jesus. As I enter this scene, I can almost hear the water lapping against the banks of the Jordan....

From out of the crowd standing along the shore, a man strides forward and into the river toward John. A hush falls upon the throng, as though it has sensed something unusual about this man.

"I have need to be baptized by *You*," John declares to Him, "and yet You come to *me?*" Jesus smiles at him and nods, and in one quick and mysterious moment, He is baptized by John the Baptist.

With this act something momentous is inaugurated into the world: Jesus' public ministry. As He wades away, the waters of the Jordan lapping about His legs, I notice from the corner of my eye that a dove is descending from the sky. It circles His head, and then a voice from Heaven pierces every heart: "This is my beloved Son."

I think now of how—on this day of Holy Week—His public ministry came to an abrupt end. On this Tuesday He finished His last public appearance in the temple and walked back to the Mount of Olives. There would be no more teaching the crowds, no more laying hands on the sick, no more feeding the hungry masses on a hillside. As He quietly walked away from it all, I wonder if perhaps there wasn't a dove winging through the darkening skies of Bethany. I would like to believe that the same symbol of God's love and nearness was present at the end of His Son's ministry as it was in the beginning.

As I reflect on the sweep of Jesus' ministry, I gaze at the stained-glass river and am reminded of my own baptism. And suddenly I am struck with the realization that it, too, was meant as another beginning for Jesus...for whenever one is baptized, His ministry is launched anew.

I turn away and leave the church, the new-found challenge of my own baptism resounding within me. Outside I cast a smiling glance toward the sky and seem to hear the echo that lies deep in the heart of every Christian: "Thou art my beloved…."

May I be a swift channel for the living waters of Your love, Lord Jesus. —SUE MONK KIDD

---

18 WEDNESDAY
…The good shepherd giveth his life for the sheep.
—JOHN 10:11

The last Wednesday of Christ's life was a day of quiet preparation. In only two days He would be gone, and He used this precious time to ready His disciples for His departure from the world. But I wonder how prepared they really were. And, more to the point, on this day of preparation how can I prepare *myself*? These questions fill my mind as I make my way to the stained-glass window in the far back corner of the church.

Of all, this one tugs at me the most. Possibly it's the gentle expression on the face of Jesus, or the way he holds the lamb on his shoulder, or the peacefulness of the wide green pasture that seems to slope on endlessly in the background that beckon to me.

The window depicts those remarkable words that Jesus proclaimed at the height of His ministry: "I am the good shepherd." As I recall this loving assurance, I imagine that I am right there, standing on the green hill in the midst of the sheep. Up ahead, Jesus—shepherd's crook in hand—carries a tiny lamb. Perhaps the lamb is wounded, or simply so small that it is in danger of becoming lost. Either way, Jesus carries it on His shoulder, and the sight makes me smile. As He moves across the soft pasture, His white robe fluttering in the breeze, the sheep nudge one another after Him. It is a tender scene, one that vibrates with love.

And, as I ponder it, the rest of Jesus' words come back to me: "The good shepherd giveth his life for the sheep." Here is a Shepherd Who so loves His flock that He will willingly die for it! I wonder whether on that Wednesday long ago, as He tried to prepare His disciples for His death, those close to Him really understood the portent of His words.

Perhaps.

I only know that now—right here—I have come upon the way to prepare myself for the agony that lies just ahead, and to hear anew His words that summon me. I take a step forward...I move with His flock...and together we follow with close steps behind Him.

Loving Jesus, I am prepared to follow You wherever You lead me.

—SUE MONK KIDD

19 MAUNDY THURSDAY
Then cometh Jesus with them unto a place called Gethsemane... —MATTHEW 26:36

Night has fallen upon the church. A lone street light filters through the stained-glass window that depicts Jesus as He kneels in Gethsemane.

The little garden seems to be gripped in an ominous quiet. Only the brook of Kidron gurgles black and swollen in the ravine below. Above, a Passover moon glides high over the olive trees. I steal along the garden path and almost fall over three figures huddled on the ground. Peter, James, John. Each sound asleep.

I walk on for a stone's throw, then stop. There before me He is kneeling beside a boulder, a terrible agony filling his face. "Oh my Father, if it be possible, let this cup pass from me; nevertheless not as I will, but as thou wilt," He pleads. He sags across the boulder, His whole body, it seems, crushed by this awesome moment of refusing to save Himself. Drops of sweat and blood bead His forehead. For an instant I cannot but think that He resembles a child caught in a nightmare.

I run, stumbling toward Him, forgetting my place on this fateful night. Then I do something that I have always longed to do, I lean over and gently wipe His brow. He stares at me with gratitude in His eyes as I back away into the night, into the deep silence of the garden. But as I pass through the gate, I hear His voice moving out of the trees to His sleeping disciples. "Could ye not watch with me one hour?"

Now, sitting here before the darkly glowing window in the empty and silent church, I open my Bible and come to this verse: "And there appeared unto him an angel...strengthening him" (Luke 22:43). And I wonder whether God might not be reminding me of a role that He long ago gave me and that I have been neglecting, for I know that often I am like the three disciples asleep on the path—I fail to keep the watch. Inwardly I may be slumbering when those around me need me most.

All my senses alert, I hear plainly the question that comes rolling out of the mists of Gethsemane toward me: "Will you henceforth stay awake to the suffering of others...and strengthen them in their despair?" I glance up at the window once more, pondering. This is not the lesson that I had expected, but I know that it has been there all along, hidden deep within the lines of agony on His face, waiting for me to reach out to it. *Yes, I will keep the watch from now on*, I answer eagerly. And maybe there will come a time when I too may serve as an "angel" and strengthen one of God's children in a season of agony.

After all, I think as I turn and leave the window, *had I not gone to Him there in the garden of Gethsemane, I could never have wiped His brow.*

Dear Jesus, please let me help You today.　　　—SUE MONK KIDD

20　GOOD FRIDAY
...And they crucified him.　　　—MARK 15:25

I sit alone, staring at the stained-glass window that pictures the Crucifixion. Jesus hangs upon the cross, a somber, red-glassed darkness draped about him. The window radiates suffering. I am reluctant to enter this scene. Nevertheless, I step through the window, not knowing where this journey will lead me....

I stand beneath the nailed body of Christ, my gaze fixed on the ground where a pair of dice have left their mark. A mysterious darkness has fallen across the earth, as though God has momentarily closed His eyes. Under the cloak of this strange eclipse, I gather my courage and look up. Jesus hangs motionless above me, stretched full-length in a shadow. Bleeding.

"Lord, come down from there," I whisper. "This is too much to bear." With enormous effort, His head turns toward me. And I know from the look on His face that He means to see it through— this giving up of His life that we might be saved. I will not watch.

But as I turn away, one single drop of blood falls at my feet. It seems to saturate the ground with His love, and at that moment I behold a fathomless truth: His sacrifice is not only for others—it is for *me*! His life's blood falls upon my path too.

And so I turn back and watch as it happens. I watch as Jesus gives Himself so that I may find my way to God. He is nearly finished. Maybe with this breath. Maybe with the next. The moment seems frozen between heaven and earth. Somewhere nearby I sense the Presence of God bending close, ready to gather up His beloved Son. Then, with all of *my* sins spilling from His heart, He dies. Just now... Jesus dies. I stand on the mound of Calvary and draw in my first breath of salvation, knowing the price that has been paid for it.

And then I let out a long breath as my meditation leads me away from the Crucifixion scene and back into the church, where all is undisturbed—except for the question that seems to echo throughout the quiet sanctuary: "Will you now die for Me?"

I think of the self-centeredness of my days. Could I die to my own desires? Could I deny my ever-demanding self? Could I sacrifice something of that self each day so that another might find the Way to God? I look to the window for strength, knowing now exactly where this journey has led me.

It is time to reach out, take up my cross—and leave.

Undo my selfishness, Lord Jesus, so I may hear the cries in the hearts of others. —SUE MONK KIDD

21

SATURDAY

*And the light shineth in darkness; and the darkness
comprehended it not.* —*JOHN 1:5*

It's a dark, gloomy Saturday, perhaps like that Saturday long ago when the crucified Jesus lay in a tomb.

I pause just outside the chapel, listening to the deep, hollow silence ringing through the dim church, and I am reminded of how silent and dark and still it was within His Saturday tomb. Low, rumbling thunder threatens the sky outside. Then I notice a passage near the stairs to the balcony. Seeking a place in which to meditate, I go through and into a small, beautifully furnished parlor. On one wall there is a splendid stained-glass window. Jesus stands there before a door, a shining lantern in His hand. Beneath is the inscription: "I am the light of the world."

Settling on a sofa behind the window, I place myself inside the scene, standing in the shadows to one side. The lantern in His hand swings to and fro gently, spreading long fingers of light into the distance. A small opening cut high in the door behind Him reveals nothing but darkness on the other side. I'm perplexed. What lies beyond this dark door? And now—but wait. Where is He going? Christ is pulling open the big gloomy door and stepping through, where He is engulfed in the darkness beyond. "Come back, my Lord!" I cry out, forgetting myself for the moment.

And then I wait, watching the door with a terrible sense of sadness. But look! Something unexpected is happening. A faint light begins to flicker from the other side. It grows in intensity until at last a brilliant radiance pours forth from that opening high in the door.

As I sit here gazing into the flood of light, my meditation gradually comes to a close. I know that this window, hidden away here in the little parlor, is a symbolic picture of that Saturday of long ago... for then too it seemed that Christ had been swallowed up in the darkness of the "other side." And what had resembled a dark and forbidding door is actually the door of hope, from which His light shines forth, just as it did from behind the stone that sealed His tomb in the garden outside Jerusalem.

I let these thoughts sift and settle in my mind as I depart into the misting rain outside. What message has this window given me? Something about hoping when there is no reason to hope? Something about trusting in the light of God that comes to us when things seem bleakest? Something about clinging to the promise of victory springing out of defeat?

Yes, all of that. And more.

Lord Jesus, I stand here before Your door of hope. May I enter?

—SUE MONK KIDD

---

22 EASTER SUNDAY

The first day of the week cometh Mary Magdalene early, when it was yet dark, unto the sepulchre, and seeth the stone taken away... —JOHN 20:1

The Resurrection window picturing the risen Christ gleams triumphantly in the little chapel. As I reflect on the radiant message etched in its panes, I place myself in that stained-glass scene...I stand at the edge of a garden.

Dawn is slowly spreading across the sky, mingling with the darkness that hovers over Jerusalem. Soft voices move along a little path through the garden, and soon three women appear in the half-light, speaking in low tones.

"Who will roll away the stone?" one of them asks.

"Perhaps the gardener will help us," another says.

As they pass by, I slip onto the path behind them and follow along unseen. The sun is burning brightly as we come upon the sepulchre. The little band halts abruptly.

"The stone," one whispers. "It has been rolled away!"

No one is in sight and there is something very strange about it all. Even the guards have disappeared. The women move toward the tomb with small, hesitant steps and peer into its darkness. Suddenly a cry shatters the stillness and startles me where I stand concealed among the trees.

"He is gone!"

They look at one another frantically, doubt and fear paralyzing them. Then, as though coming from a dream, they stumble and run away, leaving their spices spilled here on the wet grass. My heart pounds as I creep up to the opening and gaze inside. An empty linen shroud lies on the stone slab like a cocoon that has been shed. I turn and hurry after the women, only to come upon one of them standing beneath a tree, weeping. I stop at a distance, not wanting to intrude.

"Woman, why are you crying?" says a man's voice. I look up to see a figure emerging from the thickness of the garden onto the path beside the woman.

"Sir, if you have taken Him away, please tell me where He is," she pleads through her tears.

A long, silent moment hangs suspended between them. Then he calls her name—"*Mary*."

I have never heard a word shaped with such tenderness. The woman answers Him with the most beautiful word of faith ever known: "*Master!*" From my place in the garden I am filled not only with breathless wonder that He is risen, but with a yearning for this encounter to happen to me too.

The garden fades as my meditation ends and I find myself alone by the window, pondering that wish in my heart. And then I realize that my longing has been granted, for Christ is alive today and He stands upon every path and turning of my life. He comes straight to me too, His Presence so loving that I seem to hear Him speak my name.

This is God's Easter gift to each of us. Now, at this very moment, we can encounter His beloved Son just as Mary did. We can recognize Him deep in our heart and hear His voice as He gently calls our name. And as we raise our head to answer, Easter is truly born.

Master!

—SUE MONK KIDD

23
MONDAY AFTER EASTER

...He was taken up; and a cloud received him out of their sight. —ACTS 1:9

Easter has passed. But I return to the last stained-glass window in this series—"The Ascension of Christ." It marks the culmination of His life on earth. As I enter the high-arching window, the event seems to stir to life....

I join the band of excited followers gathered on a hillside to see Jesus. I push up on my tiptoes and there He is—no more than twenty yards away! In the days since His resurrection, He has made a number of appearances to this little group and they have talked of nothing else. Now they seem to be almost comfortable with Him, as though He were here to stay.

Jesus lifts His arms and a hush sweeps over us. "From now on, you will be my witnesses," He says. "Go forth to all people and all nations, baptizing them and teaching them the things I have commanded you."

A stunned whisper rustles through the crowd. "He speaks as though He is about to depart for good!" protests a man.

Many are shaking their heads. Jesus, seeing their reaction, speaks again: "But I am with you always, even unto the end of the world."

The words are lost on me. For as He speaks, a cloud comes and He is lifted away. I gaze upward for a long, unbelieving moment—transfixed. A sad, glorious miracle is taking place right before my eyes. Christ is departing the world!

"Don't go, Lord!" I almost cry out, nearly forgetting my place.

No one moves. We stare into the empty white sky. Finally I catch the echo of His last words: "I am with you always." But how? Hasn't He left? I turn and regard the little group around me, and then the mystery gently begins to clear away. *His Presence will live on in the world through us,* I think to myself, *we who have heard His words.* And with that, His commandment that we go out into the world and bring others into the fold takes on new meaning.

123

"Why do you stand looking into the heavens?" ask two men in our midst.

With the question, my meditation comes to a close. And as I gaze at and through the stained-glass window, I see beyond, far out into the world where so many still await His Presence. *Why am I sitting here*, I wonder, *staring up into the stained-glass sky?*

Then I stand up. It has been a long journey, and I am strangely refreshed. Thank you for having joined me. We have come full circle—and we can never return to the place from whence we started. We have witnessed too many miracles, too many wondrous events. As I make my way toward the door now, the lessons of this Holy Week come flooding upon me, and I pause, bowing my head in gratitude for each one...and especially for the final message I have just been given. I know now that I had been seeking it all along.

I open the door, step through, and...*out into the world*...vowing that He can forever number me among His faithful disciples.

O Lord Jesus, send me forth today, my spirit renewed, my faith strengthened, Your Word my commandment.

—SUE MONK KIDD

---

24 TUESDAY

...A man can receive nothing, except it be given him from heaven. —JOHN 3:27

I was driving south through northern Michigan on my way to spend the Easter weekend with friends in Grand Rapids.

A light snow began to fall, gradually growing heavier and heavier. At the next small town I decided I had better stop for the night. The only place that showed any sign of life was the barber shop.

"Everything's closed," the barber told me. "You can wait out the storm here if you like."

There was nothing else I could do. A couple of hours later the barber said, "Why don't you come upstairs and join us for supper?" I followed.

Late night came and the barber, apologizing for not having an extra room in which to put me up, took me down the street to a small frame house.

"Mrs. Miller," he said to the elderly woman who opened the door, "this man is stranded for the night. Do you think he might use your son's old room this evening?"

She smiled at me. "Certainly," she said. "Glad to help."

She led me to a small bedroom off the kitchen, where I spent the rest of the night. In the morning Mrs. Miller invited me to join her over a cup of coffee.

"They've cleared the road but I'll bet your car is buried. I have a shovel you can use."

My car was indeed buried and as I began to dig it out, two teenagers came along with shovels and pitched in to help. When the car was clear, I offered to pay the boys, but they refused to take any money. I returned to give Mrs. Miller her shovel and to pay for the use of her room, but she would not accept my offer. I went to the barber to thank him and to pay for my supper, but he waved my money away.

It was a few hours later, when I passed beyond the fringe of the storm and was on a clear, dry road, that I realized what had actually happened. I had just witnesed the Easter message come to pass! *I was hungry, and the people fed me; I was a stranger, and they took me in; I was stranded, and they freed me.*

Then I realized what day it was. Friday. *Good Friday.* I looked up at the clear blue sky and said, "No, Lord, You did not die in vain."

Father, every day let my actions toward others carry Your Easter message of kindliness. —GLENN KITTLER

25 WEDNESDAY
I am crucified with Christ: nevertheless I live...
—GALATIONS 2:20

Last winter a friend whose son had been killed in Vietnam said to me, "I don't know why God allows such things to happen. My son was a fine, loving person. Why did he have to die because of someone else's hatred?"

Although I prayed with Jeanette, she seemed unable to let go of the sharp-toothed resentment lodged in her heart.

Then, a few days after Easter, I received a letter from her in which she wrote: "On Good Friday, as our minister talked about God's Son having been killed for the sins of the world, it suddenly struck me that *that* wasn't fair either. Why should God's Son, Who is *perfect* love, have died for others' hatreds? And yet He did. With that in mind, I put my bitterness up there on the cross with Jesus, and suddenly all of my resentment seemed to melt under His sacrifice for us. I feel alive again—somehow resurrected."

Jeanette's letter made me think about my own pockets of bitterness and injustice that I nurse, such as the time I was falsely accused...the preferential treatment that other employee seemed to receive...the day that someone else got credit for my good deed.

No, life *isn't* always fair. That's why Jesus died for us.

Take away my bitterness, Lord, that I may truly live in Your grace. —MARILYN MORGAN HELLEBERG

26 THURSDAY
Be of good courage and He shall strengthen your heart. —PSALM 31:24

When I was about thirteen, I had the privilege of attending a small boarding school which was presided over by a white-

126

haired headmaster, Father James L. Whitcomb. He was, to me, precisely what a father should be—wise, always available, and the kind of man who'd put his arm around you and give you big grizzly hugs. He never scolded, and he had his own special way of teaching.

One afternoon I was talking with him in his study. I can't recall what drastic adolescent problem triggered the conversation, but it had something to do with how hard it is sometimes to stand up for principle against the crowd. I know this because Father Whitcomb jumped up impulsively, went to a cabinet and grabbed a ball of string and a green, dime-store kite.

"Come on, Van," he called, "let's fly this thing!"

We rushed out and up a hill to the football field where he held the string while I raised the kite over my head and ran with it. When the kite was aloft, nodding over the landscape, its rag-bag tail waving happily, the two of us stood watching, our heads tilted upwards.

"Funny thing," Father Whitcomb said, almost as if he were musing to himself, "you and I wouldn't be Christians today if Jesus hadn't stood up for His faith against those who wanted to do Him in. Don't you think that's so?"

"Yes, sir," I said, surprised that we'd returned to our earlier conversation.

"And that kite," Father Whitcomb said, trolling the ball of string, "that kite wouldn't be soaring up there now if it weren't struggling against the wind, would it?"

Didn't I tell you that Father Whitcomb had his own special way of teaching?

Heavenly Father, let me always fight the good fight.

—VAN VARNER

27 FRIDAY

Study to shew thyself approved unto God, a workman that needeth not be ashamed, rightly dividing the word of truth. —II TIMOTHY 2:15

Almost every day our high-school journalism teacher told us to "Always remember the five W's." *Who? What? When? Where? Why?* And if possible, we were to add an H for *How?*

Surely most of us have heard of these five W's through the years. Undoubtedly they're still the backbone of many a writing course— and maybe they're even used in other classes too.

But have you ever applied the five W's to your Bible reading?

Ask yourself, "*Who*'s writing this verse and to *whom* is it addressed? *What* was the occasion? *Where* was it written? *Why?*" And then, "*How* can I apply it to my own life?"

I've always found that this is an excellent way to study—and, more important, to help me remember what I've read. Why don't you look for the five W's as you go through DAILY GUIDEPOSTS this year?

For starters, try it out on the verse above!

Every day as I ponder Your Word, Lord, open my understanding.

—ISABEL CHAMP

28 SATURDAY

Watch ye, stand fast in the faith, quit you like men, be strong. —I CORINTHIANS 16:13

I want to tell you about a friend of mine. In a lot of ways Jack and I are a lot alike. First of all, Jack loves athletics just as much as I do. All kinds. In fact, given the chance, I think he'd play ball twenty-four hours a day. But a chance is one thing Jack hasn't always had.

In high school he was injured while playing football and unable to finish the season. Then in his freshman year at college a concussion ended his football season again—and after that he spent most of the basketball season on crutches. And this season—please, don't ask Jack to hang it up—he developed a rare form of arthritis after coming down with the flu. Not only couldn't he play, he had to drop out of school for a while.

Now I'm not telling you all this to gain sympathy for Jack. In fact, he would probably be embarrassed to know that I wrote this. No, I tell you because there's another way—a more important way—in which Jack and I are alike. We both know this: To play the game— the game of life—is to risk the pain and disappointment that come with injury, defeat or failure. But through faith, Jack always continues to seek the joy in life...and it's from him that I've learned how faith strengthens us to endure life's hardships.

If he possibly can, Jack will play basketball next season—because he loves life more than he fears the hurt it may bring. In a way he reminds me of the apostle Paul's words: "I have fought a good fight...I have kept the faith... (II Timothy 4:7).

What more can any of us do?

Father, thank You for those who teach us how to wage the "good fight" of faith. —JEFF JAPINGA

---

29 SUNDAY
Although the fig tree shall not blossom, neither shall fruit be in the vines; the labour of the olive shall fail, and the fields shall yield no meat; the flock shall be cut off from the fold, and there shall be no herd in the stalls: Yet I will rejoice in the Lord, I will joy in the God of my salvation. —HABAKKUK 3:17-18

My husband had been called to a new job and for this we were praising and thanking God. The job itself seemed hand-tailored for Bob, and I bubbled to everyone about the marvelous things God was doing for us.

Then a very wise man stopped me. "I deeply praise God for what He is doing in your life, Patti. But remember one thing: When God did the best thing He ever did for us, it took place high on a hill— and it was very painful."

Sometimes it is easy for us as Christians to accept God's work in our lives as a process that provides us with continual bliss. We dote on telling others about His wonderful acts of love, joy, kindness and mercy. But if we are honest, we have to admit that our lives are not free from pain, loss and disappointment. And when we pass through those times, we may be tempted to grumble or, worse, to wonder if God has deserted us.

God has not promised to make our lives easy. He *has* promised that we will never be called upon to endure more than we can bear. And He *has* promised that He will go through every day and every experience with us. So whatever comes into our lives today, let us remember: *This* is the day the Lord has made. Let us rejoice and be glad in it!

Dear Lord, we praise You for being with us in life's sorrows as well as its joys. Help us to rejoice in You whatever this day brings.

—PATRICIA HOUCK SPRINKLE

---

30 MONDAY
The Lord is risen indeed...   —LUKE 24:34

It had been a long trip, leaving home after Christmas, getting back now a week after Easter. We'd been in Singapore, on the equator, where there is no Spring. And upon returning home there were no clues to the resurrection season here in our house either.

"It's almost as though Easter never happened this year," I moped to my husband John as we pulled soiled clothing from our suitcases.

I was having my usual case of post-trip letdown. I carried an arm-load of clothes to the basement. There was no sense in getting out the Easter decorations now. "But at least," I called upstairs, "let's take that dried-out old Christmas wreath off the door!"

All of a sudden John came bounding down the stairs. "Come with me!" he said. "Out the back door!"

Silently he led me around to the front of the house. A small brown house finch and her red-headed mate scolded from a maple as we tiptoed to the door. Among the browning hemlock twigs of the Christmas wreath a tidy round nest held three speckled eggs.

All three have hatched now: three down-covered chicks many times the size of those tiny eggs. How was so much peeping energy and eagerness ever enclosed in those confining shells? How did a tomb ever contain the Lord of Life Himself?

Of course, we haven't been able to use our front door since getting home—and we're getting a little tired of those basement stairs. But they're a small price to pay for the greatest Easter decoration we've ever had.

Lord, help me to remember that my preparations, my moods, are not what make Easter... but Your unconquerable Life.

—ELIZABETH SHERRILL

Praise Diary for April

1

2

3

4

5

6

7

8

9

10

11

12

13

14

15

16

17

18

19

20

21

22

23

24

25

26

27

28

29

30

May

S	M	T	W	T	F	S
		1	2	3	4	5
6	7	8	9	10	11	12
13	14	15	16	17	18	19
20	21	22	23	24	25	26
27	28	29	30	31		

A little girl,
All dressed in pink,
Lets go her balloon
And gives me a wink!
A little boy,
That little mink,
Sneaks up on his mom
And gives her a pinch!
These scenes in the park
Remind me that May
Is a month meant for larks!
So I now salute You, Lord,
With a spirit of whimsy.
I fling my battered old hat
To the great blue beyond,
And—what marvelous luck—
It skims by a duck,
And lands in the pond!

James McDermott

GUIDEPEOPLE: A Living Parable for May

1 TUESDAY

*But thanks be to God, which giveth us the victory
through our Lord Jesus Christ.* —I CORINTHIANS 15:57

Back in 1934, Thomas Carvel was a New Yorker without a job and almost no money. What he did have was a Model A Ford, a small house trailer he'd built, and a load of ice cream he'd made and hoped to sell.

On a Friday in summer he drove out of the city, heading for a picnic ground in the country. He never got there. A tire blew on the trailer and Carvel found himself stranded at the roadside with no spare tire, no tools, no money—and a trailer full of melting ice cream.

Well, the owner of a pottery shop across the road took pity on Carvel and helped him hook up his trailer—with the melting ice cream—to the shop's electricity. Carvel started selling his ice cream from that very spot. The two men soon found that their businesses were mutually beneficial. Carvel learned the advantages of a stationary stand and, while puttering around in the pottery shop, he eventually found a device for dispensing soft ice cream—a device that became the foundation of the huge Carvel industry, one of America's largest chains of ice-cream stores.

For over thirty-five years *Guideposts* has been telling stories like that, true stories about people who have managed to see their setbacks as opportunities. "Welcome your bad breaks," "Turn lemons into lemonade," call it any cliché you like, but we know for a certainty that defeat *can* be turned into victory. We know that because Jesus suffered the worst worldly defeat and gained the greatest victory in the history of the world.

Lord, let me always find the courage in discouragement.

—VAN VARNER

2

For thou art the God of my strength...   —*PSALM 43:2*

One day I was shopping for a walking cane for my father—his step is not as sturdy as it once was—when I noticed an elderly woman tapping her way down the aisle toward me.

"Looking at canes, are you?" she asked. "Better get a good sturdy one like mine," she advised, handing me her solid, stout cane so that I could feel its weight.

We stood there, the ninety-seven-year-old lady and I, discussing the canes. And as we picked out one that would be strong enough for my father, she turned her faded blue eyes on me and instructed, "And you ask the good Lord to give your father strength each day. That's the best support he could ever have!"

She was right, of course, for isn't our Father's comforting strength the best support any of us could ever receive as we pass through this life, whatever our age?

Dear Heavenly Father, You are my mainstay... throughout all my days.   —SAMANTHA McGARRITY

3

The Lord is nigh unto them that are of a broken heart...   —*PSALM 34:18*

My daughter Karen had some unhappy news today. She learned that she will not be graduating in May because of an overlooked requirement for her degree. She was crushed. She had been counting the months, and finally the weeks, before graduation.

As I put my arms around her in sympathy, I found myself wishing that I could take on her suffering for her.

Perhaps that is the way our Heavenly Father felt when He saw the children of Israel suffering their errors. Perhaps that is why He sends His Son into the world every day—for Karen, for you, for me.

What blessed comfort there is in knowing that when we are confronted with the low periods of our lives, our compassionate Father stands waiting to enfold us in His healing love with this reassurance: "Be of good cheer; I have overcome the world."

Father, with Your love, help me to cope with my suffering—by overcoming!
—MARILYN MORGAN HELLEBERG

---

4 FRIDAY
…When I sit in darkness, the Lord shall be a light unto me…
—MICAH 7:8

We were coming in off the lake, my sons and I, after a couple of hours of "worm dangling." That's fishing—without any catching! The sun had already set, leaving a rich burgundy glow on the horizon behind us and a shore line silhouetted in mystery ahead.

Looking up at the sky, caught in transition between dusk and dark, Chris observed that there were no stars to be seen. His big brother Steve responded offhandedly, "It's not dark enough to see the stars." And of course he was right, for by the time our boat was docked and the gear unloaded, the canvas overhead had deepened and was lavishly punctuated with heavenly lights.

That little incident came back to me recently when I was reading an article by a writer who had been through a long siege of illness. For many months he had continued to deteriorate both physically and mentally. When his condition finally worsened to the critical point—when his illness reached its absolute depths, when he was totally helpless—he turned to his Heavenly Father and placed his burden in His loving care. It was not until the very extremity that he relinquished his problem—and his recovery began.

Sometimes it seems that things have to get a little darker before we can see the stars.

Lord, give us the patience to wait, knowing full well that in due time Your Light will shine upon us.
—FRED BAUER

138

5 SATURDAY
In the world ye shall have tribulation; but be of good cheer, I have overcome the world. —JOHN 16:33

It will be Mother's Day soon, and I've been thinking about the mother finch who's raising her family on our front door. She has three young ones in her nest—perhaps that's why her flittings and flutterings remind me of myself when our own three were young.

There's a deeper parallel, though. Raising a family, at the outset, probably didn't seem an especially terrifying prospect to this drab little bird. She and her handsome mate, after all, had found a nesting site far removed from ugliness and danger, a snug private world in which to bring up the children.

The truth about that world turned out to be very different. The isolated haven was revealed—on our return from a trip—to be the front porch of a busy household. Unthinkable monsters shared her children's very neighborhood.

As a mother of the Vietnam era, I sympathize with this small, nervous bird. Who had heard, when we built our nest here in the 1950's, of drugs in the quiet suburbs, student strikes in the high school? The birds aren't giving up, of course. Parents don't. But they're teaching me a secret about living in an imperfect world. Whenever they can snatch a moment from their anxious labors, the finches sing.

Lord, give me a joyful heart today, whatever comes.

—ELIZABETH SHERRILL

6 SUNDAY
Blessed be the Lord, because he hath heard the voice of my supplications. —PSALM 28:6

This month my wife Lynn is to receive her master's degree from Princeton Theological Seminary. It has been a long haul and

139

she has worked hard. We're both looking forward to Graduation Day and, as with most graduations, the center of interest will undoubtedly be the commencement ceremony.

Commencement. What a truly appropriate term! Although graduation itself signals an end to classrooms, academic schedules and many personal relationships, it's the first step into a whole new phase of life. For Lynn it's the start of her Ph.D. program in church history; for thousands of others the way is opened to countless opportunities.

I've been wondering. Wouldn't it be exciting if we could apply the refreshing spirit of commencement to each day? There *is* a way we can do it, you know, and that's through prayer—to be more specific, through our recognition of *answers* to our prayers. For what are those answers really but our Father's signal to us that one phase of our lives is finished and it's time to commence another?

So the next time you receive an answer to one of your prayers, why not regard it as a "commencement"—and "graduate" to a new beginning? You can start out with the proven assurance that He listens...He cares...He answers...and that you will have a lifetime of opportunities to begin anew in your service to Him.

Now when Lynn and I have that Ph.D. in hand—*Lord, here we come again!*

Your answer to my prayer, Father, is my summons to a new beginning. —JEFF JAPINGA

---

7 MONDAY
...Walk in the steps of that faith of our father Abraham.
—ROMANS 4:12

Many years ago, as my grandmother and I took a short cut across the pasture, we spotted a newborn calf having his first bath. The mother licked her baby affectionately and eyed us with grave suspicion.

My grandmother silenced me with a warning finger at her lips and whispered, "She's getting him ready for his first walk."

Just then the calf pulled away from its mother's tongue impatiently. Awkwardly the little animal tried to stand, fell; then tried again, made it, and walked several feet from Mother Cow. And then he began to move about clumsily.

I stifled my giggles and asked, "How did he know he could do that, Grandma?"

"He walks on the legs of faith!" she said, smiling at me.

What a wonderful thought! Even now my grandmother's answer comes back to remind me to keep on trying when a task looks near impossible.

So, today I'll "walk on the legs of Faith," God.

—JUNE MASTERS BACHER

---

8 TUESDAY
Now set your heart and your soul to seek the Lord your God... —*I CHRONICLES 22:19*

One afternoon I went for a long walk along a woodland path. Not even a bird sang and gradually I became immersed in stillness. As I rested quietly on a huge stone, I actually felt the living Presence of God surround me.

That time has passed and I realize that in these days I am seldom still; I have a husband, children and a career to care for. And yet I need to remember—

When the phone rings all day long...
be still, and know that I am God;
When the children clamor for attention...
be still, and know that I am God;
When I feel that I have not enough hours...
be still, and know that I am God;

141

When I am overwhelmed by my own inadequacies...
be still, and know that I am God;

And I have a little exercise that helps: I perch on a footstool, close my eyes and allow God's presence to fill me. Stillness surrounds me and with my spirit renewed, I'm ready to resume the tasks ahead.

How's your schedule today? Why not find your own quiet place to "perch" and—*be still, and know that I am God.*

Lord, grant me a time of stillness and fill me with Your peace.
—PATRICIA HOUCK SPRINKLE

---

9   WEDNESDAY
My soul followeth hard after thee: thy right hand upholdeth me.   —PSALM 63:8

There is a spectacular sight in Arizona—unbelievably red cliffs that are five hundred feet high. When we visited the scene recently, my husband and I approached the overhangs carefully, taking heed of the signs that warned us not to trust the strong wind that sweeps up from the canyon floor. Some people, we were told, relying on the support of that wind, have leaned too far forward, only to plunge over the edge when the wind suddenly ceased.

Standing there on those exposed cliffs, my sweater whipping back from my shoulders, I thought of the many times that we are apt to put our faith in ephemeral things such as the wind—money, pride, fame, for example—that may only topple us into the abyss.

Isn't it better to put our faith in the support of the One Who never fails us?

I'm leaning on You, Father. And the view from here is beautiful!
—MADGE HARRAH

10

THURSDAY

...The times of refreshing shall come from the presence of the Lord... —ACTS 3:19

I wasn't very hopeful that Dr. Wood could help me. All through my early years a series of doctors had tried to relieve the severe asthmatic attacks I suffered due to allergies. While they were able to counteract some of the symptoms, they couldn't prevent the sudden desperate struggle for breath that so often came in the middle of the night.

"Try to relax," they would tell me. "Anxiety only makes it worse." But how could I relax when I was scarcely able to breathe and it was nigh impossible to get a doctor at that late hour?

I was grateful that Dr. Wood didn't tell me to relax. Instead he said: "My daughter has asthma just like you do, and I know how you feel. Because an attack can sometimes be a very frightening experience, I'm going to make you a promise, which is that you'll always be able to reach me. If I'm not in the office, call my home. If you need help, I will be available—at any time, day or night."

And with those words, I began to relax. My parents never had to call Dr. Wood in the middle of the night. Just knowing that someone who could help was there, someone who understood and cared, allowed me to breathe more easily.

From time to time we all suffer from anxiety, and it comes in many forms—often in the wee, small hours of the night, when we feel especially alone and unprotected. But we are helped to overcome our fears when we put our trust in our Heavenly Father, Who understands the depths of our helplessness, Who sent His Son to share our sufferings, and Who stands ready to come to us when we call—at any time, day or night.

I know that I need only call Your name, Father—and You will be there. —PHYLLIS HOBE

143

11 FRIDAY
...He that humbleth himself shall be exalted.

—LUKE 18:14

We were a motley lot, grumbling and apprehensive, even a bit unruly. We were in the courtroom because we had been accused of breaking the law.

I, for one, anticipated the worst. I was guilty of a traffic infraction and I expected to be demeaned and humiliated in the highest tradition of the city's unfathomable bureaucracy. Instead, we were greeted by a punctiliously starched and pressed, beaming policeman. He welcomed us "ladies and gentlemen," explained court procedures, apologized for any delays we might experience, and announced that he was at our service.

He helped a young mother and her infant find a quiet corner; he reseated people so that a large family could sit together; when one woman broke into tears, he sat down beside her, put his arm around her and comforted her.

Soon people began to chat with their neighbors. The group's earlier unruliness changed to a spirit of comaraderie. *The judge may be presiding,* I remember thinking, *but this policeman is clearly in charge.*

I paid my fine contritely, as did the others, and left the courtroom with a smile on my face. And most of us had already had a nice day.

Later, I got to thinking. People in positions of authority could often give a nice day to others if, like the kindly policeman, they would try to be a little considerate of the person behind the sea of faces.

The age-old and simple words bear repeating every day of our lives: *Love thy neighbor as thyself.*

Lord, thank You that loving others never goes out of style.

—JAMES McDERMOTT

12

Lay not up for yourselves treasures upon earth...but lay up for yourselves treasures in heaven...

—MATTHEW 6:19, 20

She was in our book club and was a chronic complainer. It's true that she was raising four children in a small, rented house on a marginal income. Not easy. But her conversation always centered on "making ends meet"...the high cost of shoes...the struggle against rising prices...the latest increase in utility bills.

Then—overnight—she changed. Instead of forever broadcasting gloom, she simply radiated good cheer.

"What happened to you?" we asked, delighted. "Get a windfall?"

"No," she replied with a broad smile. "It's just that the bishop of my church pointed out to us that on the day we were confirmed, we promise to continue Christ's ministry by answering God's call to serve. He said that the 'call' would not seem like a beckoning rainbow, but more like an aching tooth. Well, my ache is for the 'new poor.'"

She'd discovered that there were twenty-eight families "right in town" that were without the basic necessities of life. Then she'd asked every parishioner to bring one item for dispersal to those in need.

"And when I make a delivery to someone," she told us, her face beaming, "I burst with thankfulness, and I feel so rich when I see how much my church family—and my own family too—is able to give away."

Lord, whatsoever I give to another, let it be a treasure...whatsoever I receive from another is a treasure already.

—ELAINE ST. JOHNS

13 SUNDAY

She openeth her mouth with wisdom; and in her tongue is the law of kindness...Her children arise up, and call her blessed... —PROVERBS 31:26,28

Last spring Culus Williams, twenty-one years old, received a degree in biology from the University of Arkansas. It was a considerable triumph for the young man and his family because Culus is the grandson of a sharecropper. In another sense it was an even greater triumph for Mrs. Alice Williams, his mother. Culus was the last of eleven children she has seen through college.

Although Mrs. Williams gives credit for her family's extraordinary educational achievements to "trusting in the Lord," she has had to scrimp, borrow and appeal to relatives and friends as well as to federal student-grant programs in order to help her children, now variously become college professors, sociologists, conservationists and nutritionists.

Culus recalls that his mother was not a strict disciplinarian. More than anything else, he says, she inspired her children by being a loving and warm "role model."

In the dawn-to-dusk, day-to-day hard work of their mother, eleven young people found the inspiration to grow into her image of them as successful college graduates. Mrs. Williams didn't push or harangue her children; instead she showed them how to live by living well.

Lord, we ask that You bless all mothers with Your love and wisdom...for they are Very Special People, especially today.

—JAMES McDERMOTT

14 MONDAY

And the earth brought forth grass, and herb yielding seed after his kind, and the tree yielding fruit, whose seed was in itself, after his kind: and God saw that it was good. —GENESIS 1:12

Unexpected guests were coming for dinner and I wanted the house to be especially attractive, with glowing candles and flowers everywhere. But the yard yielded only a few shriveled marigolds. A trip to the market proved futile, and on sheer impulse I turned into the driveway of a big estate whose flowers I had always admired. Explaining my dilemma, I asked, "Would you mind selling me a few?"

"*Sell?*" exclaimed the woman who answered the door. "Indeed not, take all you want. Flowers are for sharing."

Flowers are for sharing. The phrase unleashed a flock of childhood memories. Oh, the joy people in our small town always took in raising and giving away their flowers—flowers to carry to hospitals, flowers to bank the altar at church, memories of a dear old man who raised beautiful roses and would never let anyone pass without receiving one.

This lovely impulse manifests itself early in little children. Like bees or butterflies, children are drawn to flowers—dandelions, violets, clover. How eagerly they will squat in the damp, sweet grasses, working away as they try to gather enough to fill a tiny jelly glass for mother. Or they will rush up to an adult with one bright blossom (usually plucked too short) to show it—and bestow it. For what do children always do with the flowers they pick? They give them away!

I think God put flowers on this earth not only to adorn it for our pleasure, but to remind us of the joy of sharing His gifts with others.

How good You are to us, Father. Even Your finest gifts are free.
—MARJORIE HOLMES

JESUS, THE MASTER STORYTELLER
Parable of the Good Samaritan
—*LUKE 10:30-37*

15

TUESDAY

Where did Jesus get the ideas for His stories? I don't think He just invented all of them, marvelous though His imagination was. Rather He must have listened to the talk of people around him, in the market place, in the carpenter's shop, at the crossroads of the caravan routes—wherever people gathered. I'm sure He listened carefully, and if an intriguing bit of news or an interesting anecdote cropped up He made a mental note to use it in some of His talks later on.

You can almost tell when a story actually happened by the detail that the Master Storyteller puts into it. In the story of the Good Samaritan, Jesus begins as He so often does, with an "action lead" . . . an opening sentence that contains movement and action. "A certain man went down from Jerusalem to Jericho and fell among thieves. . . ." Instantly our attention is attracted because this opening phrase triggers a question in the hearer's mind: "What happened next?"

Jesus tells how the bandits beat the man and stole his clothing "and departed, leaving him half dead." Here he introduces the most powerful of all narrative themes: man against death. Will the traveler survive? In a single sentence Jesus has captured the attention of everyone within hearing distance.

As always, Jesus challenges His hearers. The priest hurried on, uncaring. The Levite "came and looked on him and passed by on the other side." Only the Samaritan, a member of a race discriminated against and despised by the Jews, went to his aid.

Which are you? Jesus is asking us. How likely are you to be the one to stop and help? Have you averted your eyes from someone in trouble and then passed by on the other side?

The parables are not just stories. They are invitations to self-examination. Sometimes they may arouse great self-dissatisfaction.

148

That's what He meant them to do—for He never gives up believing that we're capable of the highest good.

Now isn't that some compliment?

Lord, help me measure up to Your standards in loving others.

—ARTHUR GORDON

---

16 WEDNESDAY
Now then we are ambassadors for Christ...

—II CORINTHIANS 5:20

Have you ever seen that little distinctive red dot on the foreheads of Hindu people? It's called a *pundra*, and it's worn as a symbol of their obedience, somewhat like the ashes on the foreheads of Roman Catholics during Lent.

Lately I've been noticing an upsurge in the numbers of people wearing crosses and Stars of David, and to me this is comforting evidence that we Americans are growing in spiritual depth and commitment to our beliefs.

But the symbol that I like best of all — the only symbol that is truly universal and bridges all faiths — is the human smile. The warmth of the smile that tells another "I like you!" is God's Word in the flesh. And although the message it bears is priceless, it is a gift so easily given.

Today smile at yourself in the mirror. Doesn't that make you feel better? Then just think of how much better a smile from you will make those around you feel. A smile is the most endearing way I know of expressing your faith in yourself, your fellow man and your God.

Help me always to remember, Lord Jesus, that when I can give nothing else, I can always give a smile.

—RUTH STAFFORD PEALE

17 THURSDAY
Go ye into all the world, and preach the gospel to every creature. —MARK 16:15

Have you ever received a traffic ticket? If so, you know how my heart jumped when a patrol car's red light suddenly flashed in my rear-view mirror. It seems that I had just made a left turn into the bus lane of a newly converted one-way street. Eager to make amends, I hurried over to my automobile club and paid the fine.

Ten days later I received a notice from the Municipal Court stating that I must appear. *Whatever can be wrong?* I wondered. Anxiously I telephoned the court. In answer to my nervous question, a man asked me to wait while he looked up the citation number. After what seemed ages, he returned to the phone.

"Don't worry, Miss," he assured me. "The record shows that you're clear. The notice was just a formal reminder."

"Oh, thank you!" My gratitude and relief spilled over.

"That's all right," he answered sympathetically, and then...just before I hung up...he added, "God bless you."

Now you may think that it's a little far-fetched, but that experience reminded me of my relationship to God. My record is "all clear"...only because Christ has atoned for my sins. And my gratitude spills over every day.

Yes, Mr. Court Secretary, God has indeed blessed me—may He bless you too.

Often, Father, I will speak Your Name on my daily walk...that all may hear. —DORIS HAASE

18 FRIDAY

Beloved, I wish above all things that thou mayes prosper and be in health… —III JOHN 1:2

I had promised to visit some friends who were in the local hospital. Since my car was out of commission and the hospital was only two miles away, I decided to walk.

After covering several steep hills, I was tired…and by the time I reached the hospital, my back was aching and my feet like lead. Oh, how I anticipated collapsing into a bedside chair!

The first friend I visited was a stroke victim. He was flat on his back and I had to stand and bend over to catch his halting words. Somehow I managed to stay on my feet during the thirty-minute visit.

My next friend was an elderly woman, prone and speechless, with little signs of life other than an occasional blinking of her eyes. I doubt that she even recognized me, but I stood at her side, took her hand and prayed with her.

As you might well imagine, all of this left me saddened. And I *still* hadn't had a chance to sit down. But as I left the hospital and took a deep breath of fresh air, I was struck with shame. *How we take good health for granted,* I thought. *Sam, you've been pampering yourself too much.* With that, I set out with a good stride and climbed the first hill I came to on buoyant feet. My backache disappeared, I felt exhilarated, and by the time I reached home, I was certain I could qualify for the two-mile cross-country race.

Father, I thank You for this body that houses me so I may carry out Your work. —SAM JUSTICE

19 SATURDAY
...Whatsoever he saith unto you, do it. —JOHN 2:5

According to a World War II story, word went out through an infantry unit that the communications office was looking for a telegrapher. Because the fighting was heavy and the communications outfit was far from the front lines, an unusually large number of soldiers showed up at the appointed time to apply for the job.

The applicants sat outside the interviewer's office for several minutes, but no one was called inside. Only the sound of dots and dashes from a telegraph machine broke the silence.

Suddenly one of the soldiers jumped to his feet and rushed into the interview room. The others were astounded, but a minute later he returned with the officer in charge, who announced that the man at his side had won the job. *Why?* the others demanded.

"It's like this," the officer explained. "While you were sitting here, I sent a message in code that said, 'Anyone who can read this, come into my office immediately.' This man understood the message, so obviously he's the best qualified for the job."

We know that God has a plan for each of our lives—the Bible tells us so. Our job is to stand ready to hear His message when He calls—and then to obey His marching orders.

Are you tuned in to receive His message today?

I'm listening, Father, ready to take on any job You offer me.

—FRED BAUER

20 SUNDAY
...While they communed together and reasoned, Jesus himself drew near... —LUKE 24:15

One day while I browsed rather aimlessly through the Metropolitan Museum of Art, the exhibits seemed to finally meld into a blur of images and pictures. And then I turned a corner....

Looming ahead, filling the entire wall, was Manet's "The Dead Christ with Angels." I saw an angel tenderly lifting the head and shoulders of Christ from the slab on which His lifeless body rested. The crucified figure was overpowering in its humanness. But it was His eyes that drew my attention. Wide open and staring, they almost seemed to be focused on me alone.

Then I noticed an elderly man walking back and forth in front of the painting. "Look!" he said, catching my glance. "No matter where you stand, Christ's eyes are directly on you."

I walked to the far side of the painting, watching with amazement as His eyes seemed to follow me across the room. What magic had the artist captured?

"I have the feeling that the artist has given us the first split second of the Resurrection," I said with awe.

We fell silent as suddenly Christ's presence filled the air between us. My eyes filled with tears. The man nodded as if to say, "I know, I feel it too." Then he turned to leave. "For where two or three are gathered..." he said simply and walked away. My mind finished his sentence. "...together in my name, there am I in the midst of them" (Matthew 18:20). Yes, I had learned something very special— whenever two or three turn in unison to gaze on Christ, He is there.

It can happen today. Even right now...as you read this page.

Lord, keep our hearts open to those unreckoned moments of communion when two or three are gathered before You.

—SUE MONK KIDD

---

21 MONDAY
And he went to him...and took care of him.
—*LUKE 10:34*

I have always yearned to be a Good Samaritan, but somehow I never seemed to have the opportunity or perhaps I simply told myself that I didn't have the time. Looking back now, you might say that I was too busy to pay much attention to distress signals—until one day....

She knocked at my door, interrupting me in the middle of a busy, hectic day. Her car had broken down right in front of my house and her young son was out there in the back seat. Could she use my telephone?

I'm fighting to meet a deadline, I thought. *Why didn't she knock on someone else's door?* I felt like Scrooge, but invited her in. But first, she ran back and fetched her little boy.

I made her a cup of tea, helped her locate a towing service and— *You're being foolish*, I told myself—volunteered to drive her home. An enormous smile of relief crossed her face. And that did it! I no longer felt like Scrooge. In fact, I began to rather enjoy the role of Good Samaritan. It made me feel good about myself.

"How can I ever thank you?" she asked as we arrived at her house. "I was really in need of a friendly hand...and you gave it to me."

You know, it doesn't take much time to be a Good Samaritan. It only takes a bit of caring. Try it today.

Father, when I hear You calling to me through another, I will run to help. —PHYLLIS HOBE

---

22 TUESDAY
...The good Lord pardon every one That prepareth his heart to seek God ... —II CHRONICLES 30:18-19

Did you know that the well Jacob dug in Old Testament times is still in existence?

I sat on the edge of the well when I visited the Holy Land, and recalled the story of the Samaritan woman who came to draw water as Jesus rested there. This woman had had five husbands and was now staying with one not her husband. Jesus spoke to her of the living water He had come to bring to the world, of eternal life, of

154

salvation. Surely there must have been others more worthy of their Lord's attention.

But this story has always brought me special comfort when I have stumbled in my life and caused myself shame or have failed to live up to His commandments. At such times I have asked myself, *How can God possibly love me?*

And then I look at the woman of Samaria, who after listening to Jesus' words, ran shouting to her friends, "Come, see a man which told me all things that I ever did...," and went on from there to joyously spread the Good News that brought the multitudes to Jesus' side.

O Lord, who sees into my soul and loves me yet, I will spread Your Good News today. —ISABEL CHAMP

---

23 WEDNESDAY
...He that gathereth not with me scattereth abroad.
—MATTHEW 12:30

A lopsided map. A child's dissatisfaction with it. It seems strange, when I look back, that it took such a small incident to set my spiritual bearings on course again.

Jason, my little eight-year-old neighbor, held up the map before me. "Does it look like Texas?" he asked anxiously.

It did not.

"I lost the outline Miss Suthers handed out and I tried to draw it from memory. Anyway," he went on, "this is the only paper I had and it wasn't big enough. I had to scrunch up Texas to make it fit."

The drawing was "scrunched up" all right. *Like some of my days*, I thought, *and some of my ways.* Lately I had allowed my life to become so hectic and overcrowded that it was as far off the mark as Jason's map was. Suddenly I saw that all the many commitments I had made—to church, to school, to community—were going to have to be scaled down in size. The needs of my family and others dear to me were being "scrunched up" to fit into my busy pattern. *Why?* I wondered, *has this happened?* Because I, just as my young neighbor, had lost the outline—and my priorities were all askew. Thank you, Jason, for the lesson your funny little map taught me.

Sometimes we need to retreat from our busy lives—sit quietly with Him—and listen to His priorities for us.

What does the "map" of your life look like today? Can you find your way by it?

Dear Lord, help me to plan my days around Your purpose for me.
—JUNE MASTERS BACHER

---

24 THURSDAY

...The mountains and the hills shall break forth before you into singing, and all the trees of the field shall clap their hands. —ISAIAH 55:12

"The chief end of man is to glorify God and enjoy Him forever." I was raised on the Westminster Confession but not until recently did I begin to ask, *What does it mean to "enjoy God"?* Then one morning last fall my son and I had a wonderful experience in which we did just that.

It was a rare, golden morning with a deep blue sky. We were at the playground when he cried, "Look!" and pointed upward. Above us floated five small clouds. One of them suddenly disappeared, only to reappear in an entirely different position. Astonished, we sat down on a bench to watch. It happened again...and again. For over twenty minutes we applauded while Someone put on a marvelous cloud show up there.

Do you ever take time just to *enjoy* God? Someday soon go outdoors and chase the leaves as they scurry in the wind. Trace the patterns of silvery raindrops as they slide down your windowpane. Look deeply into the heart of a newborn flower.

Jesus said that we must become like little children to enter the Kingdom of Heaven. It's only as His children that we are aware of the magnificent playfulness with which He has showered the earth. Wherever you are today, search out this special quality—and then take pure delight in the blessings of joy that follow.

Dear God, thank You for the gift of playfulness—and for the playful creation You have placed around us.

—PATRICIA HOUCK SPRINKLE

---

25 FRIDAY
Casting all your care upon him; for he careth for you.
—*I PETER 5:7*

We gave the matter a lot of careful thought and then decided to add a new category to our prayer group's intercessory prayer time. We call it *Christ's Circle of Love*, and it works this way. After we've been praying for a person for a considerable length of time, we release him and his problem to Christ, asking the Lord to hold that person's spirit in His arms and surround him with a circle of love.

Then we simply let go.

Originally our reason for letting go was that we had received so many prayer requests that it became impossible for us to pray through the whole list in a single session. But we soon discovered an amazing thing! People whom we had released in this way began to report that our prayers for them had been answered—often on the very day we released them, or soon thereafter.

Suddenly we realized that we were experiencing a vital principle of prayer, which is that after we have prayed intensely about something, we are to LET GO...and trust the outcome to God.

If you have been praying for a long while about a stubborn problem, perhaps it's time that you release it to *Christ's Circle of Love*...for He knows best!

Lord, I now release this problem to Your loving care.

—MARILYN MORGAN HELLEBERG

26 SATURDAY
Take therefore no thought for the morrow...
                                    —*MATTHEW 6:34*

Some years ago my wife and I spent an afternoon with Shirley Temple. Her movie career was behind her; she was Mrs. Charles Black, mother of three attractive children, occasional actress on television, an obviously contented, well-balanced individual.

She told us an anecdote about her mother-in-law that I think reveals the secret of her contentment. It seems that when Charlie was a little boy, he asked his mother to name the happiest moment of her life.

"Why, right now," she said.

"But what about the day you were married?" Charlie wanted to know.

"Well," she replied, "my happiest moment was right then. You can only live the moment you're living in. So to me that's always the happiest moment."

Live the moment you're living in. Wasn't Jesus urging us to do just that when He told us to take no thought for the morrow?

Lord, help me ever enjoy each moment to the utmost as a gift from You.   —ARTHUR GORDON

27 SUNDAY
So we, being many, are one body in Christ, and every one members of one another.   —*ROMANS 12:5*

In her eighties, too frail to attend church services, Miss Minnie Woods lives alone and "attends services" by radio every week.

"But I miss the people," she told me. "It's not the same when you worship alone."

I thought then of my own church services. How I too would miss the warm feelings of support and love that radiate throughout the congregation. While praying alone has its very own special meaning, praying with others provides a Oneness with God and community that He spoke of when He said: "For where two or three are gathered together in my name, there am I in the midst of them."

So now I join Miss Minnie every week for her half-hour of radio time, and we "attend service" together. We are each other's community. Just the two of us—and Him.

Need I say more?

Lord, lend me to communion with others. —ZONA B. DAVIS

---

28 MONDAY
Seek, and ye shall find... —MATTHEW 7:7

To me faith is such a personal matter that sometimes I find it difficult to talk about casually. But every now and then my friend Emma draws me into a discussion about whether or not God exists. The outcome is always the same— Emma can't convince me that God doesn't exist and I can't convince her that He does.

Often I would end up with the feeling that our discussions were a waste of time. Until the day I was desperately searching for a beautiful old quilt that my grandmother had made. It was an irreplaceable family heirloom that had been entrusted to me...and now I couldn't find it. I had looked everywhere.

Emma happened to drop by that afternoon and after hearing about my futile search, she asked, "Sam, why don't you ask God to help you?" I looked at her quickly to see whether or not she was joking—but no, she was dead serious. So right then and there, with Emma watching on, I earnestly asked God for His help. A short time later the quilt turned up in someone else's hands and was promptly returned to me. You can imagine my relief.

But more important than that was the message I had received

from my unbelieving friend when she reached out in my time of need. It told me that faith is a continual search in which we *all* share...and that it comes to us when we least expect it. Since that day I have never again regarded Emma as a nonbeliever—but simply as a fellow searcher.

Did You know, Father, that my doubting friend is seeking You?

—SAMANTHA McGARRITY

---

29 TUESDAY

Therefore, brethren, stand fast, and hold the traditions which ye have been taught... —II THESSALONIANS 2:15

In Joseph Conrad's classic short story, *Typhoon*, the redoubtable Captain MacWhirr must make a difficult choice when his steamship runs into a monstrous storm—either try to outflank the big blow by sailing around it, or point the bow straight into the heart of the storm and try to fight it through.

MacWhirr, whom the author paints as a rather ordinary, unimaginative man, decides on the latter course, reasoning "that a gale is a gale, and a full-powered steamship has got to face it." As a result of his resolve, the ship, although badly battered, makes it safely through the typhoon and the captain emerges as the hero of the story.

Into each of our lives there come moments when we too must choose between two courses. Often indescribable courage and faith are required. What comfort it is to read the stories of others who, in the face of conflict, have not taken the easy way out but have fought on to victory.

Although David did not *have* to fight Goliath, he volunteered, assuring Saul that "The Lord who saved me from the paw of the lion and the paw of the bear, He will save me from the hand of the Philistine."

If we find that today, like MacWhirr, we are called to sail into the heart of the storm, we have His assurance that He will be there should we flounder. So let's face our problems squarely. We have nothing to fear but fear itself!

Lord, when we would shy away from a problem that needs to be confronted, remind us that Your presence will see us through.

—FRED BAUER

---

30 WEDNESDAY
And all that believed were together… —ACTS 2:44

Once again I stand over my mother's grave, the scent of fresh peonies gracing the air.

And I remember… the sound of her approaching footsteps down a hospital corridor, singled out from many by her sick child… her soft voice reading "Alice in Wonderland" in front of the fire… her tears of joy falling on my wedding veil… her gentle, aging hands patting my baby's back… red geraniums, hand-knit sweaters and black-bottom pie.

I miss her, but remembering no longer brings tears. Coming here no longer makes me sad. In fact, it seems to put me in touch with reality beyond my physical senses. And it helps me to face the fact of my own mortality.

When I entered this life, my mother received me with love, cared for me, introduced me to her Friend, Jesus. I have no doubt that she will do the same for me in the next life.

On this day set aside for remembering, Lord, I thank You for the touch of my loved ones' lives on mine… and for Your promise that we will meet again. —MARILYN MORGAN HELLEBERG

31 THURSDAY

Keep thy tongue from evil, and thy lips from speaking guile. —PSALM 34:13

I broke my right arm when I was in the sixth grade, and only with the help of my wonderful teacher was I able to keep up with the classwork. One day while my arm was still in a cast, a friend and I chatted about school while we waited our turns in the orthodontist's chair.

"You've got it made," she teased. "No reports to write, no written tests to take."

"Yes," I laughed. "And when this heals," I lifted my cast, "I might just break it again!"

"...and all that special attention you get from the teacher."

"You're being jealous," I joshed. "After all, I'm unique!"

Two little girls, joking together. Yet the next day the principal told me in stern tones that a woman who had been in the reception room at the same time we were had telephoned the school to report that I considered myself unique, deserving of special attention from the teacher, and that I planned to break my arm again to get out of doing written assignments.

At first I was too stunned to speak. But then I realized that the woman had not deliberately lied. She had only repeated our words out of context and in a manner that totally changed their meaning.

What about that something you've recently heard and plan to tell a friend? Are you sure that you have it right? Will the tone of your voice or its inflection amend the real meaning? Will your repeating it embarrass or hurt someone else?

If so, it's best to leave it unsaid.

Today, Jesus—and every day—help me to guard my busy tongue lest I do harm to another. —DRUE DUKE

Praise Diary for May

1

2

3

4

5

6

7

8

9

10

11

12

13

14

15

16

17

18

19

20

21

22

23

24

25

26

27

28

29

30

31

June

S	M	T	W	T	F	S
					1	2
3	4	5	6	7	8	9
10	11	12	13	14	15	16
17	18	19	20	21	22	23
24	25	26	27	28	29	30

Tender are the twilights now, Lord,
Lingering long and lovingly
After soft blue afternoons.
The grass springs ardently
From spongy earth,
And rabbits dart and swallows swoop
Surely downward,
Coursing along my
Freshly planted garden rows.
A breeze soughs softly through
The nascent trees
Fluttering luminous blossoms
To the still warm ground.
My heart swells round and full,
Tight in my grateful chest.
It always has and always will
As I watch You cause the earth
Turn sweet-sixteen
Each June.

James McDermott

GUIDEPEOPLE: A Living Parable for June

1 FRIDAY

Thou shalt love the Lord thy God with all thy heart, and with all thy soul, and with all thy strength, and with all thy mind.
—LUKE 10:27

We've found at *Guideposts* that the stories people are inclined to remember the best—and put to use the most—are often the simplest ones. For instance, I myself know that many years ago my prayers to God tended to resemble letters to Santa Claus—long lists of things I wanted Him to do for me. Nowadays, however, I seldom close my eyes to pray that a simple little anecdote from a *Guideposts* story doesn't flash across my mind. It was one that actor Robert Young told.

He was listening to the bedtime prayers of one of his four little daughters and she, like me, was going through her list of wants and "gimmees." But then she stopped, raised her head, opened her eyes to heaven and said, "And now, dear God, is there anything *I* can do for *You?*"

Ah, there it is again. The unvarnished faith of little children. And did I call that a "simple" anecdote? It's not. That one tender question goes straight to the mark of what God expects of His children, big and little: to be mindful of Him. After all, that was His first—and greatest—Commandment.

And now, dear God, what can I do for You?   —VAN VARNER

---

2 SATURDAY

...Come, ye blessed of my Father, inherit the kingdom prepared for you from the foundation of the world...
—MATTHEW 25:34

In yesterday's mail there was a lovely wedding invitation.

"Come," it urged. "Come—and celebrate." And at the bottom was the usual R.S.V.P. *Respondez s'il vous plait.*

As I held the creamy vellum card in my hand, admiring the fine, feathery script, I was reminded of the many invitations that God, in His love for His children, continually extends to us. One of my favorites is: *Come unto me, all ye that labour and are heavy laden, and I will give you rest* (Matthew 11:28).

As a child, I thrilled to *Suffer the little children to come unto me . . . for of such is the kingdom of God* (Mark 10:14).

Do you remember the parable about the great supper? Jesus told of the man who sent out his servant with the invitation to *Come; for all things are now ready* (Luke 14:17). But this person had just bought a piece of ground and didn't have time...that one had purchased a yoke of oxen and was occupied...another was newly married.... The invited guests dilly-dallied. They made excuses. And, at last, the door was no longer open to them.

R.S.V.P. Respond if you please. Oh, I do please! I do answer. Any time He beckons me to "Come," I don't tarry for a second.

Yes, Lord, I accept Your invitation.   —JUNE MASTERS BACHER

---

3 SUNDAY

And as ye would that men should do to you, do ye also to them likewise.   —LUKE 6:31

The small acolyte could not light her altar candle because only a tiny bead of flame glowed at the end of her torch. As she struggled, her little face getting redder, her classmates sitting in the front pew tried to stifle their giggles.

Then the choir director moved forward, gently took the torch, turned the wand to supply more fuel to the flickering flame and returned it to the child, who deftly accomplished her task.

You should have seen the beautiful look of gratitude on that little girl's face! You could hear a rustling murmur of thankfulness float through the congregation.

You know, I thought, *it's not only the big and spectacular acts that let others know we care.* We can say "You're important to me" or "I'm on your side" by a simple touch on the shoulder, or the sharing of a tissue when another is in grief, or by giving a smile instead of a glare when someone who's already contrite or embarrassed has made a mistake.

The admonition to "Do unto others as you would have others do unto you," surely deserves its name: The Golden Rule. Let's use it to-day to light the altar candle in our hearts and show that we truly care for one another.

The more we follow your Golden Rule, Father, the brighter it seems to glow. —ISABEL CHAMP

---

4 MONDAY
But God hath chosen the foolish things of the world to confound the wise; and God hath chosen the weak things of the world to confound the things which are mighty... —I CORINTHIANS 1:27

Do you remember Zacchaeus? Zacchaeus dared to appear foolish so that he might better see Jesus. He was a man of wealth and position—and surely of some dignity, for he was "chief among the publicans." But he was short and the crowds blocked his view of Jesus. So he abandoned dignity and climbed up into a tree, from where he had a good view.

Jesus, passing by, looked up and saw Zacchaeus, called him down and went home to dinner with him. Because he dared to appear foolish—and probably to feel foolish too—Zacchaeus enjoyed closer fellowship with Jesus than anyone else in the whole crowd.

There are times when I do well to remember Zacchaeus:

...when I've said a thoughtless word and have to decide whether to call and apologize. How foolish I am going to feel!

...when I have yielded to a small temptation and have to choose whether or not to confess. How foolish I am going to feel!

...when a rift has fallen between my friend and myself and I wonder if I should make the first move. How foolish I am going to feel!

We have an idiom in English: "to go out on a limb." Zacchaeus certainly went out on a limb. It cost him his dignity, but it brought him closer to Jesus. What about us? When all that stands between us and Jesus is our dignity, isn't that a small price to pay?

Dear Jesus, help us to cast aside the dignity that narrows our vision. —PATRICIA HOUCK SPRINKLE

---

5 TUESDAY
...That men ought always to pray... —LUKE 18:1

Because my daughter Karen operates a sign-painting business from her home, she receives many telephone calls. She said that she used to dread the ring for fear it might be someone calling about an order she didn't yet have ready, or someone wanting a large number of signs "right away," or a customer questioning a bill. Karen's solution? She decided to hear the ring as a call to prayer.

On the first ring she offers a word of praise to God. On the second ring she asks the Lord to bless the person calling. On the third ring she asks for His blessing on the conversation.

"It's really amazing," says Karen, "how much more confident I feel when I answer the phone now. The right words just seem to come to me. If it's a friendly customer or a social call, a warm feeling is transmitted between us—right over the wires!"

Do you sometimes dread receiving a phone call? Karen's idea of praying before answering the phone might be a blessing to you too. And just think of all those words of praise to God and the blessing of others that would otherwise go unspoken. Yes, our common every-day telephones can really be wonderful instruments of prayer!

I ask Your blessing, Lord, on all who reach out and call me today.
—MARILYN MORGAN HELLEBERG

---

6 WEDNESDAY

Blessed are the peacemakers: for they shall be called the children of God. —MATTHEW 5:9

I had ridden in planes many times—but it was during a long, seven-hour flight to the coast that I suddenly asked my husband: "Plaford, is there any danger of an engine getting tired and playing out, especially during seven hours of continuous operation? Seems to me there should be some way to check and see whether the fan belt is getting too hot."

"Zona B., big motors are made to work, not rest," he assured me. "Instruments warn the pilot if the fan belt's getting hot. It isn't the long hauls or the hard work that wear out motors. *It's friction.* Big dynamos run day after day, year after year, stopping only at long intervals for minor repairs. It's friction that cripples an engine."

Just like human engines, I thought as the plane droned peacefully on its way. Then I began to make notes of the things that create friction in my life: petty jealousies; envy; stubbornness; lack of cooperation; distrust; dislike of a job; no job; criticism; falsehoods; failure to forgive; lack of appreciation; just plain orneriness.

Observing me, Plaford asked, "Why all the little "g"s scattered through your notes?"

"Guilty," I confessed.

Anoint my heart with Your love, dear Father, so my journey will not cause friction. —ZONA B. DAVIS

7 THURSDAY

For whatsoever things were written aforetime were written for our learning, that we through patience and comfort of the scriptures might have hope.

—*ROMANS 15:4*

I have a secret vice that I might as well confess. I love to read other people's books. If I'm left alone for even ten minutes in a friend's house, I'll pull a book off a shelf and start to read it. My wife takes a rather dim view of this. She says it isn't polite. Maybe not, but I can't seem to help it.

While indulging myself the other day, I came across a little volume by Carolyn Coats with a wry title: *Things Your Mother Always Told You But You Didn't Want to Hear.* It was full of pithy little sayings that compressed a lot of wisdom into a few words:

"A clean conscience is a soft pillow."

"A baby is God's opinion that the world should go on."

"If you trust, you don't worry; if you worry, you don't trust."

"To belittle is to be little."

"The trouble with trouble is that it starts out as fun."

And so on. Sometimes droll, sometimes shrewd, always readable. Perhaps my favorite was a little four-line item that went like this:

> When you pray
> Claim what isn't
> As if it were
> Till it becomes.

Books—what precious possessions that span the generations with their wise, eternal truths!

Lord, thank You for Your very special gift of books, especially Your Book. Let me heed Your words wisely, to grow in compassion and understanding. —ARTHUR GORDON

8 FRIDAY

For God hath not given us the spirit of fear; but of power, and of love, and of a sound mind. —II TIMOTHY 1:7

When my husband was seriously ill and undergoing surgery, I was filled with anxiety. "Oh, I'm so afraid!" I cried to a friend who waited with me.

She nodded and then gave me a knowing smile. "Do you know how many times the Scriptures say, 'Fear not,' or 'Do not be afraid'?"

I shook my head.

"It's a very curious number," she continued. "Three hundred and sixty-five times."

"But that's—"

"Yes, one for each day of the year," she said, finishing my sentence.

A coincidence? Perhaps. But I learned something then that I've never forgotten. God wants so much for you and me to get the message that He tells us over and over again—every day of our lives—"Fear not, I'm here."

On that day in the hospital those words had a tremendous calming effect on me. And isn't it marvelous that we can turn to them for comfort at any time, on any day? They're always right there before us—on every page of the calendar—where they echo down through the years to gently ease our fears and our trials. All we have to do is claim them.

Help me, Father, to remember that I need never fear when I take Your hand.
                                                    —SUE MONK KIDD

9 SATURDAY

The Lord shall rule over you.   —JUDGES 8:23

Some years ago I went to Africa on a writing assignment. I was constantly on the move, never knowing where I would sleep that night, rarely collecting my mail from home, spending my time among strangers. A six-week trip extended into six months, and I became awfully homesick.

Then one bright, brisk afternoon in the city of Leopoldville, in what was then the Belgian Congo, I rounded a corner into a wide boulevard and there—fluttering on a pole atop an office building—I saw the American flag. I stopped in my tracks, stunned.

It had never looked more beautiful than it did there, waving in a blue sky atop the American embassy in the heart of Africa, thousands of miles away from all that it symbolized and promised.

I had already seen a great deal of Africa, then in the restless throes for independence, self-government, civil rights and progress—seeking blessings America already had and was striving to impart to others. Suddenly I was very much aware of those blessings, and flooded with gratitude.

Now whenever I see the American flag, I am reminded of the moment I came upon it so unexpectedly thousands of miles away in a foreign land. I recall the thrill that went through me as I realized what I already knew, but had taken for granted: our great good fortune in being Americans, one nation under God, one people under one flag.

Father, we ask for Your continued blessings upon this country and all its peoples. —GLENN KITTLER

---

10 SUNDAY

As every man hath receiveth the gift, even so minister the same one to another, as good stewards of the manifold grace of God. —I PETER 4:10

Tomorrow is St. Barnabas' Day.

Barnabas never wrote a book, never preached a sermon, never experienced a dramatic conversion or received miraculous healings.

So why do we remember him? Because Barnabas encouraged others. He demonstrates

...*material encouragement*: When the church was barely established, Barnabas was among the first to sell a field and give the money to needy believers;

...*risky encouragement*: When Saul of Tarsus claimed to have had a dramatic conversion, no one believed him until Barnabas brought him back to the church;

...*humble encouragement*: When the Gentiles in Antioch needed a leader, Barnabas left home to lead them, but soon he became convinced that Paul should be leader and he himself took second place;

...*forgiving encouragement*: When once young Mark's courage failed, Paul sent him home in disgrace. Barnabas gave the lad a second chance and so encouraged him that Mark eventually wrote a Gospel.

Barnabas' name means "son of encouragement." That's all he ever did of note—*encourage*.

Who knows what may happen in the Kingdom of God if we follow Barnabas' example? It isn't something just to *think* about....

Father, show me ways in which I may offer the gift of encouragement to others on this day. —PATRICIA HOUCK SPRINKLE

Celebrating Fathers:
SEVEN FATHERLY VIRTUES

In last year's Daily Guideposts, *Fred Bauer wrote a special seven-part series about memorable mothers of the Bible. This year we asked Fred to give equal time to fathers.*

"All parents long to give their children the tools with which to live life successfully," he says, "but what are the really important gifts we can give, the most valuable legacies we can pass along to our young people?"

This week, in anticipation of Father's Day on June 17, Fred shares his unique insights on parenting as he sets forth "Seven

Fatherly Virtues"—seven special strengths that children every-where love in their fathers and will treasure the rest of their lives.

---

11 MONDAY
A FATHER'S *EXAMPLE*

In his book, *Fearfully and Wonderfully Made*, Dr. Paul Brand, world-famous surgeon and Professor of Orthopedic Surgery at Louisiana State University, writes about his father, who was a medical missionary.

Dr. Brand recalls that when he was seven years old, he observed his father treating lepers. Now Paul Brand's father could have talked to the lad at length about his work or about the urgent need for more doctors to treat the dread disease, but he didn't. He simply went on quietly working—consoling, ministering and tending to these suffering people with utmost compassion. And it was this picture of his father, indelibly printed on the boy's mind, that shaped the course of Paul Brand's life so that later he returned to India, where for eighteen years he conducted the pioneering research that has so greatly advanced the treatment of leprosy.

From this little story it's plain to see that it was the *example* Dr. Brand's father set that had the deepest and most lasting effect of all on the young, impressionable mind.

Help us to live our lives, Father, by the examples You have so generously set before us. —FRED BAUER

---

12 TUESDAY
A FATHER'S *SUPPORT*

A friend of ours had been chosen along with several other men to receive a highly prestigious award. But when I mentioned the forthcoming event to him, he told me that he would not be there in person to receive the honor.

"Why not?" I asked incredulously, finding it difficult to believe that he would forego such an exciting occasion.

"Because Julie [his sixteen-year-old daughter] will be swimming in the district meet that night," he explained. "She's facing some tough competition and she'll need the whole family's support. The folks at the banquet won't miss me, but Julie would."

His answer surprised me, but upon reflection, I understood. I have long observed this man has always made it a point to put his family first. And, with further reflection, I realized that a man who sets that kind of priority in his life is thereby giving his children an everlasting gift—that of lifelong *support*. He blesses them with a healthy confidence and a strong self-esteem that will sustain them no matter what the future brings, for they have experienced in countless ways through the years their father's supportive love and care.

And for the father who sees his children daily grow in strength and assurance, there is no greater award.

Teach us to be supportive to our young ones, Father, as You are to us.
                                                              —FRED BAUER

13

WEDNESDAY
A FATHER'S *FAITH*

The little daughter of Jairus, one of the rulers of the synagogue, was desperately ill. "Come and lay thy hands on her, that she may be healed," Jairus begged Jesus, and Jesus went with him.

But on the way another brought word that they were too late. The twelve-year-old daughter had died. "Be not afraid," Jesus told Jairus, "only believe."

When they arrived at the ruler's house, mourning was already in progress. Jesus entered the door and asked, "Why make ye this ado?" and told those present that the girl was not dead, but sleeping.

Then he took her by the hand and told her to arise, and "straightway the damsel arose" (Mark 5:22-24, 35-43).

We are not told any more about Jairus and his daughter, but surely they must have been spiritually changed. A brush with death had brought them face to face with the living God, but only because of the father's *faith* in God's great works. About to lose his only daughter, he had turned to God's only Son for help. And he received it! Such faith is a living legacy, passed on as a lifeline from one generation to the next.

Blessed indeed is today's child who receives from his father the gift of *faith*—strong, vital—Jairuslike.

Father, teach us to pass our faith to those coming after us, as we were given faith by those before us. —FRED BAUER

14 THURSDAY
A FATHER'S *COURTESY*

The story is told of a courtly gentlemen who was walking down the sidewalk of a busy city street with his son. Coming upon a blind man with his cup extended, the father gave the man a coin and doffed his hat.

As they proceeded down the street, Dad chastised the lad for not also tipping his hat. "Very rude, young man," he said. "Very impolite."

"But, Father," the boy protested, "the man was blind."

"Ah, but *you* are not," replied the father.

A good friend of mine once described a mutual acquaintance as being full of "the courtesy of Christ." I liked the expression then and I like it now, because surely courtesy has at its heart the godly grace of honoring the dignity of all men.

Fathers who would instruct their children in gracious behavior would teach them that *courtesy* is not a mere exercise in manners, but an attitude toward others. Courtesy smooths the way and opens the door to friendship. It does not know how to offend, to be rude or to act with arrogance. Instead, courtesy provides the means by which we can better appreciate our fellow man and act with consideration and concern toward him.

The father who is himself observing "the courtesy of Christ" in his everyday life is thereby teaching it to his children...every day.

Fill our hearts, Lord Jesus, with Your courtesy toward all.

—FRED BAUER

---

15 FRIDAY
A FATHER'S *EMPATHY*

Son Number 3, Christopher, got his driver's license recently, and he's very competent behind the wheel of a car. But while he was learning to drive, he backed into a post and blinded our station wagon in the left rear taillight. I was ready with a few strong words about being careful when I caught myself and instead uttered some long-planted phrases from the past: "If nobody was hurt, it isn't serious. Cars can be repaired a lot easier than people."

Then I told Chris about a slight mishap that I had had shortly after I began driving. And suddenly I realized that I was copying a performance of *my* dad's many years before. Instead of dressing me down, my father had told me about driving *his* father's new Model A into the door of a meat-packing company! Now I don't know what my grandfather said, but I can guess.

One important secret of dealing with the mistakes of our children might be for us to remember our own youthful errors. And unless you didn't need pencils with erasers, you were as prone to slip-ups as the next. Unintentional mishaps, the errors of inexperience, the follies of youthful exuberance—it's the rare dad who can't empathize with his children as he recalls some of his own high jinks in earlier years.

Fathers who have this marvelous quality of *empathy* give their children the blessed assurance that no matter what they do, or try to do, in life, whether they succeed or fail, they are always understood, appreciated... and loved.

Father, give us the wisdom to meet innocent mistakes with loving-kindness. —FRED BAUER

16 SATURDAY
A FATHER'S *SACRIFICE*

There is an elderly man in my hometown who survived the sinking of the *Lusitania* way back in 1915. A teenager at the time of the infamous tragedy, he survived only because of an act of ultimate *sacrifice* on the part of his father.

When the British ship was struck by German torpedoes, the passengers were instructed to report to life stations. This father and son did as they were told. They made their way to a life station, but when they arrived, they found only one life preserver left. Without hesitation the father strapped it around his son. The boy survived; the father was one of 1,195 who did not.

Of course this is an extreme case of sacrifice, for not many of us are called upon to lay down our lives literally for our children. But the Bible holds up a parallel to us when Jesus says that "... I lay down my life for the sheep" (John 10:15). As Shepherd of His flock, He died on Calvary that we might live in grace.

A father is equally the shepherd of his flock, or his family, called upon to make sacrifices—of his time, of his energies, that his children might grow in grace. And again we turn to Jesus for the words that say it incomparably better than any others:

"As the father hath loved me, so have I loved you..." (John 15:9).

Thank you for Your unconditional love, Lord. Help us to emulate it in our love for our children. —FRED BAUER

17 SUNDAY
A FATHER'S *FORGIVENESS*

In the story of the prodigal son we read of the father who, upon seeing a great way off his wayward son returning home, "had compassion, and ran, and fell on his neck, and kissed him" (Luke 15:20).

I find the most touching part of the story to be that of the father on the lookout for his son's return; he was ever watching, waiting and hoping. And when on the horizon the barely distinguishable form of that "lost" youth appeared, the father ran to meet him. He didn't wait for his son to come to him. He didn't wait to hear his son beg for mercy and forgiveness. No, he was too overcome with joy to restrain himself, and so he ran to the boy and no doubt bear-hugged him, lifted him off the ground and kissed him unashamedly.

That's the kind of Heavenly Father we have and the kind of earthly father most of us long to be. For in our heart of hearts we know that there is no greater fatherly virtue than a love so deep it can *forgive* any indiscretion, any hurt and any mistake. Inwardly we repeat Mark 2:5—"...Son, thy sins be forgiven thee"—as outwardly we laugh and weep with our beloved children.

On this day, Father's Day, let all of us, across the nation and around the world, rededicate ourselves to the practice of the "Seven Fatherly Virtues" in our home and with our children.

Father, help us to give our children good examples... strong support... lasting faith... the dignity of courtesy... boundless empathy... a willingness to make sacrifices for them... and forgiveness. With these gifts we lead them into the circle of Your love.

—FRED BAUER

JESUS, THE MASTER STORYTELLER
Parable of New Wine in
Old Wineskins —MATTHEW 9:17

18 MONDAY

"Clothes make the man," goes an old saying. A public relations man for a famous men's suitmaker decided to put the adage to the test. At a national men's fashions convention in a large Midwest city, the public relations man recruited a drunken derelict to participate in a ruse.

The deal was that the disheveled man would earn one hundred dollars if he could make other conventioneers believe that he was an executive for a clothing manufacturer. He readily agreed and the plan was put into effect. After the derelict had been bathed, manicured, shaved and had his hair cut, he was fitted for a finely tailored suit. Then he was coached as to how he should act...smile a lot, wave, nod and limit your conversation to "Fine, good to see you, very interesting, fascinating."

For two days the fellow fooled everyone. By changing his appearance, he seemingly proved that good grooming and good clothes do indeed make the man.

(P.S. Reportedly, he was spotted the next day, still dressed in the expensive suit, sprawled in a doorway, drunk again. He had been transformed outside, *but inside he was the same.*)

Jesus told of the futility of such a sham. He said that men don't put new wine in old bottles "else the bottles break, and the wine runs out, and the bottles perish, but they put new wine in new bottles, and both are preserved."

The point is: Through Christ we become new creatures...first on the inside, then the outside.

Help us remember, Lord, that it is only through Your Grace and the power of Your Holy Spirit that we can hope to change.

—FRED BAUER

181

19 TUESDAY

Thou shalt guide me with thy counsel, and afterward receive me to glory. —PSALM 74:24

The law-enforcement officer certainly made his point with my fourth-grade classroom—and with me as well. He had brought along a big picture poster on safety.

Entitled "His One Mistake," the poster read like this:

> He wore his rubbers when it rained.
> He brushed his teeth twice a day.
> The doctors examined him twice each year.
> He slept with the windows open.
> He always had plenty of fresh fruits and vegetables.
> He golfed—but never more than eighteeen holes.
> He slept at least eight hours every night.
> He never smoked, drank or lost his temper.
> He did his "daily dozen" daily.
> He was all set to live to be a hundred.
> But the funeral will be held next Wednesday. He is survived by eight specialists, three health institutions, two gymnasiums and numerous manufacturers of health foods and antiseptics.
> You see, he made one fatal mistake. One day he forgot to look when he crossed the street!

Powerful, isn't it, especially when one thinks in terms of the one fatal mistake we might make if we forget to look to God at life's intersections?

Lord, watch over me. Guide my path in Your ways.

—JUNE MASTERS BACHER

20 WEDNESDAY

For the kingdom of heaven is as a man travelling into a far country... —MATTHEW 25:14

I could feel it happening to me. Despite the schedule I had set for myself for further spiritual growth—Bible reading, meditation, prayer—I was having trouble staying with my plans. Concerned, I wrote of my problem to the man who had been pastor of our church for many years before his retirement. He replied that although St. Paul tells us to pray without ceasing, this does not mean that we should pray to the exclusion of other efforts.

"Instead of dedicating *parts* of your day to God," he wrote, "dedicate the *whole* day to Him. Meditate while you travel to work. On the job, offer up your efforts for His glory. Keep God's love in your heart in your relations with others, asking forgiveness when you offend, granting forgiveness when you are offended. Let God be your partner in all you do at *all* times."

His words made me think, and then I remembered that the Lord said He would be with us *always*—not just in church on Sundays.

Adjusting to this constant companionship with the Lord has required considerable effort and frequent reminders, but with Him at my side every step of the way, I am traveling on the right road again—a road without any more detours.

Father, stay close that I may walk with You today—all day.
—GLENN KITTLER

21 THURSDAY

Seek ye first the kingdom of God, and his righteousness; and all these things shall be added unto you.
—MATTHEW 6:33

Several years ago I spent four months traveling through France and England, Ireland and Scotland. With a pack on my back, I hiked along miles of sunny country roadways, accepting lifts only when the weather was too wet for walking.

As I journeyed, I had time to reflect on my two selves—my traveling self, who had barely enough to get by on, and my settled self, who, back home in New York, had a house overlooking the Hudson River, rooms filled with furniture, closets full of clothes and several cars. Yet here I saw my happier self was the traveling self, the one free of the burden of possessions, all of which would count for little in the end. None of those things meant that I had done anything worthwhile with my life.

Long after, that trip stayed with me. And my circumstances changed—my earthly possessions were fewer, I felt strangely and wonderfully free. And today I concentrate on projects that mean more to me than mere *things* ever could.

Do you have two selves? Why not develop the happier one? And if your happier self yearns to be free of the cares that go with too many possessions and longs to focus on the deep-down creative and spiritual goals that lie in your heart, then reduce your circumstances—and gain the world!

Dear Father, please help me to free my life of its inconsequential clutter so I may come straight to You.

—SAMANTHA McGARRITY

22 FRIDAY

Brethren, be followers together of me, and mark them which walk so as ye have us for an ensample.
—PHILIPPIANS 3:17

Early one morning while driving to work, I saw a young mother out jogging with her small son. The child trotted proudly beside her, wearing a blue-and-white outfit that matched hers.

What a good mother she is! I thought as I drove by. *She isn't just telling her son about the importance of fresh air and exercise. She's showing him by her example.*

Then my fingers happened to touch the cross that I always wear on a silver chain around my neck. And there in my imagination I saw Jesus, the greatest Living Example of all. He did not just tell His disciples about the love that's so basic to humble service. He showed them.

We are all teachers. We teach by the manner in which we live our lives as Christians, thereby showing others our faith and its relevance to the world. And I wondered: *What kind of example for Christ am I?*

With that, my foot relaxed on the accelerator. First I must drive more courteously. And when I get to work, I will greet my coworkers warmly. I will work extra hard, follow directions more carefully, take time to listen more willingly, offer to help where I can.

By the pattern of my days, Father, that I may be a worthy example.   —DORIS HAASE

23 SATURDAY

...Though your sins be as scarlet, they shall be as white as snow... —ISAIAH 1:18

When my son John went on a Boy Scout canoe trip, he left me in charge of his two salamanders, Dino and Saurie. He had carefully fixed up a large aquarium, complete with dirt for them to tunnel into, lots of growing plants and a bowl of water for them to drink and swim in.

I was squeamish about caring for the salamanders at first, but I soon became attached to the little fellows. Then, on the day before John was due home, I found Saurie dead in the water bowl. I was just heartsick! I couldn't sleep that night, knowing how upset John would be. I was sure that he'd blame me. When he got home, I told him about it as gently as I could. He rushed upstairs to his room. I gave him a few minutes and then went to his doorway. He was sitting on the edge of his bed, Dino in his hand, the tears running down his cheeks.

"I'm so sorry, honey," I said as tears started down my cheeks too. "Are you mad at me?"

Without a word, John gently placed Dino back in the aquarium, dried his eyes on his sleeve, walked over and gave me a big hug. "How can I be mad at you when you're so sorry, Mom?"

I've never loved John more than I did at that moment.

That must be the way Jesus feels about my sinfulness. I know it makes Him unhappy, but when I tell Him I'm sorry, His heart runs over with compassion. He is always ready to forgive...we have only to stand before Him and ask.

I'm so sorry, Lord, for the wrongs I've done—and so thankful for Your forgiveness. —MARILYN MORGAN HELLEBERG

24 SUNDAY

O when wilt thou come unto me? —PSALM 101:2

The congregation was gathered in the small church for worship. While waiting for the service to begin, I let my thoughts roam. In front of me a little girl, maybe three years old, hummed a Sunday-school tune to herself...Carol, a dear friend of mine, was wearing a pretty new dress...Helen's deep suntan really became her...I noticed two light bulbs out in the big chandelier up toward the balcony....

Looking at my watch, I shifted in my seat and then let my mind drift again...until the child in front of me, no longer humming, suddenly shouted out in excitement, her shrill little voice striking like a clap of thunder in the quiet church: "Look, Mama!" She pointed to the Good Shepherd stained-glass window above the altar. "There's Jesus. Hello, Jesus! Jesus, hello!"

For me it was a moment of pure illumination. Here was the smallest one in our midst teaching us that waiting-time in church is precious time...not a time to fritter away our thoughts on idle trivia. The tot's attention had been focused on thoughts of Him... she had been *expecting* to meet Him...and, in her own way, she did!

We too, while we wait in church, should be turning our thoughts toward meeting our Lord...preparing our reception...readying ourselves to say simply, "Hello, Father. Here I am." And then we too will meet our Master.

Dear Father, I am ready. My heart awaits You. —SUE MONK KIDD

25 MONDAY

Wait on the Lord: be of good courage... —PSALM 27:14

Do you have a favorite anecdote, some special "potion" to pull you out of the doldrums?

I discovered mine on the streets of New York one day. I was walking to the bus station, tired and frazzled after a week of solid frustration. And then I saw—next to the entrance to the library—a little girl in a wheelchair, singing a soft song with a woman I guessed to be her mother. As I listened to their voices, I was reminded of an old story, one I had heard when I was a child.

A man once went to visit a friend who had been ill for many, many years and was now dying of an incurable disease. He took with him a book of cheer for those in trouble, a sunny book, a happy book.

"Thank you very much," the friend said, "but I know this book."

"You've read it already?" asked the visitor.

The friend answered, "I wrote it."

Now whenever I find myself getting down in the dumps, I whistle the tune and recall that old story—for truly they go hand in hand. In those who suffer and sorrow, we so often find a special kind of fortitude—that special kind of courage that serves as an antidote to the world's pain.

It was first given to us by the most courageous of all—our Lord, Jesus Christ.

Dear Jesus, thank You for a love that overcomes and a courage to go forward. —JEFF JAPINGA

---

26 TUESDAY
…We have this treasure in earthen vessels, that the excellency of the power may be of God…
—II CORINTHIANS 4:7

One day when we arrived at his home, Ben Winter was carefully studying an ugly old stump that had just been dragged out of a hog wallow. I wondered aloud what on earth he saw in that sodden, begrimed chunk of wood.

Then he took us into his workshop and brought out the plant

stand we had commissioned him to make. "Just look at the burl on that top," he said proudly. The wood revealed a beautiful curling of grain, with golden shadows and highlights that amazed even me, a cabinetmaker's daughter.

Then Ben showed us other lovely pieces he had made—smooth, satiny boxes, a little cherrywood bookstand, sleek candlesticks of walnut.

"Only a stump good and seasoned by water and the elements can produce grains like these. There's little in this world that can't be salvaged," he smiled, "and transformed into something useful and beautiful."

I learned a lesson that day, and I'd like to pass it on to you: It's worth our time and effort to dig for the buried treasure. Even in those situations—and, yes, in those people—we consider the least salvageable, there is a hidden core of usefulness and beauty, if we are but wise enough, patient enough and concerned enough to bring it to the surface.

Give me the wisdom and compassion, Father, to find the beauty and goodness in others.   —ZONA B. DAVIS

---

27 WEDNESDAY
...He that refraineth his lips is wise. The tongue of the just is as choice silver...   —PROVERBS 10:19-20

Albert Einstein was not only a scientific genius, a Nobel Prize winner and the father of the theory of relativity—he was also a man of great simplicity. One evening at a dinner party given by the president of Swarthmore College, Einstein was the guest of honor. During the affair, he was called upon for a speech.

"Ladies and gentlemen," he greeted the guests politely, paused for a moment, and went on... "I am sorry but I have nothing to say." With that, he sat down. Then he arose and added, "In case I do have something to say, I'll come back."

Six months went by and one day Einstein wired the president of the college, announcing, "Now I have something to say." So another dinner was arranged and Einstein made his speech.

When I discovered this little story, I was reminded anew that talking—whether or not we have anything to say, speaking without forethought or restraint just to fill up silent spaces—can be a hazard. For then we run the risk of uttering useless words that clutter the air...empty words without nourishment...words that are mere shells.

Jesus was the supreme master of simplicity of speech. He exercised such a rare economy of words that everything He said carried precious meaning and nourished the souls of those fortunate enough to hear Him. And, equally as important, He was unsurpassed in the fine skill of knowing when to remain silent.

Enough said....

Lord, teach me to speak only when my words will improve the silence. —SUE MONK KIDD

---

28 THURSDAY
Lord, teach us to pray... —*LUKE 11:1*

"Did you say your prayers today?" a member of my prayer circle asked me in a teasing voice.

Obviously, she assumed I had. But the truth was that I'd let another day slip by without fulfilling my commitment to intercessory prayer. Filled with shame, I vowed to do better.

It was then that I remembered the way in which my mother had trained me to practice the piano when I was young. She had placed a large calendar beside the piano. Every day that I practiced, I was allowed to paste a big gold star on that date.

Thinking now of her method, I decided to start a "star calendar" for prayer. I wrote in large letters at the top of the page the time that I planned to pray each morning, and I hung the calendar in a prominent place in the kitchen. After fulfilling each daily prayer assignment, I drew in a star.

Soon I no longer needed that childhood reminder. Just as long ago I came to enjoy playing the piano so much that I practiced without the aid of the calendar, so have I come to cherish my daily prayer time with the Lord.

If you're sometimes forgetful or fall behind in your prayer schedules, why don't you try using a "star calendar," and become your very own "star pray-er"?

Lord, keep me ever faithful in prayer and in my walk with You.
—MADGE HARRAH

29 FRIDAY
Therefore we were comforted in your comfort...
—*II CORINTHIANS 7:13*

"Bob was the most handsome man I ever dated," Nancy told her friend as they reminisced over college days. "And he was certainly one of the most intelligent. But it was his effervescent personality that made him so utterly irresistible."

"Then tell me," her listener asked, "why didn't you marry Bob instead of Chuck?"

"Because," Nancy replied with a sparkle in her eye, "Chuck made me feel that *I* was irresistible."

It's not strange that we are drawn to people who make us feel good about ourselves—for in the doing, they are *confirming* us. Telling us that we're important, our feelings matter, our words and opinions count. Their undivided attention reminds me of the old song—"I only have eyes for you...."

The Bible tells us that as we sow, so shall we reap. It seems to me that if we want a harvest of true friends, we must genuinely focus on the interests, aspirations and needs of others. Today let's make an extra effort to let someone else know of our approval. Surely we can find the means of encouragement, of affirmation, of sharing—even if all it takes is a smile, a little pat, a phone call or a note.

And really to put the point across, here's a small poem to remember about first meetings:

Those launched by criticism are sure to sour...
Those begun with compliments can't help but flower.

Dear Father, help me to see others through Your eyes—and with Your concern. —FRED BAUER

---

30 SATURDAY

And he called unto him the twelve, and began to send them forth by two and two... —MARK 6:7

One morning a police station in a small Midwestern town received a call from an elderly woman who lived alone.

"My wheelchair is broken," she said, "and I don't have the money for a new one." She went on to explain that she could take care of herself quite well—but not without the aid of her wheelchair. "I don't know who else to call," she apologized.

The men and women at the police station were so touched by the woman's plight that they took up a collection among themselves to buy her a new chair. But since they found that a new chair would cost more than they could manage, they decided to repair the broken chair themselves.

That very night, the necessary tools and parts in hand, they went to her home, set to work, and soon the old wheelchair was as good as new. Smiling broadly, they watched as the grateful woman wheeled herself around in her kitchen, made a steaming pot of tea and brought out cookies for everyone.

Now I call that a *miracle*. And I see now that a miracle doesn't have to be a big, spectacular event. It can be something very small, very loving and simple, such as doing the best we can to help another person.

Father, if two are needed, let me be the other. —PHYLLIS HOBE

Praise Diary for June

1

2

3

4

5

6

7

8

9

10

11

12

13

14

15

16

17

18

19

20

21

22

23

24

25

26

27

28

29

30

July

S	M	T	W	T	F	S
1	2	3	4	5	6	7
8	9	10	11	12	13	14
15	16	17	18	19	20	21
22	23	24	25	26	27	28
29	30	31				

How sweet the water was
This noon, dear Lord, burbling
From my garden hose.
How close in harmony I seemed to You
Beneath a ripe orange July sun,
Pulling weeds so more tender shoots could grow.
How good is work that makes me
Breathe deeply in the summer air
And filter earth between my fingers.

Now in my bed,
My limbs lying loose and spent
In a fluid balm of weariness,
A righteous part within me knows
That this toil-gained lassitude
Before I sleep
Is dearer than the silkiest sin.
Good night, dear Lord.
Thank You.

James McDermott

GUIDEPEOPLE: A Living Parable for July

1 SUNDAY

Therefore if any man be in Christ, he is a new creature: old things are passed away; behold, all things are become new. —II CORINTHIANS 5:17

Molly—wherever you are—I think of you often.

They called you Big Molly, didn't they? You were big, all right, and loud and rough. The meanest gal in town. A man who worked in the same industrial plant said you had the foulest tongue he'd ever heard, female or male. And when I went out to the Midwest to do your story, a judge told me about your drinking and rough-housing; and about your husband Arthur and how you'd divorced him and had him thrown into the workhouse for not sending money to support your little boy, Dickie. No, Molly, you didn't present a pretty picture.

You'd been an overhead crane operator, hoisting pipe and scrap iron—man's work to most people, child's play to you. You were fighting angry the night you let a ton of metal crash into a turning machine, ripping it to smithereens—and getting yourself fired. Then you got sick, and you tried to contact Arthur again, so he could look after Dickie while you were in the hospital. That was the beginning.

Dickie played on the swings in the Salvation Army's playground while Arthur watched. Then Arthur started helping the Army people, and when you came out of the hospital a Captain went out to see you and care for you. You were surprised at such unsolicited kindness. When you got better you attended some of the Army's Home League meetings.

Do you remember the day we met? You and Arthur had remarried. I found you in a bright kitchen making sandwiches and stuffing eggs for a picnic. You were still big, with great clumsy, gentle hands, but you were not the Big Molly I'd heard about. You were soft-spoken, almost timid.

Why the change? You told me in one quiet sentence: "I found the Christ that was in me all along."

So that, Molly, was a young editor's first encounter with a fact that he's seen repeated over and over and over again: no matter who you are or what you've done or how late it is, through Jesus Christ you can change your life.

Change me, Lord. Change me even now.   —VAN VARNER

2

MONDAY

Thou…shalt quicken me again, and shalt bring me up again from the depths of the earth.   —PSALM 71:20

I hadn't seen my dear friends Alma and Calvin Hardy since they retired and moved to the country. When Alma called and invited me to dinner, I was delighted…but a little worried too. I had known several men who had retired and they had become cranky, bored, restless. Now I had some trepidation about how I might find Cal.

To my great joy, both Alma and Cal looked fit and healthy. The twinkle in Cal's eyes was brighter than ever, and it was obvious that he wasn't wasting away with boredom.

"What are you up to?" I asked, curious.

With a sly little smile on his face, Cal led me to the garage. And there instead of a car was a small, tidy workshop, fragrant with the aroma of herbs hanging in bunches from the ceiling. Small jars glistened on shelves around the walls, and labels proclaimed "Hardy Spices." Cal and Alma were in business for themselves…and doing very well indeed! They were growing their own herbs, drying them and selling them to food shops all around the country.

Cal laughed at my astonishment. "You know, I thought my life was over when my job ended," he told me. "Then I seemed to hear God saying, 'Cal, why don't you try to be like those herbs you like to grow? Even when you take them out of the garden and dry them, they still have plenty of flavor." And He was right of course. Retirement doesn't have to be the end. It's the beginning of something new...maybe something even better than before!"

With this day, Father...and every day...let me begin anew with You.   —PHYLLIS HOBE

---

3 TUESDAY
Save me, O God! For the waters have come in to my soul. I sink in deep mire, where there is no standing...
                                                        —PSALM 69:1-2

The term *salvation* has a very concrete meaning for me.

As a college student eager to impress my friends, I once "borrowed" my parents' hibachi without permission and took it on a beach picnic. When we dumped the coals after eating, the bottom grill fell into Biscayne Bay with the charcoal.

"The hibachi's no good without it," my father sighed, and drove me back to where the grill had fallen in. Unhappy and repentant I slipped off my sandals and slid over the sea wall. Then I screamed. The bottom of the bay at that point was covered with barnacles and rusty cans that cut into my feet.

Instantly two arms reached down and hauled me over the seawall to safe ground. Then as I sobbed, Dad took his shirt off, dried my feet, and carried me to the car, never mentioning the grill again.

What does salvation feel like?

To me, it is the incredible feel of two strong arms hauling me off the razor-edged results of my own behavior, comforting me and carrying me in love to a place of safety. Salvation? A Father's forgiving love.

Dear God, today I thank You for Your eternal love that stands ever ready to forgive, restore and save me.

                                                        —PATRICIA HOUCK SPRINKLE

4 WEDNESDAY

Mine eyes shall be upon the faithful of the land, that they may dwell with me... —PSALM 101:6

I never cared for hoopla. During my high-school years, I used to dread the excitement of the big proms, with their attendant kings and queens, parades and floats. It all seemed so unnecessary, such a waste of time.

But the other day I read about a town in Nebraska that set aside a Saturday on which to honor local couples who had been married for fifty years or more. Last year the king and queen for the day were a husband and wife who had been married for nearly seventy years! The town staged a big fancy parade, and there were floats, bands and a lot of hoopla. *Well, how about that?* I thought. *How nice!*

It took that little town in Nebraska to straighten out my thinking about hoopla. How wonderful it is to live in a country so free and joyous that its towns can stage celebrations as they please—to honor whom they please, even that battered but still vigorous institution of marriage! Is a parade necessary? Of course not. But it's a fine example of the enthusiastic and indomitable American spirit upon which this country was founded.

Today's a great day for hoopla all across this land of ours. I hope that all the bands are out, that there's a parade in every town, with lots of floats, and that—flying high over all—the red, white and blue of Old Glory will wave in the breeze from coast to coast!

I thank You, Lord, for our glorious country. Help us to preserve freedom and justice for all. —JAMES McDERMOTT

---

5 THURSDAY
Thou hast appointed His bounds that He cannot pass.
—*JOB 14:5*

While in Singapore last year, they were celebrating the Year of the Pig, here at our house it seems to be the year of the bird. Not only are finches nesting on the door, a robin is trying to get through the window.

Over and over he hurls himself at the glass, beating the invisible barrier with his wings. A score of times a day I'll hear his frantic flappings—at the kitchen window, up in the bedroom—startling me in my study as I type. What does he see? What does he want, that he expends his energy and batters his wings?

It's started me thinking about obstacles at which *I* have strained in vain. Goals toward which I make no progress. Prayers where the answer always seems to be "no."

That objective that looks so alluring from here...I wonder. Might it be as dismaying, if I actually achieved it, as the other side of the window would be to the determined robin? Because I could open the window, of course, and let him in. I've even considered it, as a cure for foolishness, before he exhausts himself striving for an illusion.

Then I picture his bewilderment, his terror at finding himself trapped, the risk of doing himself worse harm trying to get out. And I keep the window closed.

Lord, show me when the obstacle across my path is a challenge to overcome—and when it is the shield of Your mercy barring the way.   —ELIZABETH SHERRILL

6 FRIDAY
The just shall live by faith. —*ROMANS 1:17*

In recent years the effects of Parkinson's disease have severely restricted my father's activities. Most of the time, because of the constant tremor in his muscles, it is difficult for him to do even simple things such as replacing a fuse or changing a spark plug.

The last time I visited my parents Dad and I were out in the back yard, where I was taking photographs. Suddenly he said, "Sam, I want to take a picture of you." I gave him the camera and then for long minutes stood watching as he tried to hold it steady enough so that he could see through the lens.

Although his hands shook uncontrollably, he just wouldn't give up. Finally he looked around, sat down on a nearby stump and motioned for me to sit on the ground in front of him. With his elbows braced against his knees, the camera fairly steady, he snapped the shot. "Click!"

It had taken fully ten minutes, but Dad had been determined to figure out the solution and to follow through. His courage and resolve make me proud—and sometimes ashamed—of how easily I tend to give up or shy away from tasks that I'm not certain I can do. How much better it would be if I could learn to follow my dad's method—to stick to the job, believing and trusting that a way will be opened.

That's what I call *real faith.*

Dear Heavenly Father, please strengthen my will as You show me the way—the Way of faith. —SAMANTHA McGARRITY

7

SATURDAY

And walk in love…   —*EPHESIANS 5:2*

My husband and I took a nice gift to the wedding. But the gift I brought home from the church was greater.

I will always remember the minister's words to the bride and groom: "This ceremony makes you husband and wife. This is a wedding. The *marriage* comes later. Its success depends on an ever-growing love."

How true, I thought, remembering back over the many compromises and sacrifices my husband and I had made for each other during the course of our own long marriage. For, yes, it has *become* a marriage. Hour by hour—day by day—year by year.

And isn't this true of every relationship? We acknowledge an introduction and then gradually that stranger becomes a friend. We bring a child into the world and this tiny bit of humanity widens our circle of love. And once, long ago, I met Christ as my personal Saviour because He loved me. But, oh, how I have since grown because now I know what it is to love Him in return!

Yes, it was indeed a beautiful gift—a promise—that I brought home from the wedding. Ever-growing love.

Lord, may I be worthy of it. Hour by hour—day by day—year by year.
                                                        —JUNE MASTERS BACHER

8

SUNDAY

He that is of God heareth God's words…   —*JOHN 8:47*

The highlight of my visit to Greece last summer was the morning I spent on the Acropolis, where I was fascinated as the guide recounted the history of those ancient ruins. Then someone pointed out the *agora*, the ancient Athenian marketplace, and just above it Mars Hill, where Paul is said to have preached. A gold cross marks the spot today.

My mind, which had been focused on the giants of Greek history, suddenly turned to dwell on a giant of Christian history. I found myself trying to imagine the courage it must have taken for St. Paul to have spoken out in that intellectual center of the world about the risen Christ. Certainly his audience of skeptics was unreceptive (they called him "babbler"), but that fact did not deter Paul one bit.

"...In all things ye are too superstitious," he told his listeners. "For as I passed by...I found an altar with this inscription, TO THE UNKNOWN GOD. Whom therefore ye ignorantly worship..." (Acts 17:22-23). Paul went on to witness earnestly to the *known* god—"For in him we live..." (Acts 17:28). Paul went on to witness to a known God, one who doesn't dwell in temples and was not made by hands.

When we review the history of the Christian church, men like Paul remind us of what a great heritage we have. The buildings that once graced the Acropolis—the Parthenon, the Propylaea, the Erechtheum—have all fallen, but the God about whom Paul spoke still lives, still rules.

We thank You, Father, for sending us the inspiration and wisdom of Your great teachers. —FRED BAUER

---

9 MONDAY
For the preaching of the cross is to them that perish foolishness; but unto us which are saved it is the power of God. —I CORINTHIANS 1:18

"Take a good look at that plus sign," my husband said one night as we were working on our accounts. "It's the sign of the cross."

"You're right!" I exclaimed, and then drew it—(+). "Something that *adds* rather than subtracts."

"Now look at the minus." His fingers moved the pen—(−). "A small horizontal line. Negative, lying down. The only way we can get over this is to pull ourselves to our feet, stand up—and open our arms wide. When we do, we are turning the minus into a plus. We have become a plus sign—like the cross."

"And that makes you the kind of person who *adds* to other lives! You want to help, to encourage, to give."

"You got it!" My husband laughed. "Hey, we've had quite an arithmetic lesson in love."

Dear Lord, help me to stand up in the strength of the cross, to be a positive (+) instead of a negative (−), a sign that will add to other lives. —MARJORIE HOLMES

---

10 TUESDAY
Pray without ceasing. —I THESSALONIANS 5:17

I have a new goal in life these days—keeping up with the Jones'.

That's Marge Jones and her gang of four, times two. Marge is Mom to all eight of them. Quite a unique family, wouldn't you say? But it's not just the size of this clan that's unique. All of the children are handicapped, and each one has been adopted by Marge, who, by the way, isn't married and never has been. "With a crew like mine," she says, "I probably never will be."

Oh, and Marge smiles a lot—even when the bank account is empty, as usual. All she says is, "Sure I worry some days, but it's a lot easier to trust in God."

I've often wondered where that deep trust of hers comes from. Sometimes when I'm fussing about things, I picture Marge out camping with the kids, or at a Wednesday-night church service, or singing "Jesus songs" around the dinner table.

So that's why I'm trying to keep up with the Jones'. Recently I let Marge give me a little motherly advice. "Once last spring," she said, "the kids got halfway down the drive on their way to the school bus and Laura yelled, 'Mama, we forgot to pray!' So I yelled back, 'Lord, please be with these children today', and one of them yelled back again, 'In Jesus' name, Amen.'"

Mama, we forgot to pray! Marge, I want you to know that I won't forget. Not any more. And thanks—for showing me not only where that trust comes from, but how.

Today, Lord, with a little help from a big family, I learned a little Bible verse with a big message..."Pray without ceasing." *And I will.*
                                                        —JEFF JAPINGA

---

11 WEDNESDAY
O clap your hands, all ye people...   —PSALM 47:1

My visit to Carmel, one of the loveliest spots on the California coast, coincided with a rock festival in nearby Monterey. Late on a sparkling afternoon, my hostess and I went down to the beach to watch the sun-spectacular. We were dismayed to find the usually placid beach aswarm with noisy, brawling, long-haired youths, all of them drinking, smoking, wrestling, shrieking. It was quite a sight and we were about to retreat—but suddenly the glorious sunset swept over us. And over them.

For almost an hour, as kaleidoscopic streamers of red, gold, rose and lavender streaked across the sky, we sat there enthralled. A deep hush fell over the throng, the raucous voices settled into a gentle murmur and an unbroken peace descended upon all. Finally, as the last little rim of the brilliant red ball dropped below the horizon, a great wave of spontaneous applause burst from the rock crowd.

"What do you know?" my friend exclaimed in astonishment. "They're applauding God!"

"No," I countered rather bluntly, "they're applauding nature."

She smiled at me. "Somewhere I read these words," she said. "'A sunset is nature. The beauty is God.' I don't think you can love the one without the Other, do you?"

Heavenly Father, may our hearts join as one in gratitude and praise for Your magnificent works.   —ELAINE ST. JOHNS

12 THURSDAY
Do all things without murmurings and disputings...
—PHILIPPIANS 2:14

I grumbled out loud as I took from the sink a knife heavily smeared with peanut butter. How many times had I told the children not to leave knives there coated with peanut butter? A thousand maybe? Still muttering to myself, I wiped the knife clean and started to put it in the dishwasher.

Then a startling thought popped into my mind. Suppose there were never any peanut-butter knives in the sink? Suppose the house was absolutely spotless three hundred and sixty-five days a year—a real showplace? I wondered, *How many women would give anything in the world to have children, even if they left peanut-butter knives in every room in the house?*

And after that an even more sobering thought startled me, so that I stood motionless at the dishwasher, the knife still in my hand. Suppose I lived entirely alone...in an entirely perfect house?

I shuddered, put the utensil in the dishwasher and then bent down to pick up tiny particles of dry mud that had fallen from one of the boys' tennis shoes. My grumbling had suddenly stopped. This time I wasn't even going to ask, "Which one of you boys tracked mud through the kitchen?"

Father, I thank You for the joyous blessing of others—both family and neighbors—to look after. —MARION BOND WEST

13 FRIDAY
...A man of understanding walketh uprightly.
—PROVERBS 15:21

Marion Wade was one of the most devout men that I have ever known. He always carried the New Testament in his pocket and was quick to tell anyone, at any time, that it was his faith that had helped him to succeed in the business world.

He had absolutely no qualms about mixing religion and business and often said, "If you don't *live* it, you don't *believe* it."

It was this firm conviction that helped him to build a one-man rug-cleaning enterprise into a gigantic maintenance corporation, with thousands of employees throughout the world. He called it ServiceMaster—in the service of the Master.

"I have never tried to take a step forward in the business world without first spending time on my knees asking for God's guidance," Marion once told me, "and He has always given it to me."

Marion Wade will forever be a reminder to me that in business or pleasure, I too shall strive to be guided by God first, last and always. It's the only lifestyle that never lets you down—nor lets you let anyone else down!

Lord, in all that I do and all that I am, You come first.
—GLENN KITTLER

14 SATURDAY
...And honour him, not doing thine own ways, nor finding thine own pleasure, nor speaking thine own words... —ISAIAH 58:13

Today the newspapers are filled with stories of wrong-doing and corruption at all levels, but it seems that we hardly ever read stories of people who in every walk of life thwart temptation every day. Recently I thought of three friends who might be called unsung heroes for their staunch honesty and integrity.

— Helen's husband is away from home for weeks at a time. Sure she gets lonely and misses companionship. But she never complains and says very simply, "I honor my marriage vows."

— Bert recently purchased a new car that can travel at speeds of over one hundred twenty miles an hour. But he says, "The speed limit is fifty-five. I honor it."

— Bill night-watches at a food-processing plant, where he has the keys to all the freezers. "Sure I have access to everything in there," he says. "But I honor the confidence my boss has in me."

Now maybe my friends' comments seem rather matter of fact, but stop and think a minute. Haven't we all heard these lines: *A little flirting won't hurt—Going sixty or seventy is no big deal—They'll never miss it, they have more than they need.*

As Christians we have been given a set of commandments to guide us in all our ways and to show us the path of righteousness. When we learn the joy of being able to say, "I honor His trust," we know that we have obeyed.

Father, help me to live up to the trust You have placed in me.

—ISABEL CHAMP

JESUS, THE MASTER STORYTELLER
Parable of the Sower

—MATTHEW 13:3-23
—MARK 4:3-20
—LUKE 8:4-15

15 SUNDAY

All storytellers wonder sometimes whether they're getting through to their audience, and perhaps there were moments when Jesus Himself wondered. Many people came to hear Him, and yet... how many were really understanding Him? How many were doing what He advised them to do? How many lives were being changed?

He put those questions into a parable so simple and so brilliant that it appears in three of the four Gospels in almost identical form. It is the parable of the sower.

Jesus did not grow up in a farming family, but Nazareth was a small village and many of its people must have been farmers. So the sight of the sower striding along in the spring, casting handfuls of seed must have been familiar.

The sower scatters his seed. Some of it falls on hard-packed ground where the birds come and eat it. Some lands in shallow soil where it germinates quickly, but is scorched by the sun and dies because it has no established root system. Some starts to grow but then is beset by weeds and thorns and briers that choke it. And some lands on good ground, and brings forth fruit, "an hundredfold."

One would think the message in the story is unmistakable, but Jesus patiently spelled out the meaning for his own disciples. The seed is the Word of God. The devil, like the birds, comes and takes it away before it can take root. Some people reach with enthusiasm, but then fall away. Others are distracted by too much trouble—or too much money. Then finally the message does get through to some, with wonderful results.

Which category would you put yourself in? A sobering question, but precisely the one Jesus wanted His hearers to ask themselves. I think the truth may be that most of us belong in more than one category. Few are so stonyhearted as to reject the whole Gospel out of hand. But certainly there are times when fits of enthusiasm and dedication die away. Times when thorns—the cares of the world—crowd out everything that's important. And there are periods when this temporal world is so satisfying that the eternal one is blotted out.

To be fair, there are times when the seed really has fallen on good soil, too. But it's an uneven terrain at best. One that can be improved.

Help me improve my soil, Lord, and transform my life into rich, fertile ground. —ARTHUR GORDON

16

MONDAY

...So will I save you, and ye shall be a blessing...

—ZECHARIAH 8:13

They say his name was Dismas. He was a thief. One of three men crucified on the same day as Christ on the hill outside Jerusalem. I have always wondered what he stole, and why. And who had told him of Jesus.

For Dismas was a believer. He called Him by the name of Lord. He knew that Jesus would be resurrected, for he said, "...remember me when Thou comest into Thy kingdom."

And Jesus said to him, "Verily I say unto thee, Today shalt thou be with me in paradise." What a promise!

Today there is a memorial dedicated to Dismas in the state prison in Dannemora, New York. It is called the Chapel of the Penitent Thief. It tells every sinner—and that means you and me, all of us—that it is *never* too late to turn to Jesus and join Him in paradise.

Lord, forgive me my sins and show me Your Way.

—ZONA B. DAVIS

17

TUESDAY

Pray for them which despitefully use you, and persecute you... —MATTHEW 5:44

Some years ago a woman in our town seemed to take joy in criticizing people behind their back, including members of my family.

At first I let that woman and her wagging tongue really disturb me. One day I complained bitterly about it to a friend, who gently urged me: "Don't criticize. Pray."

Reluctant to pray for this bothersome woman, I decided to take my friend's advice anyway. *It won't hurt to try,* I told myself. But what happened next took me by surprise. No, my prayers didn't cause the woman to change. They changed *me*! I simply couldn't bring myself to hate someone for whom I was praying. And at last I felt peace within myself because I was no longer having to deal with all those bad feelings.

Have you ever tried praying for someone who has used you poorly? Try it and see what happens. I wager that you'll be every bit as surprised as I was. Don't pray for the other person to change, but for God to bless that person, always remembering that the other is one of His children too. Then you'll find it easier to let go of the ill will that has been destroying your happiness and taking away your peace of mind.

Today's a splendid day to set out in search of peace, don't you agree?

Dear God, help me to understand that while hatred works only against myself, prayer works for us all.

—SAMANTHA McGARRITY

---

18 WEDNESDAY

I beseech you therefore, brethren, by the mercies of God, that ye present your bodies a living sacrifice, holy, acceptable unto God, which is your reasonable service. —ROMANS 12:1

When I was a child, I heartily disliked Bible study but my grandmother would insist on it with the words, "Let's get cookin'!" Finally, after years of persistent study, the Word came alive to me.

Grandma is gone now but one of my most treasured possessions is her large pewter spoon that for fifty years of marriage she used for stirring, wearing it away until amost a whole half-inch is gone from the tip.

When I look at my grandmother's spoon, resting now on a shelf in the breakfront, I wonder—if God had given me a spoon when I first set out to serve Him, how much wear would it show today?

I don't want the measure of my life's work in His service to be like a little-used spoon. I want it to be like a beloved and well-worn utensil, mellowed and molded by everyday use, yet strong and ready to be handed on to the next in line.

And if that's the case, I had better "get cookin'" right away!

Heavenly Father, use me this day to Your glory.

—MADGE HARRAH

---

19 THURSDAY

My little children, let us not love in word, neither in tongue; but in deed and in truth. —I JOHN 3:18

Legend tells us that once a zealous young man went to St. Francis of Assisi and implored the saint to teach him how to preach.

"Gladly," said Francis. "Come with me."

All afternoon the young man followed Francis about, waiting eagerly for his lesson. They paused beneath a tree, and Francis stooped to return a young bird to its nest. They went on and stopped in a field crowded with reapers, and Francis bent his back to help the laborers load the hay onto a cart. From there they went to the town square, where Francis lifted a bucket of water from the well for an old woman and carried it home for her.

Each time they stopped, the young man was certain that a sermon would be forthcoming—but no words of great truth or wise discourse issued from the saint's mouth. Finally they went into the church—but Francis only knelt silently to pray.

At last, they returned to the place from whence they had started. "But when," the young man, by now thoroughly perplexed, asked the saint, "are you going to teach me how to preach?"

Francis smiled. "I just did."

Dear Lord, make my life a sermon—this day.

—PATRICIA HOUCK SPRINKLE

20

Be not overcome of evil, but overcome evil with good.
—ROMANS 12:21

Whenever someone refers to a "four-letter" word, we usually think of it as being an ugly word. But do you know that there are literally hundreds of very beautiful "four-letter" words?

Love is a four-letter word. And *kind* is a four-letter word. In I Corinthians 13, the Bible's "Love Chapter," St. Paul tells us that "Love is kind."

Why don't we try using these lovely words of Paul's to counteract some of the ugly expressions we hear from time to time? For instance, whenever we hear someone else use a four-letter word that offends us, we can show *love* by being *kind*. Now I don't mean that we act in a self-righteous manner, or in a namby-pamby way, but that we quietly set an example of just plain, everyday courtesy.

In John 17:8, Jesus tells our Father that He has given us "the words which thou gavest me...." With that glorious gift—the Word of our Father—can we do less than try to bring it forth by our actions and let it shine, even under the least of circumstances?

—Or *especially* under the least of circumstances?

Father, teach us to show love *and to be* kind *to those who have offended us.*   —ISABEL CHAMP

21

Let every man be fully persuaded in his own mind.
—ROMANS 14:5

I couldn't wait. As soon as I arrived at the mountain cabin, I dashed down to the lake for a swim. My dog Trooper followed, his tail waving in exuberant circles as he eagerly sniffed the fresh country air.

Plunging into the water, I swam out to an old wooden raft to sun myself. But Trooper stood uncertainly at the water's edge.

"Trooper—come!" I called. It wasn't like him to hesitate. "Good boy, come on!"

He cocked his head questioningly and then ran in the opposite direction, disappearing into the thick bushes along the shore. I didn't like that and was about to tell him so when suddenly he leaped out of the bushes and plunged into the water, swimming straight for the raft. He climbed aboard and stood wagging his whole body as though he expected me to praise him. *For what?* I wondered.

Then I studied the shore again and saw that the bushy area was much closer to the raft than the sandy beach from where I had entered the water. Trooper hadn't been disobedient after all—he was simply looking for a shorter route.

"Good boy!" I said, patting his head. "Good, *good* boy!"

Dear Father, help me to remember that we each travel our own path to You. —PHYLLIS HOBE

---

22 SUNDAY
The people which sat in darkness saw a great light...
—MATTHEW 4:16

All during the church service a nagging thought kept going through my mind: *Introduce yourself to the woman next to you and invite her to join your Sunday school class.* I felt shy about it and ignored the urging. *Invite her*, the Silent Voice repeated. *She probably already goes to a class*, I argued. The urging and my disobedient attitude went on all through the sermon. The woman turned and looked at me once. I smiled and she returned the smile.

After the closing prayer, I leaned over, introduced myself and said, "I'd like to invite you to our Sunday school class."

"Oh," she beamed, "I'd love to go with you."

And after that Shirley continued to come to our class. As we got to know one another better, she confessed, "That Sunday my son was praying that just the right person would invite me to just the right class. I'm a new believer and I didn't know anyone in the church."

As it turned out, Shirley and I were almost neighbors, and on that first Sunday we had each driven alone twenty-five miles downtown to attend the same church. And in a church of over ten thousand members, we had sat next to each other! I had been stubborn about speaking to her, but her son must have been a stubborn prayer too.

Have you ever felt the urge to speak to someone who "happened" to be sitting next to you in church, or anywhere? If so, don't be stubborn.

Dear Father, teach me to reach out to those whom You place beside me. —MARION BOND WEST

---

23 MONDAY

Remembering without ceasing your work of faith, and labour of love, and patience of hope...

—I THESSALONIANS 1:3

For me one of the most fascinating exhibits at the 1982 World's Fair, held in Knoxville, Tennessee, was the China Pavilion, which featured a panoply of beautifully crafted art works. Everyone in our family especially enjoyed the pavilion.

Although there were so many pieces to appreciate, I think that my favorite was a magnificent ocean liner carved out of ivory. Measuring at least three feet long, the multi-decked ship and its hundreds of passengers standing at the rails were accurate replicas, each fashioned in intricate detail. The project, a sign explained, represented a lifetime of work on the part of the artist. *Such grace! Such beauty!* I thought.

"Can you imagine all the patience and dedication it took?" I asked my wife.

"And love and vision," she added.

Yes, it took all of those gifts, I am certain. But upon reflection, I believe that all such dedicated undertakings require artists who have a great sense of the present and an enjoyment of the moment, those who understand that life is a journey, not a destination—a passage, not a port. With this kind of insight, wouldn't it be possible for each of us to carve out small daily joys in our lives that, when added together, might transform God's gift of life into the manifold blessing He intended?

I think I'll start today off as the artist of my own life—the first step in a lifetime's project for Him!

Lord, teach me the art of living in the here and now—not the there and then. I would like to make each moment a gift to You.

—FRED BAUER

---

24 TUESDAY
...I will never leave thee, nor forsake thee.
—HEBREWS 13:5

One time when I was a little girl, I was deeply frightened by an event far beyond my comprehension. My father's oldest sister was seriously ill and the family had gathered at her bedside. We children were instructed to remain outdoors.

Not understanding the situation, but sensing its gravity nonetheless, I huddled alone beneath the shade of the big pear tree in the front yard—until suddenly the quietness seemed overwhelming, and I panicked. Crying out in utter terror, I ran toward the forbidden parlor and its bleak gloom. Immediately I felt a warm, familiar hand close reassuringly over mine. My father scooped me up into his arms and I knew then that, no matter what, everything was going to be all right—Daddy was with me.

To this day, it is not the grief on the faces of those around me at that time that I best recall. It is the tender memory that my father was with me in my time of deepest need. He heard my cry and he removed my fear.

And today I treasure that same assurance from my Heavenly Father. You have it too should you cry out for comfort. Will your burdens be eased? Not always. But, blessed assurance, you will find that you are no longer alone.

Walk with me, Lord. All the way!   —JUNE MASTERS BACHER

---

25 WEDNESDAY
And Enoch walked with God...   —GENESIS 5:24

She lay with her nose resting on her paws, apparently asleep. Che'la was her name, poodle was her breed, gray her color.

And my friend Sue was the one Che'la loved most of all. This was evident in the way Che'la's shiny black shoebutton eyes peered up from under a fringe of hair and followed my friend every time she stood up and moved about the room. When Sue led me into the dining room, Che'la trotted at her heels. When we went out on the patio, Che'la followed. Wherever Sue went, Che'la was always nearby. And whether the small curly dog was playing with the new kittens or drinking from the water dish, she always seemed to have one eye fixed on her master.

In Genesis 5 a man named Enoch is said to have "walked with God." I have long pondered over the exact meaning of that phrase— and now I think that at last I understand it. I believe that Enoch walked through life in constant devotion for his Master—just as little Che'la's days are spent in following after my friend Sue. To and fro, here and there, Enoch went about his daily business, ever alert to follow God's commands, ever rejoicing in God's Presence, always choosing to stay close to God.

I would like to "walk with God" too, to share with Him every moment of sunshine that crosses my path, each shadow of uncertainty, the least thought in my heart.

Father, can You hear my footsteps today?   —DORIS HAASE

---

26 THURSDAY

He that giveth, let him do it with simplicity; he that ruleth, with diligence; he that sheweth mercy, with cheerfulness.   —ROMANS 12:8

How well I remember one of my first jobs in a commercial art studio. A customer came in one day angry berating my supervisor over a botched illustration. *Oh-oh,* I thought, *someone in this studio is in big trouble!*

When the supervisor approached my table, I realized that *I* was the culprit. I braced myself for a tongue-lashing—or even dismissal. Instead, the supervisor calmly explained my error and told me how to correct it. When I asked why he hadn't scolded me, he replied, "Anything produced in this studio is my responsibility. If it's wrong, I take the blame." Then he grinned. "And if it's right, I take the credit."

A simple declaration, but to me through the years it has come to represent the epitome of fairness in an employer.

And as a Christian I know that my work, my life, my relationships with others, all reflect my Lord and my faith—whether I do well or poorly. I guess that like everyone else, I'm bound to make mistakes now and then. But I will always try to be faithful and true—and honor as best I can in my life the One to Whom *all* credit is due.

Help my life reflect Your highest calling for me, Lord.

—MADGE HARRAH

27
FRIDAY

Behold, I stand at the door, and knock: if any man hear my voice, and open the door, I will come in to him…

—*REVELATION 3:20*

One day King Edward VII and his wife went for a long walk in the country. Dusk came upon them quickly and as they were hurrying to return to the palace, the queen turned her ankle and was unable to walk farther. They stumbled toward a farmer's cottage nearby.

The king knocked at the door and the farmer called out, "Who's there?"

"It is Edward," the king replied. "My wife is injured. Kindly let me in."

"Go away," the voice inside the cottage said. "I don't let strangers in."

"I am your king," Edward called. "And I require your assistance. I need to come in."

The farmer stomped to the door, determined to get rid of the intruder. But when he flung open the door, he saw that it was indeed his king standing there. Quickly he welcomed the royal couple to his home and provided cloths with which to bind the queen's ankle.

In the years that followed, the farmer told the story time and again, always saying, "And to think that I almost didn't let my king in!"

Are you heeding the call of *your* King? Will you open your heart and let Jesus in?

Come, Lord Jesus, be my Guest.   —DRUE DUKE

28
SATURDAY

Ye know that every one that doeth righteousness is born of him.   —*I JOHN 2:29*

Today marks the opening of the 1984 Summer Olympics

219

held this year in Los Angeles. I've always marveled at Olympic athletes, what it is that distinguishes them.

One of the best insights I ever received was from Jim Denney, the United States' top ski-jumper at the 1980 Winter Olympics in Lake Placid. When I asked him what it really took to be an Olympic athlete, he replied, "Talent of course, then hard work, faith in yourself and—most important—faith in God's Presence. And above all —*concentration*. You need your mind and your muscles going in the same direction."

While I'll never be an Olympic athlete, I learned something special from Jim's words that I've been trying to apply in my everyday life: concentration. So often I *think* I'm going to do something—and then I let myself be sidetracked and go off in a totally different direction. Like I *think* I'm going to send a card of sympathy...or make that phone call to a shut-in...or volunteer time for the Boys' Club...and then suddenly time has gone by— and I'm still standing at the gate!

We can't all be Olympic heroes, but maybe we can be "Christian" heroes if, like Jim said, we *concentrate*—point our actions in the direction of our thoughts and carry out our good intentions.

What are you thinking of doing today? Will you *do* it?

Yes, Father, I will do it today. —JEFF JAPINGA

---

29 SUNDAY
...Pray for one another, that ye may be healed.
—JAMES 5:16

Recently when I had to be hospitalized for a minor problem, many friends called or wrote to say that they were praying for me. I appreciated every call, every card, but one friend's letter stood out in particular.

She wrote: "This is the prayer I pray for you every morning at eleven o'clock: *Blessed Lord Jesus, shine Your healing light on Marilyn, gently removing the cause of her illness. I now affirm, in the name of Jesus Christ, that Marilyn is strong and healthy and that her mind is at rest. Amen."*

It wasn't just the words that touched me. By telling me *when* she would be praying for me and *what* she would be praying, my friend gave me something specific that I could really hold on to. Every day I knew just when she was there with me—I could *feel* her very presence.

After this, when I write to someone who needs my prayers, I will remember that warm, glowing touch of extra love.

Thank You, Lord, for strengthening us with the loving prayers of our friends.   —MARILYN MORGAN HELLEBERG

---

30 MONDAY
They shall run, and not be weary...   —ISAIAH 40:31

Fatigue—just plain physical tiredness—is a problem for many people. Did you know that there is a spiritual remedy for it?

One day Roy Lawrence, an English minister interested in spiritual healing, went to visit an old lady in Cornwall named Carrie Oates. Carrie, spry as a cricket at the age of eighty-two, had been healed of glaucoma by the laying on of hands, and she herself possessed a remarkable gift of healing.

"My gift," she told Roy Lawrence, "is to draw people into the stillness of God's presence. The highest form of prayer is contained in the words, 'Be still and know that I am God.'"

About fatigue, Carrie Oates had this to say: "When you're tired, sit down for a few minutes, close your eyes and think of the presence of God, because He is everywhere. Dwell on the words, 'made in the image of God', and 'the life of God in every cell'. There is no weariness in God—and if you let His strength flow into you, there will be no weariness in you either!"

Can your mind tell your body how to behave? Of course it can, and if the harmony of God dwells in your mind, it dwells also in your body.

Lord, fill me with the healing Presence of Your harmony today.

—ARTHUR GORDON

---

31 TUESDAY

He answered and said unto them, When it is evening, ye say, It will be fair weather: for the sky is red. And in the morning, It will be foul weather...for the sky is red... —MATTHEW 16:2-3

When I was in junior high school, we girls always toted around autograph books. On pages decorated with flowers and curlicues, friends would write their favorite sayings or sentiments and then sign their names.

But occasionally trivia made way for a message that stood out way above the rest. Such was the treasure that my English teacher, Mrs. Brand, wrote in mine. My autograph book disappeared ages ago, yet I can still see her fine Spencerian script on a bright pink page in my book.

"Always remember, Isabel," she wrote, "that it takes a few clouds to make a beautiful sunset." I knew that she was referring to my difficulty in differentiating between adjectives and adverbs. This weakness was hindering me in my desire to become a writer, and at the time I was almost despairing.

But today I can see how right she was. Completely cloudless skies are rare for any of us. There is always something we have to contend with or overcome. But we *do* have the ability to set those clouds in any perspective we choose. We can see them as a necessary part of a beautiful and colorful sunset, as Mrs. Brand said, or we can narrow our vision and see them as part of a threatening and storm-laden sky.

Lord, help me to live this day so that I see the lovely colors instead of the threatening storm. —ISABEL CHAMP

Praise Diary for July

1

2

3

4

5

6

7

8

9

10

11

12

13

14

15

16

17

18

19

20

21

22

23

24

25

26

27

28

29

30

31

August

S	M	T	W	T	F	S
			1	2	3	4
5	6	7	8	9	10	11
12	13	14	15	16	17	18
19	20	21	22	23	24	25
26	27	28	29	30	31	

Today, Lord, remember when I
Picked my garden's first lush-red
Ripe tomato? How—holding it in my palm,
Heavy as a stone, warm as a puppy,
Round, rich, full—I cried out:
"Praise You, Lord! Praise Your bounty"?
My back prickling in the August sun,
My feet rooted in mystery of warm brown earth,
My heart was swimming in love for
        Your abundance.

Now it is evening, Lord, and in this cool air
I recall my motive for the garden.
And I am ashamed.
"Let's plant a garden this year,"
        I said.
"Vegetables are so expensive,
And we could save some money."
A mean little reason for a garden…
I wasn't praising You then, Lord.
So I'm asking You now
To lengthen my vision that
I will see Your bounty always
Looms larger than my lack.

James McDermott

GUIDEPEOPLE: A Living Parable for August

1

WEDNESDAY

There is no fear in love; but perfect love casteth out fear.
                                                                    —I JOHN 4:18

The distinguished writer Helen Worden Erskine once amused us at *Guideposts* with a story about a lizard. Mrs. Erskine was an animal lover, but she drew the line at crawling reptiles. She was afraid of them.

Years ago, on a magazine assignment in what is now Pakistan, Mrs. Erskine had to stay several days in an old Karachi hotel where the service included a white-turbaned Moslem man-servant who slept on a mat outside her door. In the middle of the first night she awakened suddenly. A large lizard with a green back and a yellow belly was on the wall watching her intently.

She rushed to the door. "Help!" she screamed to the man-servant. "There's a lizard in my room."

"Yes, Madam," he replied, "there's a lizard in every room."

"I'm afraid of it. Kill it. Get rid of it."

"But, Madam," said the servant, "if I do remove the lizard, you will be plagued by all types of insects. Learn to live with your lizard. He is your friend. Once you realize this, your fear will vanish."

Mrs. Erskine suddenly felt ashamed of her fears and went back to face the lizard. Thinking of St. Francis and his love for all living things, she vowed to accept that ugly little creature as just as much a part of God's world as she herself was.

By the third night, Mrs. Erskine was bringing a few grains of sugar from the dining room and gingerly offering them to the lizard. And by the time she left Karachi, she and the lizard were friends. She no longer feared him.

So we see it: the sage advice that Emerson gave so succinctly: "Face the thing you fear the most, and the death of fear is certain."

You've told us, Lord, that perfect love casteth out fear. Help me to practice that love this month.   *—VAN VARNER*

2 THURSDAY

I will offer to thee…thanksgiving, and will call upon the name of the Lord. —PSALM 116:17

I'm a daytime person and I'm almost always up when the sun rises. But I don't always notice it. Until—every now and then—something special happens.

This morning I was standing at the kitchen sink filling a kettle with water and absent-mindedly looking out the window, not actually seeing anything at all. Then, across the grassy hill and just beyond the tall evergreens, the leading rays of the sun seemed to mushroom across the skies and the heavens began to glow with a tenuous blush…until, as though by magic, a sea of burnished apricot and gold swept across the hill and down the valley.

Standing there, I was overwhelmed by the power and majesty of God, Who fashioned this marvel of beauty, and yet could create something so practical and essential as light. I lowered my head. *Father*, I said, *good morning*…and my eyes filled with tears.

God expresses His love for us in so many beautiful ways and we don't always take note of them. But when we do, when we take time from our own busy pursuits, we can only wonder at ourselves and what we have been missing.

Did you see the sun rise today?

Dear Father, I come to You with the dawning of each new day.
—PHYLLIS HOBE

3 FRIDAY

As we have therefore opportunity , let us do good unto all men… —GALATIANS 6:10

Alexander Bryan and Cortland Heyniger were partners in a modest company that manufactured small, flat-decked sailboats during the late forties and early fifties. When Aileen Bryan, Alexander's wife, became pregnant, she complained that the little boat's flat deck was extremely uncomfortable for her to sit on. As a result, the two men designed a boat that had a well for her feet. They called the new boat a *Sunfish*.

So far, thousands of *Sunfish* have been sold, making it the most popular class of sailboat ever designed. Yet it is a simple fact that the sole idea behind the now-successful boat was that of making a pregnant woman more comfortable! As I look around, it seems to me that many of our finest enterprises have been built by those who put the wellbeing of others first.

So if really spectacular financial and material success is your goal, don't ask youself, "What's in it for me?" Instead, ask, "What's in it for *others*?" Then go one step farther. Ask yourself the same question about every facet of your life.

Then you'll *really* be successful!

Dear Father, I am successful only when I serve You by serving others. —JAMES McDERMOTT

---

4 SATURDAY

Hearken unto this... stand still, and consider the wondrous works of God. —JOB 37:14

One evening we were walking along the beach with friends. When the sun reached the horizon, it spread a crimson glow into the sky that was truly breathtaking.

"Magnificent!" someone breathed.

"Simply beautiful!" another murmured.

Then an elderly woman spoke up. "On a scale of one to ten, I'd give it a five," she said. After a pause, she sighed and added wistfully, "I don't think that sunsets are as beautiful as they used to be."

The conversation drifted on to other things, but my thoughts kept returning to her observation. I could hardly believe that sunsets had really changed over the years. No, it was the woman who had changed. Her husband was gone, her hair was silvered, her walk had slowed down. Once, when she was young and seaside sunsets still fresh to her eyes, she had seen beauty more vividly than she did now, in the twilight of her life.

"Beauty is in the eye of the beholder," the poet tells us. And youth is a state of mind. We are never old unless we allow our thoughts and attitudes to become so wrinkled that we can no longer appreciate the endless beauty of God's handiwork all about us. Some people never lose their childlike sense of wonder.

Lord, rekindle in us daily, a spirit of adventure and an enthusiasm for living. —FRED BAUER

---

5 SUNDAY
And the inspiration of the Almighty giveth them understanding. —JOB 32:8

All during the Sunday-morning service I was irritated by the jingling of the charm bracelet on the woman seated behind me. Then as I turned to leave the pew, I noticed that she was wearing a "Visitor" label. Forgetting my annoyance, I put forth my hand and introduced myself, welcoming her to our church.

"Oh," she beamed, "the pastor told me that I should meet you. We've just moved to your neighborhood." As we walked out of the church together, she said, "I hope my bracelet didn't disturb you. I hadn't intended to wear it today but I couldn't unfasten it and my husband Pete had already left for work."

"There are quite a few charms on it," I commented.

"I call it my 'miracle bracelet,'" she confided. "Each charm tells a story. See, this is the date we bought our first house, this one is Pete's promotion, and this one is for the birth of our grandson." Then she stroked one of the charms lovingly and said, "This one is from Katie, my dear, dear friend. We cried when Pete and I had to move away."

She looked up and although she was smiling, there were tears in her eyes. New in town, her husband working, lonely for her friend Katie. Quickly I tucked her hand in my arm. "You're coming home for dinner with my family," I said. "I want them to see your bracelet!"

Arm in arm, we went down the street. My impatience in church was something I'd have to settle with God later. Meanwhile, perhaps she and I could become friends. Perhaps someday, God willing, I might even earn a place in that circle of love that she wears around her wrist.

Teach me, dear Lord, the wisdom of tolerance that I may not be blind to Your blessings. —DRUE DUKE

---

6 MONDAY
Then shall the righteous shine forth as the sun...
—MATTHEW 13:43

On a damp, rainy Monday morning I stripped the beds as I went about my household duties. Later when I put clean sheets on the bed where my husband and I sleep, the unmistakable aroma of sunshine and fresh air seemed to fill the room. It was so sweet and refreshing and surprising that I bent over the bed for a better sniff. Just outside the rain was beating against the windowpanes. The day was gray, uninteresting, depressing. Yet inside, our bedroom seemed to be just flooded with sunshine.

Then I remembered that several weeks earlier on a bright, sunny day I had hung the sheets outdoors. It was the kind of day that simply beckons you to put sheets out on the line, where they can be whipped dry by a warm breeze and perfumed in the sun. It would have seemed almost criminal to have put them in the dryer on such a day.

Smiling as I went from the bedroom, I thought that I would like to be like those sheets—giving out a warm, sunny radiance even when everything around is dark and gloomy. Maybe *especially* then.

Father, help me to bring sunshine to others on a rainy day.
—MARION BOND WEST

7 TUESDAY

For ye were as sheep going astray; but are now
returned unto the Shepherd… —*I PETER 2:25*

Our visitor from London was telling us about a British cat named Rupert, who lived in a suburb of London with a family named Robinson. Rupert, it seems, had a way of disappearing for a day or two, sometimes three. Then he would come back as though he had never left.

One day Rupert reappeared wearing a brand new collar. A bit suspicious, the Robinsons attached to the collar a note that said: "My name is Rupert. I live at 22 Lansdowne Place with the Robinsons." Then they waited.

Pretty soon Rupert vanished again. This time, when he finally returned, another note was attached to his collar: "At 84 Bainton Road, where I live with the Cromwells, my name is Blackie."

"Smart cat," said one of our other guests with a laugh. "He had the best of both worlds."

But the oldest (and wisest) lady present shook her head. "Not so smart," she said. "He didn't know who he was. And he didn't know where he belonged."

Think about it. How smart are you?

Whenever we seem likely to stray, Lord, remind us to Whom we
really belong. —ARTHUR GORDON

8 WEDNESDAY

…The gift of God is eternal life through Jesus Christ
our Lord. —*ROMANS 6:23*

On a summer day filled with the fragrance of wildflowers, I was walking through an Indiana meadow when I came upon a little cemetery that belonged to the monastery perched at the top of the

231

hill. It was a small brown plot, stretched across the earth like an old monk's robe. I could not resist. I slipped through the gate and strolled among the rows of timeworn headstones, stopping now and then to read the ancient inscriptions. Then, unexpectedly, I came upon a grave still fresh, its headstone new and unweathered. Not a single blade of grass yet graced its neatly packed soil.

Suddenly the reality of death seemed very close... intruding into the present from out of the mists of the past. Standing there alone in the quiet little cemetery, I felt a deep twinge of sadness.

But as I turned to leave, I paused and looked back. Fluttering through the graveyard, dipping and dancing over the tombstones, was a small yellow butterfly. It was in sight for only an instant, but that one quick glimpse brought back to me a glorious truth: Life continually flows from the death of life. With the metamorphosis of the bright-winged butterfly from the tomb of the cocoon, isn't God showing us this? And I knew that it was but one more example of the eternal life He gave us with the death of His only Son.

As I left the cemetery, remote and quiet in the sunny meadow, I was flooded with new hope and joy—for after all, a grave is simply the doorway that welcomes us to God's Kingdom of Heaven!

Thank You, Lord, for giving us small, bright-winged reminders of the eternal life promised us through Your Son.

—SUE MONK KIDD

---

9 THURSDAY
He that dwelleth in the secret place of the most High shall abide under the shadow of the Almighty.

—PSALM 91:1

For nearly three years a huge black German shepherd roamed our neighborhood, until one day I brought him home. Despite his ferocious appearance, George, as I later named him, was extremely shy and it took me the next two years to convince him that no one wished him harm.

He was a gentle dog, loved and admired by everyone in the community, and eventually he became very docile and obedient. He took up the back seat of my VW whenever I went on trips or shopping forays. He loped along behind my bicycle, plunged into the Croton River with me in the summers, paddled behind when I went canoeing or rowing, took hikes with me, from his corner in the kitchen watched me cook...and invariably ended up in the center of things whenever I gave a party or invited friends in for dinner.

I guess you could say that George was like my shadow. He had needed someone to love him and care for him. Now that he belonged to someone, he had found his purpose in life—that of being *my* dog and *my* companion.

Now whenever I look at my contented canine friend, I find reflected in his eyes the same security I find within myself when I turn to *my* Lord and Master. And I would know then that just as George's days of loneliness and seeking are past, so are mine!

Dear Father, wherever You lead, I follow as Your grateful shadow.
—SAMANTHA McGARRITY

---

10 FRIDAY
Depart from evil... —PSALM 34:14

Ordinarily I am a cautious driver, but on this day someone had been tailgating my car, barreling past me to change lanes, then slowing down in front of me on purpose.

I was annoyed, so annoyed that the next time he began to tailgate, I found myself—for the first time in my life!—deliberately putting on the brakes. The furious glare he cast in my direction as he responded by roaring past me at rocket speed was truly frightening. Suddenly I had a strange feeling of menace and sobered immediately. In a situation like this, reciprocal anger might lead to real trouble. Furthermore, this was a dangerous freeway and we were approaching merging traffic just ahead.

That's when I saw the signs: "KEEP RIGHT." And soon thereafter: "YIELD, PROCEED WITH CAUTION."

Most of us who drive know and obey the vehicular laws—and most of us who are Christians know and obey God's laws. Should we ever be tempted to bend either set of rules, it is well to think: "KEEP RIGHT." And my goodness! When dealing with others, what better guideline do we have than to "YIELD, PROCEED WITH CAUTION"?

The Psalmist advises us to depart from evil, yes, but he has more to say. The rest of the verse above reads: "...and do good. Seek peace and pursue it." Today if someone would "tailgate"—whether by car or by an annoying habit or comment—I will remember to yield and to proceed with caution—in pursuit of peace!

Lord, I know I'm "right" when I follow Your Golden Rule.

—JUNE MASTERS BACHER

---

11 SATURDAY

For as he thinketh in his heart, so is he...

—PROVERBS 23:7

Mother Teresa of Calcutta, when asked for some special words of wisdom, replied, "Smile at those you live with." And Plato tells us that "the face is the mirror of the soul." And another writer states, "Each of us is a living advertisement of how we think and feel. Others are 'reading our ads' all the time."

Lots of people know that I'm a Christian. I wonder what kind of "advertising" I'm doing for Jesus....

I'm going to try to make my "ad" for Jesus more positive and appealing. Will you join me? As you go through your morning grooming routine, try to keep your heart focused on Him. Repeating a one-sentence prayer or a Scripture verse will help. You may be surprised at the light that will shine from your face as you go about your daily work. Even strangers may take notice of it—but best of all, you will find it a real joy to smile at those with whom you live as your outward actions mirror your loving inner thoughts.

Yes, it's true. Each of us can set up our own advertising campaign for Him!

Lord, I pray that Your light may shine through me for all to see.
—MARILYN MORGAN HELLEBERG

---

12 SUNDAY

...The kingdom of God cometh not with observation: Neither shall they say, Lo here! or, lo there! for, behold, the kingdom of God is within you. —LUKE 17:20, 21

Recently in our Sunday Bible class a young man raised the question: "Just how do we *find* the Kingdom of God? We live in a *worldly* kingdom. It takes *money* to live. Unemployment is high. We suffer from the effects of inflation, from crime, from wars. I know that Jesus has told us not to worry about our lives, but how can we possibly not worry?"

How indeed? I wondered, sitting there silently.

"Luke seventeen, verses twenty and twenty-one," answered our teacher promptly. "They tell us to look no further for the Kingdom of God, it is *here*. And they mean *here*, right in the very *midst* of the unemployment, the inflation, the crime and the wars. You find the Kingdom by surrendering all your doubts to God. Search the depths of your heart. What do you find reigning there, fear or faith? If your answer is *faith*, you have found the answer to both questions."

As the young man's face lit up with comprehension, he smiled and slowly nodded. "I get it."

So did I.

Let me spend today, and all my days, in Your Kingdom, Lord Jesus, now and forever. —DORIS HAASE

13 MONDAY
For the wind passeth over it, and it is gone…

—PSALM 103:16

Judy and I had planned our trip to Spain for over two years, and now—at last—we were leaving the plane just after our arrival at the Madrid airport.

"Hold it right there," I called to Judy. "I want to get a picture of you and the plane." I also took a shot of her getting into the taxi, then stepping into the elevator of the hotel and later in front of the Prado.

"You're wearing me out," Judy laughed after she had paused in mid-stride for the umpteenth time.

"Well, I want to record as much as I can so we'll have something to remember the trip by," I replied.

The next day we took a bus tour to Toledo, and our guide, who noticed my busy, clicking camera, said to me, "If you spend all your time taking pictures, you're never going to *see* anything."

How wise that guide was! I had been trying to capture—to possess, really—every moment. And indeed all that remains from our first days in Spain are some dusty photographs tucked away somewhere in a drawer. But there are priceless moments for which there are no photographs: standing arm in arm with Judy atop the Giralda tower in Seville, lazily picnicking in a sunny hideaway cove of the Mediterranean, strolling in the Moorish majesty of the Cathedral at Cordoba.

No, our best treasures can never be captured on plastic or tape or film—they lie deep in our hearts.

Lord, let me not try to possess the riches of life. Teach me instead to enjoy them to their fullest as they arrive.

—JAMES McDERMOTT

14 TUESDAY

Charity suffereth long, and is kind; charity envieth not; charity vaunteth not itself, is not puffed up…
—*I CORINTHIANS 13:4*

One evening recently when my husband arrived home from the office, I was all set to give him an account of my day's problems. The words were right on the tip of my tongue, ready to spill out when I noticed the weary lines on his face. *He must have had a really hard day*, I thought.

Then I remembered a question one of my high-school friends sometimes asked when she wanted to "put down" someone who was talking on and on about his or her troubles:

"Are you bragging or complaining?"

It struck me then and there that a recital of my day's woes would indeed be both bragging *and* complaining. It would be a deliberate effort on my part to get my husband's undivided attention and to engender his sympathy.

Quickly I pushed the words of complaint way in the back of my mind, gave my husband a kiss and hurried off to finish preparing supper. His look of love and gratitude, when we sat down at the table with the children for the evening blessing, more than made up for any satisfaction I might have felt in unloading my problems on him and presenting myself in the role of brave martyr.

When I'm tempted to put myself first, Father, first let me ask if I'm being kind. —MADGE HARRAH

JESUS, THE MASTER STORYTELLER
Parable of the Mustard Seed
—MATTHEW 13:31-32

15

Of all the major sporting events I've attended—the World Series, the Indianapolis 500, the all-star games, the Kentucky Derby, the college bowl games—the most stirring by far was the 1980 Winter Olympics at Lake Placid. Watching colorfully uniformed men and women from all over the world pit their athletic skills against each other was both moving and exciting.

Of course, the big story out of the 1980 games was the U.S. hockey team's surprising gold-medal victory over the heavily favored Russian team. All the world loves an underdog, a person or group of people who courageously battle great odds.

Maybe that is another reason for the Bible's popularity; it's penchant for stories about successful underdogs—David against Goliath, Daniel against the lions, Shadrach, Meshach and Abed-nego against the fiery furnace, the Israelites against the Egyptians. Drawing upon this identification with and love for the underdog, Jesus often championed the small over the large, the last over the first, the sinful over the pious, the poor over the rich, the weak over the powerful.

In His parable of the mustard seed, the Kingdom of Heaven is like a mustard seed, "which is the least of all seeds, but when it is grown, it is the greatest among herbs...." Though Jesus was giving us a prophetic message about what was to come from His ministry, it nonetheless expressed the theme that from little acorns, great oaks grow. He referred to the mustard seed later in Matthew 17:20 when he told his disciples that with the faith of a mustard seed, they could move mountains.

Literal mountains? No, those are the easy kind. He meant figurative ones—flesh-and-blood mountains that require an unshakable belief in the face of overwhelming odds. Such faith can bring to fruit the hopes and dreams and visions of the suffering, the defeated and the disillusioned. As the old hymn says....

> Got any rivers you think are uncrossable,
> Got any mountains you can't tunnel through,
> God specializes in things thought impossible,
> He does what others cannot do.

Lord, fill us with a trust unquestioning and a faith unflagging.

—FRED BAUER

---

16 THURSDAY
...For he (the Spirit) dwelleth with you, and shall be in you. —JOHN 14:17

"Listen!" my father said. "Listen to the song of the Spirit!" Daddy and I were standing in a pine forest, where our family was camping one summer night. And I did hear a song! It seemed to echo across the centuries on the wings of the wind, and there was something in my child's heart that answered back. Some years later, as we watched a mountain waterfall together, Daddy said the words again—and suddenly the rushing waters became a symphony. Then one breathless day during World War II, I stood aboard a Navy ship, tears streaming down my face, and kissed my father good-by. He winked, chucked me under the chin and said, "Listen! Listen to the song of the Spirit!" As I looked out over the rolling sea to the edges of space, I heard it again—*the song*.

Even today, the song of the Spirit comes to me in varying guises— in the mourning dove's soulful call, or the sound of rain on a cabin roof, or the moan of the winter wind in the fireplace flue. But now I know a secret that I didn't know as a child. The Spirit *never stops*

239

singing—and He sings within me! All I have to do is to be still and listen.

I will take time today, Lord, to pause and listen for the song of Your indwelling Spirit. —MARILYN MORGAN HELLEBERG

---

17 FRIDAY
...The way of transgressors is hard. —PROVERBS 13:15

Sometimes people come to me and say that their prayers seem to receive no answers. They pray and pray, they say, but never see any results. So sometimes I tell them this little story.

I grew up in a series of small towns in Ohio, where my father was a Methodist minister. This meant that I was a "preacher's kid," always afraid of being labeled a sissy or a namby-pamby. One day when I was about fourteen, I decided to dispel this reputation for good by walking down the main street smoking a cigar.

I bought a five-cent cigar, lighted up and started down the street. I hadn't gone fifty yards when suddenly from around a corner came my father. I snatched the cigar from my mouth and hid it behind my back as he approached me. I looked around wildly for an avenue of escape, but there was none. Then I saw a poster across the street announcing the arrival of a circus in our town, and in a frantic effort to create a diversion, I cried, "Look, Dad, the circus is coming! Will you take us to it?"

My father looked me right in the eye. "Norman," he said, "never ask for favors while you're holding a smoldering disobedience behind your back." With that he walked on down the street.

See what I mean? God's laws are plainly set forth in the Bible. If you are breaking one or more of them, why should He grant you any favors? Think about it. Get rid of those "smoldering disobediences" before you ask for help. Do it today.

Lord, I seek You at all times in all truth and honesty.

—NORMAN VINCENT PEALE

18

The heavens declare the glory of God   —PSALM 19:1

What an enchanting way to spend a summer evening! When I was a child, my mother would spread out an old quilt on the side lawn just before dark. Then she and I and some of the neighborhood children would lie down on it and gaze up at the heavens. Sometimes for hours.

"There's Orion," someone always observed. "Look, a falling star!" someone else marveled. "I used to look up at the very same stars when I was a little girl," my mother often told us. And then we would mull over all the people in the past who observed the same celestial glory. "Even the Lord Jesus Himself, when He was on earth, saw the stars just as we see them now," the elderly woman from next door pointed out. We never tired of it—lying on the old quilt and looking up into the silent, starry night.

The other evening I walked out of our air-conditioned den, away from the television, and spread out an old quilt on the lawn.

"What are you doing?" one of our teen-aged sons asked nervously as he rode up on his bike. He glanced around cautiously to see whether any of the neighbors might be watching. "I'm going to look at the heavens," I announced calmly. He sat down beside me and followed my gaze upward. Our other son soon joined us. And my husband, who understands all about looking at the stars, quietly came from the house and sat down on the quilt. And after that, lo and behold, our nineteen-year-old daughter and her boyfriend plopped down beside us.

"There's Orion," my daughter said.

"Did you used to do this when you were a little girl, Mama?" one of the boys asked.

Deep, deep satisfaction and a wondrous sense of worship filled my heart.

Thank You, Father, for being the same yesterday, today and forever.   —MARION BOND WEST

241

19 SUNDAY

...Thy rod and thy staff they comfort me.

—PSALM 23:4

In my church, we kneel at the altar to receive the Lord's Supper. I was in meditation, waiting for the elements to come to me, when a few feet away a small commotion began. I turned my head slightly and peeked to see the cause.

A child, less than three years old, who had apparently been left alone in the pew, had found his way to his parents and was trying to squeeze in between them. Worshipers kneeling on either side of the parents were moving over to make room, and as the toddler snuggled close against his father, his small face beamed with the satisfaction of being with him, safe and secure.

There at the Lord's table I too smiled—for I am like a child in my Father's world. I am such a small part of His great creation, yet so many have moved in so many ways to make it possible for me to get closer to Him.

And—with Him—I am joyously safe and secure.

Such joy, Lord, to lean on You!

—DRUE DUKE

20 MONDAY

For it is God which worketh in you both to will and to do of his good pleasure. —PHILIPPIANS 2:13

Recently I read a story attributed to Rabbi Joseph Liebermann. In the tale, the rabbi falls asleep one night and has a dream. In the dream he dies and goes to stand before the Judgment Seat of God. As he waits for God to speak, he fears that the Lord will ask him, "Why weren't you a Moses...or a David...or a Solomon?" But God surprises him. He simply asks, "Why weren't you Rabbi Liebermann?"

242

Now I've read a lot about Mother Teresa and her selfless work in India; I've noted the lives of dedicated Christians throughout the world; and I've observed those around me who seem to accomplish so much for God. And next to all these I've felt myself ordinary and inadequate.

Sometimes I've even longed to do as they have done.

But the rabbi's story has set me straight. When my life is over, perhaps God will ask me why I wasn't Mother Teresa. But he might ask, "Why weren't you Sue Kidd? Why didn't you offer the world that special gift I gave only to *you*—the gift of yourself?"

I don't think I'm going to wait for Him to ask the question. Instead, I'm asking it of myself today.

Each of us has his own unique song to sing, his own particular gift to bring to the world. Even me! Even you!

Yes, Father, You can count on me.   —SUE MONK KIDD

---

21 TUESDAY
And Jesus said unto them, I am the bread of life…
— JOHN 6:35

I had to be out on an errand early this morning. I overslept a bit and didn't have time for breakfast, so when I returned to the house, I automatically hurried to the kitchen for a cup of tea and a muffin.

Upstairs a pile of unanswered letters, a mound of laundry, a half-written manuscript, and a list of phone calls to be made awaited me.

Soon it would be time to pick up the children.

Do I have time to read my Bible? I wondered. I felt so duty bound to the chores of the day.

Then my eye fell on the teacup and the muffin crumbs on the table. On coming in, hadn't my first priority been automatically to feed my body? Then wasn't my next priority to feed my *soul*? I did just that. I took up my Bible and discovered once again what I should have known all along — that both bodies and souls function best when they've been nourished!

Dear Lord, I will partake in the Bread of Life through the reading of Your Word today. —PATRICIA HOUCK SPRINKLE

---

22 WEDNESDAY

And God saw every thing that he had made, and, behold, it was very good. —GENESIS 1:31

Late one summer our family visited Zion National Monument. We stayed in a campground surrounded by ancient apple orchards that had been planted by Utah's early pioneers. The gnarled trees sagged under their heavy loads of fruit, and windfall apples covered the ground in great golden drifts.

We asked the park ranger for permission to pick up a few apples. He begged us to.

"Most of the fruit goes to waste anyway," he said. "Campers don't seem to know that apples found anyplace but in a supermarket are fit to eat."

I was amazed at his words. And then I thought of my weekly dependence on the grocery store—and my grumbling over the high price of applesauce.

Later that evening, while stirring a fragrant pot of my own spicy apple concoction over the campfire, I mused: It's ironic that today we seem to trust more in the supermarket manager for our provender than we do in the Lord!

Isn't it time that we get back to basics?

From now on, Lord, I will delight in the earthly abundance with which you have blessed me. —MADGE HARRAH

23 THURSDAY
...With what measure ye mete, it shall be measured to you... —MARK 4:24

The tale is told of a child who lived high in the Smokey Mountains. One day when she was being naughty, her mother spanked her.

The little girl ran to the edge of a precipice and shouted at her mother, "I hate you! I hate you!" And an echo came back from out of the valley, "I hate you! I hate you!"

Frightened, the child ran to her mother, sobbing.

But her wise mother led her back to the rim of the ravine and said, "Now call out, 'I love you! I love you!'"

The child did so, and a clear, sweet voice came back—"I love you! I love you!"

Taking the little girl in her arms the mother said, "My dear, always remember that in life we get what we give."

Heavenly Father, help me to give my best. —ZONA B. DAVIS

24 FRIDAY
And whither I go ye know, and the way ye know. —JOHN 14:4

It seems to me that every now and then some of the most cherished lessons in life are derived from the most unlikely of situations.

The other day a man told me about a drive he and his son had taken from Long Island to Connecticut. They took the ferry across Long Island Sound and when they debarked, evidently took the wrong road. They drove for a long, long time—too long—without reaching their destination. Finally, totally confused, they pulled up at a garage for directions.

245

"We're lost," they announced to the mechanic.

"Nope," he said, "you're not lost. You're *here*." Then he told them how to find the road they wanted.

Now whenever I feel really confused and bewildered by the burdens of everyday life, when I feel that perhaps God has forgotten me and my problems as I grope for guidance, I find myself remembering that little story. And then I can hear my Lord saying, like the kindly garage-keeper, *"No, you're not lost, Jeff. You're here."*

What greater comfort in all the wide world than to know that we can "be here" with Him—especially when we think we're lost! For hasn't He told us over and over again that He is with us always?

Wherever we are, Father, You have promised to be also. May that promise never be lost on us. —JEFF JAPINGA

---

25 SATURDAY
O God, my heart is fixed; I will sing and give praise…
—PSALM 108:1

How easy it is to put off cleaning the attic. Only this past week my husband descended the attic steps umpteen times—each time with some cherished, half-forgotten item: scrapbooks and annuals from high school and college, his swimming medals, a collection of antique coins. But the thing that thrilled both of us the most was an old album of Grace Moore recordings.

"What a beautiful singer she was!" he said.

I awoke the next morning to the magnificent voice of Grace Moore singing *Ave Maria*. I hurried through my shower and began to exercise to her song, bending and stretching at the bannister that serves as barre. And my husband, looking up from the foot of the stairs, began to sing with her, his voice blending with the rich, sweet sounds from that gifted throat.

It was truly a moving experience for both of us.

Since then we have listened to our other Grace Moore recordings, and we never cease to marvel at the miracle of those records that bring back a treasured voice from out of the past.

It often reminds me of a voice of Another that can be heard without the miracle of electronics. The voice of Jesus speaking... the gentle voice that heals and gives us eternal words of hope and promise... the voice that has never been silenced. All we need to do is to listen for it in our hearts.

Lord, I'm listening and singing for You. —MARJORIE HOLMES

---

26 SUNDAY
...Lo, these many years do I serve thee... —LUKE 15:29

"Better *is* than *was!*" read the safe-driving poster. And suddenly I was reminded of a dilemma I had recently been trying to resolve.

I had been feeling, perhaps somewhat justifiably, that I had "served my term" in church group activities and taught enough Sunday-school classes over the years. *After all,* I asked myself, *isn't it time the younger ones took over?*

But then an inner voice would argue that if I withdrew, wouldn't I run the risk of becoming a "was"? And those around me—at home, at church and at work—still needed me to be an "is." And, oh, I had to admit, how good it was to be needed! All at once my dilemma was resolved by the message on that simple poster.

Would you like to have a tried-and-true rule for driving safely through life? No matter how long your route may seem or how tempted you may be to turn off, keep on going—straight ahead— and be an "is" for the Lord. Don't stop mid-course, for we are meant to serve Him *all* the days of our lives.

I want to work for You today, Lord... and tomorrow... and...
—JUNE MASTERS BACHER

247

27 MONDAY

Now the God of hope fill you with all joy and peace in believing, that ye may abound in hope...

—ROMANS 15:13

One August day in 1948—when I was still just a tyke—word got out that Dan Topping, the glamorous owner of the New York Yankees, had docked his yacht at the marina in Westhampton. I pedaled my bicycle so quickly to the site that not even our nimble little beagle, Tagalong, could keep up with me.

The Topping yacht was big, but its size was only a fraction of its magnificence. Its splendor lay in the harmony of its every gleaming fitting and contour. Although the boat was made of wood, its quality was more that of finely sculptured marble. I walked back and forth along the dock, studying it over and over again, fascinated by every little detail.

Suddenly there was a man on deck, wearing a blue blazer and elegant white flannel trousers, a silk kerchief tied casually at his neck.

"You like it, don't you?" he asked in a way that made me know, even at ten years of age, that he himself liked it very much indeed.

"Yes, sir," I breathed. "It's the most beautiful boat I've ever seen."

"Well," he smiled, "if you feel that way, you ought to get one like it for yourself when you reach my age."

"Oh," I said, awe-struck, "I could never hope to have a boat like this!"

"Well, son," Dan Topping told me, "if you don't *hope* to get one, you never will."

A lesson, I think. Not for boats, maybe, but... isn't it true? *If you don't hope....*

Lord of all possibilities, help me to keep my sights raised high.

—JAMES McDERMOTT

28 TUESDAY
*Wherefore, my beloved brethren, let every man be
swift to hear, slow to speak...* — JAMES 1:19

I used to think that I was a good listener. You could talk to
me about any of your problems and I would understand. In fact, I
would even tell you how I felt when the very same thing had
happened to me. "I know just how you feel," I always said. And I
meant it.

But I'm not that way any more, not since a dear friend once had
the courage—and the love—to interrupt me and ask, "How can you
possibly know how I feel? You're not *me*!" At first I was hurt. Then,
when I had thought it over for a little while, I *truly* began to
understand.

We really can't know how the other person feels. If someone else
is expressing sorrow, we can acknowledge the feeling of sorrow, but
it isn't *our* sorrow. The same is true of joy, or anger, or despair. We
can share these feelings with each other, but only so far. Then we
have to let go, and simply listen with love.

Nowhere in the Bible does Jesus say, "Yes, I know just how you
feel," nor does He ever ask us to know how another feels. His
commandment is that "Ye love one another; as I have loved you..."
(John 13:34). And this means that we listen, not that we put
ourselves in the same place with another.

Some call it sympathy. Some call it compassion. I call it *love*.

*Father, teach me to listen to others as You listen to me—with
love.* —PHYLLIS HOBE

29 WEDNESDAY
...Not my will, but thine, be done. —LUKE 22:42

Last summer when I was struggling with a particularly
stubborn problem, I tried everything that I could think of, but

249

nothing worked. In fact, the harder I attempted to work things out, the worse they became.

Then one day a tiny yolk-yellow butterfly flew into my car and in its attempt to get free, it kept flying into the windshield blindly. Even though I opened the window and gently tried to brush it out, the little creature was too frantic to let me help. When I got home, I left the car window open, thinking that it would find its way out, but the next morning I found it dead on the dashboard, only a few inches from freedom.

Something clicked in my mind. I had been attacking my problem in the very same way that the little butterfly had attacked the windshield. Even my prayers had been frantic pleadings. What I needed to do was to stop beating my wings, to relax and put my trust in God's creative power to lead me out of my dilemma.

And when I did just that, God showed me the way—in a completely unexpected manner!

Yes, there *is* a solution to every knotty situation. If you have been praying about a problem but have found no answers, perhaps you too need to stop trying to force your own resolution—and let God lead you to His.

Thy will be done, Lord.   —MARILYN MORGAN HELLEBERG

---

30 THURSDAY
And the Lord answered me, and said, Write the vision, and make it plain…   —HABAKKUK 2:2

I was attending my first alumni banquet since graduation many years earlier. During the course of the evening I was introduced to a man whom I hadn't met before and in the conversation that followed, I asked, "What is your work?" He replied that he had been at the college for the past several years.

"Oh, how nice," I said. "In what capacity?"

"Why, I'm the president," he replied.

Well, I tried to make excuses for myself, but it was obvious that I had not read the material sent to me by my alma mater.

Now someday I hope to sit at Heaven's banquet table. After the above experience, I have a fear of turning to someone nearby and saying, "Hello. What's your name?"

"Habakkuk."

"Glad to meet you, Mr. Habakkuk. What was your earthly work?"

"I was a writer."

"Oh, how nice. What did you write?"

"Habakkuk."

"Habakkuk?"

"Yes. It's a book in the Old Testament."

I'd probably try to make excuses for myself, but it would be obvious that I had ignored the material sent to me by God.

Will you join me today in becoming acquainted with Mr. Habakkuk by reading his book? It's only three chapters long.

Help me to be faithful to Your Word, Father, as revealed to us by Your holy scribes. —ISABEL CHAMP

---

31 FRIDAY

These things I have spoken unto you, that in me ye might have peace. —JOHN 16:33

One Sunday long ago our pastor spoke to the congregation about faith and "everyday miracles." I have never forgotten that sermon, because its message has helped me so many times through the years.

"Once I lost a very important letter," he said, "that the bishop had given me to answer. I searched everywhere for it. I turned the place upside down, to no avail. At last, disturbed and tense, I was forced to give up. But before going to bed, I prayed. 'Dear Jesus', I said, 'please help me find that letter.'

"Then a great sense of peace came over me. I relaxed and fell asleep instantly. In the morning, refreshed, I walked into my office, pulled the desk out from the wall and looked behind it. There, wedged between desk and wall, was the letter. Now, two miracles had taken place. Which was the greater? Finding the letter? No, it was the peace-filled sleep. You see, by turning the problem over to Jesus, I was able to rest in faith."

Today whenever a problem causes me to toss and turn in my bed, I remember that sermon, and I practice its lesson.

"Dear Jesus, help me..."

And when I do that, I too am blessed by that "everyday miracle." My heart is at rest in faith, and I relax and fall asleep.

For faith and the miracle of peace it brings, we thank You, Dear Jesus. —DORIS HAASE

Praise Diary for August

1

2

3

4

5

6

7

8

9

10

11

12

13

14

15

16

17

18

19

20

21

22

23

24

25

26

27

28

29

30

31

September

S	M	T	W	T	F	S
						1
2	3	4	5	6	7	8
9	10	11	12	13	14	15
16	17	18	19	20	21	22
23	24	25	26	27	28	29
30						

It is said they come,
Each one an individual,
Across two thousand unseen miles
To crest, climax, and find finality
Against this windswept stretch of beach.
Waves: surging in battle gray under leaded skies,
Spitting hissing spume
Into a stinging howl of wind,
Smashing the seething, shuddering surfline.

I come to this sparse-grassed dune to relearn
The truth that seems to ring so clear
In the bleached tang of salt air.
I too am created individual.
I am more than just a grain of sand
Crushed ignorantly from grinding rock.
But, to grow precious in Your sight,
I must seek You, seek You, seek You
With the ardor of September's questing waves.

James McDermott

GUIDEPEOPLE: A Living Parable for September

1 SATURDAY

When a man's ways please the Lord, he maketh even his enemies to be at peace with him. —PROVERBS 16:7

Some people make the mistake of equating kindness with softness.

Entertainer Gary Moore told us at *Guideposts* about an old Chinese man named Ling Toy who for twenty years had owned a restaurant in Gary's neighborhood. One day a young man named Wong opened a restaurant across the street. Ling Toy was distressed about the possible competition and he began to spread false stories about Mr. Wong—how his kitchen was "dirty" and how Wong was too young to know "the *real* art of Chinese cuisine."

None of this, however, seemed to disturb Wong. Whenever someone told him what the old Ling Toy had said about him, Wong would reply, "You must be mistaken. Ling Toy could not possibly have said that. From everything I know about Ling Toy, he's much too fine a man."

Well, slowly Wong's good words filtered back to Ling Toy, and he was dumbfounded. The old man walked across the street and introduced himself. It marked the beginning of a long friendship.

What was the wisdom that Wong put to use? In Wong's kitchen, hanging over the door where he could see it every time he came under attack from Ling Toy, was a placard with these words: "The enemy is best defeated who is defeated with kindness."

I will practice kindness, Lord, in the face of friend and foe alike.
—VAN VARNER

256

2

SUNDAY

...And a word spoken in due season, how good is it!
                                        —*PROVERBS 15:23*

I had planned to attend a Bible-study class this fall but, weary of Old Testament studies, I chose to take up golf instead. What did I need all that extra Bible information for anyway?

At the golf club I watched the players work up a sweat as they made their way on the course. The game looked really rugged. *But why on earth*, I wondered, *do they pack around such big, heavy bags of clubs?*

When one of the men paused nearby before teeing off, I asked him, "Do you actually need so *many* clubs?"

"The irons?" He smiled. "I suppose it doesn't make much sense to an onlooker. But you see, we have to prepare ourselves for whatever challenge we might face out there on the course."

"So you use *all* of the clubs?"

"Oh, no, not in every game," the man replied. "The fact is, some of them I've never used. Still, I may need them someday, especially if my ball lands in a sand trap—or in the creek!"

You know, on second thought, I might just need the "iron" that Bible-study class offers. Who knows the lay of the course ahead, what unexpected challenges may have to be faced? I'm going to rearrange my schedule today.

I will go the length of the course, Lord, prepared with Your Word, for all life's challenges.   —JUNE MASTERS BACHER

3

MONDAY

For we are labourers together with God...ye are God's building.   —*I CORINTHIANS 3:9*

I grew up on Duke Ellington's music—*Take the A Train, Satin Lady, I'm Beginning to See the Light*—and I was fortunate enough to have heard his sacred music performed in cathedrals across the country from New York to San Francisco.

But there was one thing about Duke that I never knew in all that time…not until one day a friend informed me, "Duke was a very spiritual man. He once told me, 'My music is the way I pray.'"

Today—Labor Day—I have found myself thinking about Duke's remark. His music made him wealthy and famous and gave a lot of happiness to a lot of people at the same time. And yet, music was Duke's job, his work. It was the way he earned his livelihood.

This morning I imagined how wonderful it would be if each of us could feel about our jobs or our work as Duke did about his. What if our labor to earn our daily bread were to become a prayer—a prayer wherein we acknowledged the Source of our talents and the Judge of our efforts?

Work would be a positive joy! It would be a loving offering to our Lord and an ongoing prayer of praise. Today at work, let's dedicate our labor to Him. I wager it won't seem like *work* at all!

Lord Jesus, You dignified labor when You served as a carpenter. Inspire us to honor You in our labor as we do in our prayers.

—GLENN KITTLER

---

4 TUESDAY
Use hospitality one to another without grudging.
—I PETER 4:9

My husband and I were traveling across the country and decided on the spur of the moment to drop in on some old friends, only to find that they were in the midst of packing for an imminent move! Boxes were stacked high in all the rooms, trash was strewn over the floors, unkempt children dashed about the halls.

Nevertheless our friends greeted us joyfully. They seated us without apology on crates in the midst of the chaos and served us fresh-baked cherry pie and steaming coffee while giving us their undivided attention for a full hour. Seldom have I felt so royally treated.

The memory of that day has since helped me through many a household crisis of my own. Among other things, it has taught me that I need never be embarrassed over a messy house or a chaotic situation. To throw a damper over what could be a happy occasion just because I'm not happy with the current state of disorder is selfish. It only serves to focus attention away from the guests and onto my tension and discomfort. Yes, the annoyance that petty problems may present is certainly trivial when we consider that what *really* counts is the joy we find in one another's company.

After all, aren't we familiar with the blessed comfort we feel when our Heavenly Father welcomes us into His house, at any time, under any circumstances?

Father, You always make me feel welcome. Help me to pass Your loving hospitality on to others. —MADGE HARRAH

---

5 WEDNESDAY
We are troubled on every side, yet not distressed; we are perplexed, but not in despair; persecuted, but not forsaken; cast down, but not destroyed...
—II CORINTHIANS 4:8,9

I have a friend who lost her son in an accident almost thirty years ago. You can still see the bitterness in her face. She turned away from God and nothing seems to console her.

I have another friend, Ruth. She's a retired missionary who recently lost her son in an airplane crash. There were lines of pain on her face when I last saw her, but also lines of deep compassion and an expression of new-found joy.

"How have you been dealing with your loss, Ruth?" I asked her.

"Well, for one thing, I've become mother to one hundred boys!" she said.

259

"A hundred!" I exclaimed.

"Yes. The boys at the nearby Boys' Town desperately need love and attention, and I have it to give. I've signed up as a volunteer. It's difficult to dwell on your own pain and loss when you are helping others."

Whatever life brings my way, I hope I have the courage to turn my face *away* from the bitterness of loss and grief and *toward* the life-giving flow of love...by reaching out to others.

Father, help me to view life as a glass half full *of water, rather than half empty.* —MARION BOND WEST

---

6 THURSDAY
He that loveth his brother abideth in the light...
—*I JOHN 2:10*

In one of his books, the late Loren Eiseley tells about a man who walked a beach near daybreak following a storm. The shore, according to Eiseley, was a beachcomber's paradise, covered with prized shells that had washed up during the night.

Most of those out at that early hour had brought sacks in which to carry the shells they found, but the shadowy figure that caught Eiseley's attention in the early morning light was empty-handed. Although the man occasionally stooped and picked up something, he quickly tossed it back into the sea. The author-anthropologist was intrigued, and he moved closer. On the individual's next stoop and throw, Eiseley discovered what he was about—he was retrieving starfish and throwing them back into the foaming surf.

Would they live? Eiseley wondered. *Probably not*, he thought—but even if the star-thrower's attempt was folly, the writer found an important lesson in it. "He had placed himself on the side of life," Eiseley wrote, "and that's where I want to be."

Among our acquaintances there are people like the shell-gatherers, focusing only on inanimate things...and then there are those who concentrate on the living, attempting to bring hope and healing, truth and love, to bear. Christ was one of the latter. He told us that He had come so that His children would have life, and have it more abundantly. The people I know who have found abundant life are those who willingly share their resources—their time, their energy, their talents—so that others may find lives of abundance too.

I would like to be a star-thrower. Wouldn't you?

Sensitize us to the need about us, Lord, and motivate us to reach out to others in love.   —FRED BAUER

---

7 FRIDAY
...The righteous shall be in everlasting remembrance.
                                                                    —PSALM 112:6

When I returned from a vacation trip through New England, I found a handwritten sign taped to my office door that read, "Sam, life ain't the same widdoucha!"

It was nice to be back, good to have been missed, and I felt a warm glow inside.

But for me there was an even more significant message in that sign. It made me realize that my life had become rather insular of late and that I hadn't stayed in touch with my friends by phoning or writing as regularly as I once did. And, due to an unexpected personal setback, I had withdrawn a bit. The message on my office door was telling me, in effect, that I was needed. And also that no matter the troubles I was going through, I was loved!

It's sometime easy for us to forget that "Life ain't the same widdoucha!" Today that sign hangs right over my typewriter, where it constantly reminds me that there is always something—even if only a smile, a touch, a word of encouragement—that I can give toward making life happier for someone else.

Yes, each one of us is a part of His plan, and we are each necessary to one another, as beloved sons and daughters of the same Father. Sometimes all it takes is a vacation to make us realize it!

Dear Heavenly Father, thank you for giving us the love that spans all time and distance. —SAMANTHA McGARRITY

---

8 SATURDAY
He is my refuge and my fortress... —PSALM 91:2

I'm learning something else as I watch that mother finch —something she's as slow to grasp as I've been. I'm getting a little annoyed, in fact, at the time it's taking her.

Can't the silly bird see that I'm her friend and protector? Her landlord, if it comes to that. That's *my* door she's squatting on, *my* front entrance she's taken over. A dozen times a day I have to trudge down to the basement and out the back way. I bang on the window at deliverymen to preserve the sanctity of her home, work with the windows closed lest the sound of my typewriter ruffle her peace of mind.

Her response? To fly away with a squawk every time she catches sight of me.

It's made me wonder about the things *I* run away from. How often, out of fear, have I fled the approach of God Himself? How often has the Owner of the place, without my knowing, safeguarded my shelter of twigs and straw? How long has He waited for a word of thanks?

Lord, thank You. —ELIZABETH SHERRILL

9 SUNDAY

*And let the beauty of the Lord our God be upon us:
and establish thou the work of our hands…*
—PSALM 90:17

On my father's last Sunday in his own pulpit after forty-three years in the ministry, I worshiped with his congregation. When the service was over, one of his members approached me, her face glowing.

"I just want to tell you," she said, giving me a little hug, "that your dad is leaving a better place than he came to."

Although I myself don't plan to retire for many years yet, her words often come back to me in the evening as I prepare for bed. After all, in the English language, "to go to bed" is also "to retire."

And what question could we better ask ourselves at the close of each day than this: "Am I leaving the world this day a better place than I came to?"

Father, I offer You the work of my hands this day, done to Your glory.   —PATRICIA HOUCK SPRINKLE

10 MONDAY

Draw nigh to God, and He will draw nigh to you.
—JAMES 4:8

I have always had trouble in carrying a tune. Only if I stand as close as possible to the piano, can I stay anywhere near key.

Last week my life seemed to resemble my singing—it was all out of tune. I had four speaking engagements and a writing deadline. By Tuesday I was tired and tense. On Wednesday I missed an interstate turnoff, got stuck in the mud, and then left out an important part of my talk.

Yes, my life was clearly out of kilter. Then it occurred to me that I

263

had been neglecting my daily quiet time with God. I had wandered away from the One Who keeps me in harmony.

That night I went into my room and closed the door, resolved to remain there until I once again felt our Lord's presence. After an hour of Scripture reading, prayer and just being with Him, I felt myself at peace again. I seemed to waltz through the rest of the week, easily and effectively. That small, quiet interlude made me realize that the busier my life is, the more I need time to spend close to Him.

If you are facing a busy week, make a resolve to stay near to your Source of harmony by spending *extra* time with the Lord. It will turn your week into a symphony!

Loving Lord, when my days are too full of busyness, hold me close that I may dwell in harmony with You.

—MARILYN MORGAN HELLEBERG

---

11 TUESDAY

Have mercy upon me, O God, according to thy lovingkindness...blot out my transgressions.

—PSALM 51:1

All summer I brooded over a misunderstanding I'd had with my favorite golfing buddy. Early in the spring I had given George a special set of irons that once belonged to my uncle, and in return George had said that he would give me a driver he had bought but never used. Then—the very next week!—he had a yard sale and sold the driver. Although he apologized later, saying he hadn't realized how much it meant to me, I stopped playing golf with him. I went out on the course a few times alone, but gradually I lost interest in the game.

Then one day in mid-August my wife Judy brought me a story about a grocer in New England whose business had been failing because his steady customers were no longer coming into the store.

The proprietor finally figured out the reason: His best customers owed him money and they were too embarrassed to come in! So he ran an advertisement in the local paper, announcing that there was no such person as a debtor in his store.

"Your bill is paid in full. Start fresh with us today," the advertisement said.

"Are you trying to tell me something?" I asked Judy.

She smiled and said, "Well, you know George would probably like nothing better than to play golf this afternoon. Why don't you give him a call?"

We had a great game together.

Forgive me, dear Father, and help me to forgive others.
—JAMES McDERMOTT

---

12 WEDNESDAY

Take therefore no thought for the morrow: for the morrow shall take thought for the things of itself.
—MATTHEW 6:34

Uncle Ned, long since past his ability to work, sat on the porch of the little country store, idly whittling.

"Tell me," said the tired farmer, wiping the sweat from his brow, "are all your days as carefree as this one?"

The aged man went on quietly whittling. "Nope," he finally replied laconically. "Just two of 'em. Yesterday. And tomorrow."

Well, that's an answer worth thinking about. Yesterday—and its "might-have-beens"—is gone. And tomorrow holds a splendid promise, but we can't yet grasp it.

And there *is* today! God's day—this day that He is sharing with you and me at this very moment. My prayer for you is that every hour of it be spent just as you and He would have planned it!

Thank You, Father, for making this day. It is truly "Heaven-sent."
—JUNE MASTERS BACHER

13 THURSDAY
And under his wings shalt thou trust... —*PSALM 91:4*

My husband and I were on our way home from an evening church service. I was driving. Halfway home a freakish storm struck. Suddenly the pounding rain turned into large balls of hail that pelted the car crazily and bounced off. The traffic that usually zoomed down the expressway slowed to a crawl. Many cars pulled off the road.

But I continued to inch along, barely able to see a few feet ahead, when suddenly we were sliding on ice—in September!

"Slow," my husband cautioned. I nodded. I couldn't go any slower ...I was creeping along in low gear. Finally my husband's voice became firm.

"Look," he pointed, "there's a bridge ahead. Pull under it and stop."

I did, and we found instant, sweet relief, crowded into the refuge area with other travelers waiting out the storm. The sudden, profound silence spoke to me and I thought about the passage in Luke 13:34: "How often would I have gathered thy children together, as a hen doth gather her brood under her wings, and ye would not!"

Sitting there under the bridge, the storm raging outside, I vowed that the next time I faced a stormy situation, I would instantly allow my Father to give me the powerful protection of His loving wings.

Even in the eye of the hurricane, Father, I will seek You.

—MARION BOND WEST

14 FRIDAY
He received them...and healed them that had need of healing. —*LUKE 9:11*

I can still hear the doctor's words: "Jeff, there's definitely something wrong with that knee. I suggest we go in and take a look."

In he went—and there's a scar on the inside of my right knee to prove it. And though painful bone chips and torn cartilage were removed, though I play basketball and ski and do everything else that I used to do, that knee will never be quite the same. There will always be that tinge of pain if I move in the wrong way, the rainy-day stiffness, the question of whether a brace is necessary in particularly strenuous situations. And of course there's the scar itself—that continual reminder that something of myself has been hurt.

My knee, though, isn't the only place I bear scars. The others are the invisible ones—those left in the heart, such as recollections of hateful words, of friends passed on, of promises broken. Each scar reminds me not only that what lies beneath will never be the same again, but—more important—of the skill of the Physician Who repaired the damage and made the part whole again.

And then I think, *Scars are Good News.* News of healing. Reminders of His love.

Touch me, O Father, with Your healing hand—and continuing Grace.   —JEFF JAPINGA

JESUS, THE MASTER STORYTELLER
Parable of Laborers in the Vineyard   —MATTHEW 20:1-16

15   SATURDAY

In the story about the laborers in the vineyard, once again Jesus is trying to make His followers understand what the Kingdom of Heaven is like. He tells of an owner of a vineyard who goes out early in the morning and hires some workers. The agreed-upon wage for each man is a penny for the day's work. Later on, at noon and again at midafternoon, the owner hires more workers, assuring them that "whatever is right, I will give thee." Finally near the end of the day he hires yet another group, saying, "Go ye also into the vineyard; and whatsoever is right, that ye shall receive."

When quitting time comes, the workers line up to be paid. Those who started work first are angered to learn that every man is to receive a penny regardless of when he came into the vineyard. "Not fair!" they complained furiously. But the owner of the vineyard will not change his mind. It's his money, he says; he can dispense it as he sees fit. And so he does. End of story.

Is the Kingdom of Heaven, then, a place of unfairness? Surely that can't be what Jesus meant. What *was* His meaning?

Some years ago I found a clue. After a family picnic at a mountain lake in North Georgia we had planned for an hour of swimming before driving home. But two of the children wandered off and did not return until it was almost time to leave. They came rushing down the hillside and plunged into the water with the rest of us.

"Where've you been?" I said a bit irritably. "You've missed all the fun. Now it's time to go!"

One of the truants splashed up to me with a sunny smile. "Never mind," she said. "We're just as wet as you are!"

And so she was—just as wet. And I saw—or thought I saw—what Jesus must have been driving at. If the Kingdom of Heaven is the love of God, then that love is absolute. Whether you accept it soon or late, you are loved with a love that is timeless and knows no gradations whatsoever. Fairness or unfairness, justice or injustice have nothing to do with it. Once you're in the vineyard, the reward is the same for everybody.

You can't be wetter than wet!

I thank You, Father, that Your love does not have to be earned— let me receive it today.   —ARTHUR GORDON

16 SUNDAY
I am in a great strait: let me fall now into the hand of the Lord... —*I CHRONICLES 21:13*

The first time I went through a car wash, I simply couldn't let go of the steering wheel. I sat there clutching it as though I were frozen.

"Let go. Let go of the wheel!" the man shouted at me as the car was pulled through on the track. But I couldn't. As the car was doused by gallons of water and swept by enormous brushes, I gripped the wheel even harder.

The wheel fought back slightly and the entire trip through the car wash was somewhat rough and jerky...and a bit frightening. I was greatly relieved when the car rolled off that track—I didn't trust it.

A few weeks later when my car was covered with grimy city pollution, I mustered up my courage to visit the car wash again. *This time,* I told myself, *I'm going to trust the men and the track...and take my hands off the steering wheel.*

What a difference! It turned out to be a smooth, almost delightful ride. I just sat back and was carried along the track slowly...and safely.

Right in the middle of the wash it occurred to me that that's how faith works—by letting God take over completely and trusting in Him to guide us safely through. Sometimes it may be difficult to do, and yet when we do let go and let God take over, life runs so much more smoothly.

Dear Lord, help me to remember that You are the One in charge.
—SAMANTHA McGARRITY

17 MONDAY

Thou shalt bless the Lord thy God for the good land which he hath given thee. —DEUTERONOMY 8:10

Whenever I have the occasion to be in Washington, D.C., I always go over to see the White House. During the years I have been doing this, eight different First Families have resided there; and although I have not always been in accord with the principles of the head of the family, I know that the majority of the people in this country elected him.

I find myself thinking about this at the moment because exactly one hundred and ninety-seven years ago today the members of Congress signed the Constitution of the United States, making it the law of the land, and the people of the United States voted to approve it. And about thirty years ago Congress passed an act declaring today Citizenship Day.

That's what I think about when I look at the White House—not the people who are living there temporarily, but the people who put them there. Us. *You and me.* We citizens. Look at it this way. Ours is the only country in the world that has undergone peaceful transitions of governments from the very beginning. No other country can make that claim. This is because the government of the United States *is* the people.

Citizenship Day, then, is not only a reminder of the privilege of being an American, but also a reminder of the obligation to participate in America. Today let us be especially grateful for both.

Heavenly Father, we thank You for the men and women who had the foresight and wisdom to place our beloved country under Your guidance. May we be worthy of their dreams.

—GLENN KITTLER

18

TUESDAY

Thou wilt keep him in perfect peace, whose mind is stayed on thee... —ISAIAH 26:3

"What happened?" I exclaimed when I dropped by to visit my friend Flo one warm spring day. Big splashes of fresh red paint speckled her white garage doors.

She smiled ruefully. "I was out here painting the patio bench," she said, "when a large moth began fluttering around. I swatted at it with my brush—and this is the result. I shouldn't have let a mere insect interrupt me like that."

The next morning I took my Bible and turned to the Scripture reading for the day. I'd barely started when I remembered that I must take the roast out of the freezer for dinner. And while I was there in the kitchen, I also boiled potatoes, mixed my husband's favorite dressing and fixed dessert. By now it was too late to return to Scripture reading. My previously quiet morning had quickly passed.

The next morning I tried again to read my Bible, and again I let various chores claim my attention. Suddenly, I was reminded of Flo's moth. *My time is positively moth-ridden!* I thought. *I'm diverted from my real goal at every step of the way. Well, no more. Scripture comes first. Chores can wait.* With that commitment, my mind stayed on course—I completed my Scripture reading—and my chores as well.

How about you? Will you be sidetracked today when you pick up your Bible? If so, just remember the lesson of Flo and the moth, and stay your course.

Thank You for perfect peace, Father, when my mind is stayed on You. —ISABEL CHAMP

19 WEDNESDAY

...But if we walk in the light, as he is in the light, we have fellowship with one another... —I JOHN 1:7

The other day a physician was being interviewed on an early morning talk show. He spoke of a most unusual piece of medical research.

He said that a group of patients were shown a film about Mother Teresa's work of love in the streets of India, ministering to the homeless, the hopeless and the hungry. Following the movie, the patients were administered a test that measured their immunological defenses. It was found that their defense levels had risen while watching the film! The doctor indicated that the evidence seemed to suggest that the feeling of compassion is good for your health.

Maybe it's unconventional, but the next time you feel a cold or an illness coming on, why not remember this line of defense and simply dose your heart with an overflowing cup of compassion? Surely God has had all along the best cure for most of the ills that beset us: Love one another.

Today, Father, please strengthen me with Your prescription for compassion... and love. —SUE MONK KIDD

20 THURSDAY

Let us not therefore judge one another any more: but judge this rather, that no man put a stumblingblock or an occasion to fall in his brother's way. —ROMANS 14:13

When I was a child, my father's broad smile as he carried in a basket filled with golden-skinned pawpaws would announce the arrival of autumn. Pawpaw trees were rare in our part of the country, but my father knew of a secret patch deep in the woods. For years he showered gifts of pawpaws on friends, never once revealing his source.

Then one fall Dad's old friend, Homer Tate, persuaded him to tell the secret. Together they stole off into the woods, only to find the fruit still green. They would wait. But when Dad returned a week later, all of the pawpaws were *gone*! Not one was left.

"Homer! That rascal!" Dad fumed when he came home. "I should have known better than to trust him. He's a downright thief!"

That same evening there was a supper at our church. When we arrived, we saw Homer's car parked out front. "Bet he has a basketful of pawpaws right there in the car!" Dad snorted. He strode over and opened the car door. Sure enough. Sitting there on the backseat was a big granite fruit canner—and Daddy just knew it was full of pawpaws. Swiftly he lifted the lid and thrust his arm in, clear up to his elbow—and deep into the hot noodles meant for our church supper!

Well, Dad's arm wasn't hurt and we never knew who picked the pawpaws, but everyone in church knew about noodles. It was an unforgettable lesson not only to my father, but to our whole family. How proud we can be—and how wrong!

Father, let me always seek the truth before jumping to conclusions.
—ZONA B. DAVIS

21 FRIDAY
I will both lay me down in peace and sleep; for there, Lord, makest me dwell in safety. —PSALM 4:8

When my neighbors received word of a family emergency, I offered to stay with their little three-year-old, Amy for the few days.

Amy and I had no trouble in keeping busy. We looked through picture books, baked cookies, repaired a teddy bear's ear and took nice, long walks. By nightfall I was so tired that I couldn't wait to finish dinner and go to bed.

But Amy couldn't fall asleep. She kept calling to me. Could she have a glass of water? Another blanket? A particular doll? I was losing patience. "Amy," I said, "it's time to go to sleep!"

She looked up at me, her wide, innocent eyes filled with concern. "You won't go away, will you?" she asked in a tiny voice.

Then I understood. Amy wanted to be sure I was still in the house. She was afraid she might wake to find herself alone.

Hugging her close, I promised, "Honey, I'm going to be here every minute...even when you're sound asleep."

As I drifted off to sleep that night, I thought of my own childlike fear of being left alone. And I thanked God for His love that constantly reassures me that He is always there.

Father, when I feel alone and frightened... I will call Your name.
—PHYLLIS HOBE

---

22 SATURDAY
But even the very hairs of your head are all numbered. Fear not therefore: ye are of more value than many sparrows. —LUKE 12:7

Two large turtles live in our greenhouse. Most of the time they just creep about, eating bugs, cat food and melon rinds. Occasionally, however, they try to climb the walls and then they topple over onto their backs. A turtle on its back can suffocate. Therefore, I check on those turtles several times a day to make sure that they are still upright. If they aren't, I pick them up and set them on their feet.

And when I do, I think of the occasions when I have stumbled and fallen spiritually, only to have God pick me up and set me on my feet. In reading the Bible, I'm continually amazed by God's love and concern for His creation. What a comfort it is to know that His eye is on the sparrow, on the turtle—*and on me!*

Today, Lord, I will share with others the assurance of Your ever vigilant love. —MADGE HARRAH

274

23 SUNDAY

But many that are first shall be last; and the last shall be first. —MATTHEW 19:30

One of my elementary-school teachers always made the children line up before marching into the classroom. The shortest (and, I thought, the prettiest) girl stood proudly in front, while the tallest (me) slouched at the rear.

"Honey," my grandmother would comfort me, "last can be *special!* Do you remember the Danites in the Bible? They occupied the hindmost place, a very important rear position among the marching armies of Israel. You see, there were stragglers to be gathered up, lost property to be retrieved, rear-guard protection to be given."

Then she would smile. "The most important thing, honey, isn't being first ... it's serving God from *wherever* we are."

I try to remember my grandmother's words when my heart is heavy with feelings of "last" and "least." At those times, when I mourn my mediocrity or sorrow over my limitations, I know that I am once again slouching at the end of the line, overcome by self-pity.

And then I recall her story about the Danites, and I realize that, like them, I have been given work to do for my Lord...and that being truly first means serving God first...*wherever* you are!

I gladly go "hindmost" for You, Lord Jesus. —DORIS HAASE

MY LESSONS IN FAITH
by Marion Bond West

Sometimes unforeseen events enter our lives and shake the foundation of our faith. Such was the case with Marion Bond West when her beloved husband, Jerry, was stricken with cancer in the Fall of 1982. She found herself inconsolable, angry, her faith ebbing. She went through phases of emotional upheaval that left her weak and wondering, until finally she was able to listen once again to God's assurance that He is always with us. In the meantime, Jerry's post-surgery treatment was successful and he was home again and back at work.

Then in a letter dated June, 1983 to Guideposts, Marion wrote telling us that her husband's illness had reoccurred. Going through it all once again, she wrote: "One of the most important things I've learned is that no matter what the circumstances, God is bigger than any fear...when my trust in Him became bigger than my fear of losing Jerry, the fear had to go."

In the next week Marion shares some of the steps she took in the first months of her long journey back from doubt and fear into belief and trust. Underlying each one is courage—the kind of courage that comes only when we accept the grace of our Lord and, holding on to faith, move forward despite our circumstances. We hope Marion's "Lessons in Faith" will strengthen and inspire you in your need.   —THE EDITORS

Editor's Post-Script:

As Daily Guideposts was going to press, we received word that Jerry had died on July 17, 1983.

We, at Guideposts, are thankful for the friendship and love the West family has shared with us through the years. We will miss Jerry, and are grateful for the warm and intimate moments of knowing him through the pages of Guideposts.

---

24 DAY ONE—MONDAY
Wherefore be ye not unwise, but understanding what the will of the Lord is.   —EPHESIANS 5:17

I was spending most of my time in the hospital with my husband. One day a new patient in a room nearby cried, "Please don't leave me. Oh, please come in here. Someone. Lord, help me."

"Someone will go to her," I assured my husband. But her cries continued. *Lord, send someone to comfort that woman, please.* But no one came and ten minutes later, to my amazement, I found myself entering her room. I remembered too late the words of a long-ago Sunday-school teacher: "Never pray unless you are willing to be part of the answer."

I looked down at the frail woman, probably in her eighties. She was staring at the ceiling, a look of terror on her face. I hesitated, not sure of what to say or do.

"Hello," I managed, leaning close to her. "Is there anything I can do for you?"

She looked at me blankly for a moment and then—a suggestion of hope dawning in her eyes—said in a weak but clear voice, "Oh, would you hug me?"

Careful not to disturb any of the tubes or the oxygen, I gently put my cheek against hers and held her for a few minutes. Then I kissed her on the forehead. When I stood up, I said, "I'll be back to hug you again in a little while."

She nodded, giving me a contented little smile and drifted off to sleep. My heart filled with renewed strength and courage. When I returned to my husband, he was asleep. Quietly I bent down placing my cheek next to his....

I know that it was really You loving that woman, Father. You just needed a pair of arms to use. I am ever available, whenever You call, for whatever service You need me.

—MARION BOND WEST

---

25 DAY TWO—TUESDAY
For the people had a mind to work. —NEHEMIAH 4:6

It was the night my husband was placed in intensive care. Even though my fourteen-year-old son Jeremy had been told that his

277

father was "doing okay now," he wasn't certain. He just looked straight ahead, tears filling his unblinking eyes. He couldn't bring himself to look at me as he asked, "Is he going to bed when he comes home?"

"No. He'll be just like he always was."

"Will he be tired and weak?"

"Of course not."

"Are you...uh, going to have...to go to work?" Now the tears brimmed over, slid down his face.

"No. Daddy will be working, like always."

"Well, I've thought about it. I know I could make the soccer team at school this year. But I'm not going out. I'd have to give up my job at the garage after school if I did. And I think I should be working— right now."

Nothing that his father or I said could convince Jeremy that it was all right for him to quit his job to play soccer. "My mind's made up. I'm going to work," he said, almost as happy—maybe even happier —than if he *were* going to play soccer.

Jerry and I have always derived such joy from our children—but Jeremy's desire to pitch in and help, even if it meant sacrificing something dear to him, is truly one of the highlights of our lives.

Thank You. Father, for those generous and loving people who work to ease our way. —MARION BOND WEST

---

26 DAY THREE—WEDNESDAY
But my God shall supply all your need according to his riches in glory by Christ Jesus. —PHILIPPIANS 4:19

I rested my head on the cold metal bars of my husband's bed in the intensive-care unit of the hospital. His condition was critical and the doctors had no answers for us. I feared that I was reaching the end of my faith.

"Oh, God," I whispered, "please send me something or someone so that I can hold on. My need is desperate."

Instantly a rich voice rang out: "I am the Lord, thy God Who strengtheneth thee. Yea, with My strong right hand I will uphold thee...."

Astonished, I raised my head, but no one was there. I hurried out of the room and looked up and down the corridor. No one. But the voice still boomed: "I will never leave you nor forsake you...." Then, following along the hall, I found the source. In a room nearby, a striking young man stood tall and erect like a mightly warrior. His face glowed as he read from the Word of God to a frail woman in the bed. Still reading, he flashed me a smile that indicated I'm available.

"I need you," I said softly, "in Room 406."

Within a few minutes he appeared in our cubicle bringing with him all the promises of hope, courage and love. When he started to read the Ninety-first Psalm, my faith began to soar.

Then I asked, "Will you sing?"

He smiled and began: "Blessed assurance, Jesus is mine—" My husband awoke and the three of us joined hands and prayed.

And when the stranger departed, it was all right. For he had left behind God's sweet Holy Spirit, Who comforted us throughout the long night.

Father, thank You for meeting us in our hours of deepest need.

—MARION BOND WEST

---

27 DAY FOUR—THURSDAY
Behold, I make all things new.   —REVELATION 21:5

It was my husband's second day home from the hospital. You know it when you've had a brush with death. We both knew it all too well.

There was a new gentleness in Jerry. Simple things made him

smile suddenly. "The sky is so blue," he said several times. The first hint of fall penetrated the September day. "I'm going out to pick butterbeans," he announced, looking out the kitchen window.

Gardening had long been Jerry's special love, and picking and shelling butterbeans he had grown himself was his special joy. I had always been careful to be occupied or busy when shelling time came around. It was something of a family joke...shelling butterbeans was far from my idea of a good time. But today I bolted out the back door and started picking butterbeans right alongside Jerry—for the first time ever. We'd been married for almost twenty-five years and I'd never before picked even one butterbean with him.

After a few moments of quietly working together, Jerry remarked, "You've never picked butterbeans with me before."

"I know. What I didn't know was how much I've missed. It's fun, isn't it?"

We just knelt there in silence for a moment, looking at each other, our hands full of butterbeans.

"It's nice to have you here," he smiled.

Father, thank You for teaching me what's really important.

—MARION BOND WEST

---

28 DAY FIVE—FRIDAY
Now therefore hearken unto me, O ye children: for blessed are they that keep my ways. —PROVERBS 8:32

For seven weeks Jerry and I went each morning for his cobalt treatments. I was quiet, but Jerry talked with everyone in the waiting room, encouraging them, sharing with them and on occasion even laughing heartily.

One day I noticed a woman in a wheelchair, and from somewhere came the desire to speak with her. She barely acknowledged my presence. Although I was a bit perplexed, her lack of response seemed to trigger a question within me and I asked her, "Do you know how much God loves you?"

She shook her head. I knelt by her side and began to tell her about His love.

"I don't believe," she murmured, her face averted.

That night I prayed for Wilma and asked God to show me a way to reach her. Very gently came the response: "Don't take her anything of a religious nature. Take the handmade shawl in the top of your closet and wrap it around her, telling her that it really isn't a shawl at all but My arms, enfolding her in My love."

The next day I placed the shawl around Wilma's shoulders and explained where it had come from and why. She touched it wonderingly and sat quiet for a moment. Then she raised her eyes to mine, and through her tears she whispered, "I do believe, and may God bless you."

With those words joy once more found its way into my saddened heart. Hearing Jerry's strong voice in the waiting room, I went and sat by him, and joined in with the conversation.

Father, never let us forget that when we help others, we help ourselves. —MARION BOND WEST

---

29 DAY SIX—SATURDAY
He healeth the broken in heart, and bindeth up their wounds. —PSALM 147:3

Could Christmas be the same this year? Wistfully I looked out our living-room windows at the festive lights across the street. I hadn't even been able to think about putting up decorations, but the children insisted.

"We'll do it, Mama. We'll even stuff each other's stockings." My husband had encouraged them and supervised the gift buying, while I withdrew deeper into my shell of fear and despair.

Then on Christmas Eve Jerry was adamant that we share our

Christmas with someone needy. "It will help us," he said calmly.

Mechanically I went along, taking a lovely floral arrangement to a lonely widow we know. Tears of joy glistened in her dim eyes when she saw us. Sitting there in her tiny den, we admired the small make-shift branches she'd tied together to form a tree. As we chatted, she wiped away the tears, expressing her gratitude for our company.

"Sometimes," she confessed, "I just need someone to hold me." Jerry gathered her frail body in his arms and held her. Then we bowed our heads for prayer and I heard my husband praising God for His unspeakable gift. A bit of the spirit of Christmas was working its way into my heart.

As we neared home, we saw that the children had lit the tree, candles flickered brightly in the windows. We sat in the car for a while and looked, warmed by the love and courage of our children. A little more of the meaning of Christmas eased into me, and then Jerry reached over and took my hand. I squeezed his back and said, "Merry Christmas, dear."

Father, forgive me when I limit You. Help me to trust my loved ones—and myself—to Your loving care.

—MARION BOND WEST

---

30 DAY SEVEN—SUNDAY
I will sing unto the Lord as long as I live: I will sing praise to my God while I have my being. —PSALM 104:33

During my husband's illness, I faced deep moments of despair...and an ebbing faith. Although Jerry and I frequently prayed together—and apart—I seemed to battle doubt continuously.

One night when I was especially restless, a dream came to me. Jerry and I and the children were pioneers stranded in a covered wagon on the prairie. The enemy—wild Indians—was attacking. There was no hope; we faced certain death. But then—just as in the cowboy movies—the cavalry appeared on the horizon. The soldiers were riding hard and fast, coming straight to our rescue even as the enemy bore down on us. And the Indians were driven off. Then the riders dismounted and embraced us, expressing great joy at finding us safe. Some of them I knew—others were strangers. My husband and I and our children cried out in gratitude to the cavalry and we all sang praises to God around the campfire.

Upon awakening, as I pondered the dream, a gentle silent Voice seemed to offer an explanation. "You really do have a serious problem, Marion. You can't handle it alone. The cavalry in your dream is the Body of Believers who have banded together to intercede on your behalf. They mean business with the enemy and their prayers are reaching Me. I know that the foe seemed unconquerable to you and your little family huddled there in the covered wagon, but remember this: The soldiers who joined together to rescue you are in My army—the army of the Lord Jesus Christ—and it is because of the Calvary two thousand years ago that they ride today, and they ride in victory.

"Never give up...for I promise you that in the midst of your very peril—in life and in death—I will always be with you now and forevermore."

Nothing can shake my belief, Father. Throughout all of my days—here and in eternity—You are my Saviour.

—MARION BOND WEST

And A Special Note To Marion:

Today we and all the readers of Daily Guideposts *send our love to you, daughters Julie and Jennifer, and twins Jon and Jeremy. God bless you.*

Praise Diary for September

1

2

3

4

5

6

7

8

9

10

11

12

13

14

15

16

17

18

19

20

21

22

23

24

25

26

27

28

29

30

October

S	M	T	W	T	F	S
	1	2	3	4	5	6
7	8	9	10	11	12	13
14	15	16	17	18	19	20
21	22	23	24	25	26	27
28	29	30	31			

At dusk last night I caught
The first tart tang of woodsmoke,
And now I notice pumpkins
That had lain fat and indolent on their vines
Beginning to congregate in topply roadside pyramids.
The barn is stuffed with fragrant hay,
And cornstalks are bunched in slender teepees on
     brown fields.
Our musty pantry's bending shelves
Now darkly gleam with mason jars—
Pickles, beets, tomatoes, strawberry jam,
     plum jelly—
Good all Fall, Winter, Spring and more!
We'll pick more apples for the cellar
And mash the culls to a frothy cider
So sweet we'll drink it all today.
Oh, Lord, how bounteous this golden month!
I am mindful, Lord, that it was November
When the Pilgrims made a day of Thanks.
But I've always known it was October
That gave them the idea.

James McDermott

GUIDEPEOPLE: A Living Parable for October

1 MONDAY

Praying always with all prayer and supplication in the Spirit, and watching thereunto with all perseverence and supplication for all saints. —EPHESIANS 6:18

One of my most beloved friends is a pickpocket. Well, a *former* pickpocket. He spent thirty years at his "trade," including three harsh terms in prison, before he met a widow who changed his life. He wrote to us at *Guideposts*, and I traveled to see him, the first of many visits over the years.

The widow had sensed good in this man, and she did the only thing within her power to turn him around: *she prayed.* Constantly. Without ceasing. Then his sister began praying for him too.

Well, my friend began to lose his touch. He'd place his fingers on a large roll of bills and it would slip from his grip...he'd lift a wallet and it would be empty...he'd hear a soft voice calling him to turn to look, spot the police before they spotted him and walk away. It was as though some strange, great power were guiding him. So great was the potency of those women's prayers that they prayed him out of business!

In time, my friend turned his life over to the Lord, and has since spent his remaining years trying to make amends for his past. He is an old man now. The widow is dead. But he was there to help her when she, in turn, needed him.

It's a bittersweet story, this one, perhaps my favorite of all *Guideposts* stories, for it not only shows me the great and mysterious power of prayer, but the possibility of redemption for each and every one of us.

Father, I know You hear when others pray for me. Help me to heed You, as well. —VAN VARNER

2

TUESDAY
Be ye therefore ready… —*LUKE 12:40*

A friend of mine in New York City told me about watching two shoeshine boys competing for business on the block outside his office window. As the day went on, Harold began to notice that one of the boys was getting far more customers than the other. Time and again a pedestrian would walk straight past the first youngster, but when he'd get to the second, he'd pass by, then slow up, turn around, come back and put his shoe out.

Harold was intrigued and before the day was out, he couldn't resist going out on the street himself.

"Shine?" asked the first boy. Harold shook his head and strode on.

"Hey, mister," the second youngster called out brightly, "get yourself a shine for Sunday!"

That one turn of phrase made all the difference. It was good salesmanship. The second boy knew that every one of us wants to dress up—and I mean spiritually too—for the Lord.

How about it? Even though today is Tuesday, don't you think you ought to have a Sunday shine?

For You, Heavenly Father, let me be at my best every day of the week. —NORMAN VINCENT PEALE

3

WEDNESDAY
Who knoweth not in all these that the hand of the Lord hath wrought this? In whose hand is the soul of every living thing, and the breath of all mankind. —*JOB 12:9-10*

My stepson and his wife are building a new home. We have enjoyed poring over the blueprints with them and visiting the beautiful wooded hillside where the house will stand. One day I remarked, "What a complicated and exciting undertaking—but it's going to be a simply fabulous house."

My doctor-husband laughed. "Not nearly as fabulous as the one you live in right now. Your own body!" And he went on to speak of its marvels.

"When a man builds a house, he has to go to others for so many things. The architect, the plumber, the bricklayer, the electrician. Other people have to dig the foundation, put in the appliances, the windows and doors. But for the human body, your parents didn't even have to order a blueprint. You were already coded and planned for by the unseen Master Architect.

"And then to make it function over such a period of time! We speak, we hear, we see—all our senses provided for us in the Master Builder's plan. It is the greatest miracle. Just to occupy the human body is to live with absolute proof of God."

His words were like a revelation. Every time I see a new house now, or a new baby—or even regard my own body—I think of them and marvel.

Blessed Creator, I am filled with awe and thanksgiving before this miracle, my body. Let me trust in Your blueprint for my life.

—MARJORIE HOLMES

---

4 THURSDAY

The Lord shall preserve thy going out and thy coming in from this time forth, and even for evermore.

—PSALM 121:8

It was that time of the year, when the sun pales and thick clouds scud across a lavender-blue sky. Still beautiful, still a few browning leaves on the trees, but—October. Winter was on the way.

From the living room I heard the geese honking high overhead, and hurried outdoors to watch them. Their annual trek south always amazes me: the precise V-formation, the commanding cries from one bird to another, the powerful, graceful, sweeping change of direction without a single bird losing its place in the group.

How is it possible? I asked myself. *How do the birds know that our land will soon be unable to offer them food and shelter? Who teaches them how to assemble? Who gives some the leadership and custody of others? Who will guide them on their return flight when the land is once more productive?* And the answer comes to me... yes, of course—God.

Gazing up at the sky, I suddenly felt foolish and humbled. I'm always concerned about the next minute, the next day, the next year. I want to know *now*—this very minute—what's going to happen next and what I can do about it. How much better to be like one of those birds winging high up there in the sky, trusting God to provide for me... even before I myself know what I need.

Father, as You say...   —PHYLLIS HOBE

---

5 FRIDAY
   ...Thy wonderful works which thou hast done...
                                          —*PSALM 40:5*

One day Peter Kilham, the ingenious inventor-designer whose cylindrical bird feeder has won world-wide popularity, showed me the little pond behind his home where he does much of his bird-watching. In the swampy ground I noticed many large skunk cabbages, their leaves a brilliant green against the rich, dark soil.

Peter noted my interest. "Fascinating plants, those skunk cabbages," he said. "They have a remarkable built-in thermostat that enables them to radiate warmth in early spring. This melts the snow around them and allows the cabbages to get an early start and have a longer growing season than the other plants. Skunk cabbages may not have the most elegant name in the world, but when the Great Designer got around to them, He gave them this special quality— and they've flourished ever since."

291

The capacity to radiate warmth, I thought. What a marvelous attribute—for cabbages…or kings…or you and me.

May we reflect in our actions toward one another, Lord, the warmth of Your love. —ARTHUR GORDON

---

6 SATURDAY
…Freely ye have received, freely give. —MATTHEW 10:8

I walked alone that first morning of the retreat. Although we had started on the silent walk as a group, the spaces between us soon widened. Suddenly I heard the crunching of dry leaves as someone stepped close to me from behind—an intrusion on my solitude.

A warm hand clasped mine, closing my fingers around something cold and round and hard. A horse chestnut! I hadn't seen one of those since I was a child. I smiled at the person who handed it to me. Then, rubbing my fingers over its cool, rippled surface, I felt as though a tightly latched door within myself had burst open, and I was immediately filled with awareness of the Lord.

I caught up with the woman ahead of me, who smiled as I placed the chestnut in her hand and moved away. Then I watched, marveling, as that little bit of caring was passed from one to another ahead of me, silently linking together people who only moments before had been as strangers. And to think that my closely guarded privacy had almost made me miss that moment of shared wonder!

Lord, help me to find You this day by reaching out to others.
—MARILYN MORGAN HELLEBERG

7 SUNDAY

For we being many are one bread, and one body: for we are all partakers of that one bread.
—I CORINTHIANS 10:17

On July 20, 1969, Apollo II landed the first men on the moon. Astronaut Buzz Aldrin requested a moment of silence from ground control in Houston. From his space suit he drew out the carefully wrapped elements of communion that he had brought with him from his church back on Earth. In the one-sixth gravity on the moon, the liquid—the first liquid ever poured on the moon—curled slowly and gracefully into the chalice. Then the astronaut broke the bread and ate it, commemorating the words of Jesus: "This is my body broken for you." And as he lifted the cup to drink, he remembered the promise: "This is my blood which is poured out for many."

Commenting on that rare moment of worship while suspended in outer space, Aldrin later said: "I sensed an especially strong unity with our church back home and with the church everywhere." This first holy communion on the moon reminds me that despite the distance of our differences, we are all one. On Earth. And beyond.

Lord, help me today—Worldwide Communion Sunday—bring Christians together, not in uniformity, but in unity.
—SUE MONK KIDD

8 MONDAY

And these words, which I command thee this day, shall be in thine heart: And thou shalt teach them diligently unto thy children...
—DEUTERONOMY 6:6,7

As one of the judges of the annual *Guideposts* Youth Writing Contest, I've noticed that often as many as twenty man-

293

uscripts will arrive from the students in one class. When this happens, I find myself thinking about the teachers of those students. Not only are they encouraging the youngsters to try to win a scholarship and to express themselves in writing, but they are prompting their students to write about their spiritual experiences and convictions.

I can look back at my own years as a student and recall several teachers who were strong influences on me in a similar way. I suppose that a couple of them probably influenced me as much as—if not more than—my parents did.

You know, every day many of us have an opportunity to be a teacher to someone—a child, a friend, a co-worker, a neighbor. What does it take to be a *good* teacher? Being genuinely interested in the other person, drawing him out, finding his own unique potential.

Isn't it true—when we bring out the best in others, we bring out the best in ourselves?

Help me to teach others, Lord . . . as You teach me.

—GLENN KITTLER

---

9 TUESDAY

. . . Watchman, what of the night? The watchman said, The morning cometh . . . —ISAIAH 21:11,12

Another dark, gray day. After a week of clouds and rain, I was feeling depressed. Then I noticed that Mrs. Damon was planting tulips in her garden next door, a smile hovering on her face.

"You actually look happy," I said. "How do you manage it in all this gloomy weather?"

"I just watch the sun disperse the darkness."

"But the sun's not even shining."

Mrs. Damon continued dropping bulbs into the ground. "It's up there though," she said.

Later that day an unexpected card arrived from a friend. Its message might well have been written by my neighbor:

> I heard a bird sing in the dark of December:
> A magical thing and sweet to remember.

Suddenly the day seemed brighter—and I too knew that the sun was still up there, right where God had hung it.

And it's there for me every day, I thought, *unless I myself allow the clouds to make me forget*. But even more than that, I think that I would like to be a lifter of darkness for those to whom depression is not just a transient cloud. A card, a visit, a phone call—perhaps a smile, a touch, a hug. Send a sunny message to someone today!

Father, let me find creative ways of revealing Your sunshine to others—especially to those who can't see that the sun still shines behind the clouds. —JUNE MASTERS BACHER

---

10 WEDNESDAY
Lord, teach us to pray... —LUKE 11:1

For four years some of my closest friends and I met every Wednesday morning to pray. Our faith soared as we saw our prayers being answered, and we grew unbelievably close to one another.

Then we fell into the habit of sharing our discoveries of how God was answering our prayers, and soon the sharing became longer and longer, the prayer time shorter and shorter. Inevitably the talking seemed to dominate our prayer meetings. We appointed a time-keeper so we could begin praying at a certain time. It worked for a few weeks, but then we were back to our chatter.

One morning I entered the prayer chapel with two friends to find that we weren't the first to arrive. Another member of the group was already there. Head bowed and hands folded, she had begun a private prayer time with God. Without a word, we quietly sat down and prayed silently for a time. Then someone prayed aloud.

Yes, we were back on the right track—talking *to* God, not *about* God.

Father, when I speak, let it be to You first.

—MARION BOND WEST

---

11 THURSDAY
...I am the light of the world...   *—JOHN 8:12*

The sky was heavily overcast that night as we stood at the Shelbyville airport, a field not yet lighted, and watched a plane attempting to land. A private craft, it carried the pilot and a Congressional candidate. Waiting with me were two party representatives who would whisk the candidate off to a local political meeting.

As the plane roared over our heads, we suddenly realized that the pilot, without ground visibility, could not possibly see the landing strip. Hastily we decided to make an "X" in the center of the runway with the headlights of our cars—and then pray the plane down.

When the "X" was formed, the pilot came in safely, but he was truly a shaken man.

"Should this ever happen again," he advised us, "drive to opposite ends of the runway and beam your headlights at each other. That will tell the pilot where the strip is, and how long it is."

Today you may meet someone, like that pilot, hunting for a landing strip in life. It's good to remember he may not need an "X" but he could surely use some light on the boundaries! Then pray him down until he lands safely.

Father, help me to light my brother's way and guide his landing.

—ZONA B. DAVIS

12 FRIDAY
For whosoever shall call upon the name of the Lord shall be saved. —ROMANS 10:13

Christopher Columbus' voyage from Spain to America (he landed in the Bahamas on this date in 1492) was an arduous one that came close to disaster. After three weeks at sea with nary a sight of land, his crew petitioned their captain to turn around, not because they feared "falling off the edge of the earth," but because they were worried about having to fight strong return winds.

However, Columbus persuaded his men to go on, telling them that he had sailed for the Indies and that he would continue until, with the Lord's help, he found them. Columbus' biographers tell us that on many days of the voyage, the great seaman's log said simply, "We sailed on."

Sometimes when in our lives we sail uncharted waters, our fears grapple with our faith and we are tempted to give up and turn back. It is then that we fully realize the strength and power of our Heavenly Father's love. He stands beside us, ever ready to support us should we falter. In Him we can always find the courage and resolve to hold to our course, to sail on—even when the seas are at their choppiest.

Let's greet today with our heads high, chins up, ready to "sail on," knowing that He has us firmly in tow.

Lord, should I falter midway, guide me with Your compass.

—FRED BAUER

13 SATURDAY
Shew me thy ways, O Lord; teach me thy paths. —PSALM 25:4

Last fall I took a trip by car to visit friends in several different cities. I didn't bother to buy a road map. "After all," I

297

reasoned, "I have a pretty good sense of direction, and there are always road signs to follow."

How did I do? On the long stretches, fine. But I became hopelessly lost in Charleston, Columbia, Statesville, Burlington and Augusta. Finally, forced to admit my inadequacies, I pulled into a gas station and bought a map. What a relief it was to at last see where I was, where I needed to go and how to get there!

And today I realize that my journey in faith is like that trip. I can get through a good bit of living by using my own understanding, my conscience and the advice of others. But when specifics overtake me—a maze of sorrows, unruly temptations and difficult decisions—I need a map. No wonder the Psalmist refers to God's Word as "light" on the pathways of life. I don't travel well without it.

Lord, make Your Way plain before me. Amen.

—PATRICIA HOUCK SPRINKLE

---

14 SUNDAY

Wherefore be ye not unwise, but understanding what the will of the Lord is. —EPHESIANS 5:17

Once, on a flaming October day, I felt especially frustrated by my inability to stamp out a particular little habit in my life. I had tried countless times to break it, without success. *What's the use? I can't change,* I thought. *It's simply the way I am.*

Later that day I took a walk and found myself beside a beautiful old church. As I looked up, filled with admiration for the graceful brick tower, my eyes fell on a tree growing just inside the church yard. It was a striking tree, half autumn red, half summer green. I had caught it in perfect transition. Reaching up, I plucked a leaf and studied it, fascinated by the process that was gradually transforming its colors. Patiently, quietly, the leaf had yielded itself to the mysterious work of God's design.

As I stood there musing, I began to gather hope. If God designed such a miraculous capacity for change into the leaf, surely He did so for me too. I also could be transformed! But first, like the leaf, I must yield myself to God—with complete trust and patience—and offer no resistance to His work within me.

There beneath the cool shadows of the autumn tree, I tucked the near-crimson leaf into my pocket, a reminder that no one should ever give up on himself. With God's plan at work in our lives, we can all be changed—just as surely as the changing of the seasons!

Help me to see Your design for my life, Father, and then follow it.

—SUE MONK KIDD

JESUS, THE MASTER STORYTELLER
Parable of the Rich Fool —LUKE 12:16-21

15 MONDAY

I know of a brother and sister who have not spoken to each other for over a dozen years because of a disagreement over the settlement of their late father's estate.

Christ dealt with such a problem. A brother, probably a younger brother, asked Jesus to intervene, and press his older brother into sharing his inheritance. Jesus declines, cautioning against covetousness. Then he tells about the rich farmer who was so prosperous that he had to keep building bigger and bigger barns to hold his grain. He was so rich, in fact, that he could retire.

"Take thine ease," he counsels himself. "Eat, drink, and be merry."

But God spoke to him and said: "You fool. Tonight your soul shall be required."

Luke concludes the passage by commenting, "So is he who lays up treasure for himself, and is not rich toward God."

Contrary to what some may think, the moral of this story isn't that money is the root of all evil. But anything that separates man from God is a sin. The farmer's mistake was that he gloried in his

299

wealth, worshipped it, idolized it. And God required his soul.
Those that have ears, let them hear....

Help me discern the lasting from the passing, Lord, and gold from the dross, and to live my days purposefully and meaningfully in Your Presence.
—FRED BAUER

---

16 TUESDAY

In the day when I cried thou answeredst me, and strengthenedst me with strength in my soul.

—PSALM 138:3

"I hope you don't mind my calling you so late," Jessie said. "I just had to talk to someone and I knew you would understand."

Jessie's husband Tom had died almost a year earlier and now she was going through a period when each day seemed to recall a painful memory: "Last year at this time Tom and I were.." "A year ago we were celebrating my birthday and.." "Last Christmas Tom was...."

"Everyone's been wonderful," Jessie said, "but it's time for me to go on alone. People have other things to do. They can't always be fussing over me."

I knew what she meant. When we lose someone close, our family and friends gather around and at first we don't realize how great our loss is—and then gradually friends stop knocking on the door and calling to ask how we are. And then the loneliness really hits us.

"I knew you would understand," she had said. But did I? Like everyone else, I had assumed that Jessie would be all right. Surely someone was looking after her. I had been meaning to call her for the longest time, but....

No, I hadn't been a good friend to Jessie—but from now on I'm going to be. With God's help, I'm going to become the friend she— and God—think I am.

Lord, I want to be the kind of friend who's always there—the kind of friend You are.
—PHYLLIS HOBE

17 WEDNESDAY

Fear thou not; for I am with thee...yea, I will uphold thee with the right hand of my righteousness.

—ISAIAH 41:10

I had an assignment in Charleston, West Virginia. Now I *knew* that my twelve-year-old Volkswagen could barely make it across the local Queensboro Bridge without breaking down. But that wasn't going to stop *me!*

I tossed my overnight bag into the car, started the engine and then shifted into reverse. Nothing happened. *Oh, no,* I groaned. *Don't let the transmission go now. I have to make this trip. Besides, I don't have the money for another big repair job.*

Well, I knew that it would be a long drive and that, in addition, I had to make a couple of stops on the way. Angry and upset, I ran around the corner to a nearby mechanic, told him where the car was and shouted over my shoulder, "If it's going to cost more than fifty dollars, don't fix it." Then I hurried off to a car-rental office.

I was pretty unhappy about the way life was treating me, but my attitude changed soon enough. Late that night I inched my way over the Appalachian Mountains and around some of the scariest hairpin turns I'd ever driven. I was so grateful not to be driving my old wreck, with its dubious brakes and lackadaisical pickup. I felt secure in the late-model rental car.

When I returned home two days later, I learned that the repair to my Volkswagen cost exactly fifty dollars. Someone had surely been watching out for me!

Dear Father, thank You for Your loving protection, especially at those times when we are not aware of it.

—SAMANTHA McGARRITY

18 THURSDAY

Behold, I have set before thee an open door, and no man can shut it... —REVELATION 3:8

The story is told that the great Houdini, world-famous escape artist, experienced only one failure. In England he was placed in a prison. Since no one had ever been able to keep him trapped for more than a few minutes, Houdini fully expected to escape in a few brief moments.

Two hours later he was still picking at the lock, sweat pouring from his face. Finally, heartsick, he had to admit that he could not escape from the prison.

When the truth was made known, it was discovered that indeed the door had been successfully unlocked by Houdini. He hadn't known it though, for he hadn't pushed against it...he simply worked away on a lock that he had already opened. He could have walked out, a free man, at any time.

I can identify with Houdini. Many times God has unlocked a door for me, yet I have continued working at the lock, begging Him to open it. All I had to do was to push the door and walk through, free of the burden that imprisoned me. But because I didn't *believe* my pleas had been answered, I remained closed in, struggling, panicky.

Doesn't this tell us something about doubt...and belief? Is there a door you have been trying to open for a long time? How about giving it a little shove today?

Father, sometimes we make our own prison. Thank You for opening the door. —MARION BOND WEST

19 FRIDAY
If thy brother trespass against thee, rebuke him; and if he repent, forgive him. —LUKE 17:3

We were student teachers, all of us in the classroom new to the methods of education.

"What do I do," someone asked the instructor, "if an experienced teacher puts me in a bad light in front of the pupils?"

"There are times," she replied, "when you must love others enough to confront them with the truth. If a person embarrasses you, say so. But gently."

Well, I have been slow in learning to follow that advice. It has always been far easier for me to ignore a wrong than to let the offender know—even in a gentle way—that my feelings have been hurt. The problem, of course, is that I have not really ignored the hurt—I've just pushed it way to the back of my mind. Then one day it's likely to surface, blown all out of proportion. And, even worse, I've been harboring resentment.

Yes, it's best to talk over a hurt, as my instructor of long ago prescribed. And I agree with her reason—love. And I agree with her manner—gently. And, one more step. I agree with Jesus' admonition—*forgive!*

Do you have a hurt that you're trying to ignore? Bring it out in the open today—lovingly, gently, forgivingly.

Lord, I would ask of You three qualities in overcoming a hurt received from another: the courage to speak out, a gentle manner and a forgiving heart. —JUNE MASTERS BACHER

OCTOBER 1984

20 SATURDAY

Who hath saved us, and called us with a holy calling, not according to our works, but according to his own purpose and grace, which was given us in Christ Jesus before the world began... —II TIMOTHY 1:9

While playing for the Baltimore Colts, football star Ken Hall cracked a neck vertebra in five places and never seemed to regain his playing coordination. In the three years following his injury, he was traded to three different teams. Because it seemed that his career was floundering, he decided to quit. At the ripe age of thirty, he found himself working as a tour guide in a sugar factory.

But today Ken Hall is a successful business executive. When recently asked about his early spate of bad fortune, he said, "There's a lot of positive in any negative situation.... Really, there are no negatives."

No negatives? Well, obviously there were plenty of negatives in Ken Hall's life. But he overcame them by his simple refusal to measure himself by others' standards. Of all his high-school trophies and awards—and there were hundreds of them, a whole garage full!—not one remains. Just as he didn't take people too seriously when they said he was the greatest, so he didn't pay too much attention when he was judged a failure. He simply picked himself up and kept going, believing and trusting that he could be whatever he wanted to be.

Ken Hall's victory confirms the trust that Jesus has placed in us, for His love continually assures us that we *can* overcome if we but have faith and believe wholeheartedly in our Heavenly Father's purpose for us.

Father, uplift my thoughts today. —JAMES McDERMOTT

304

21 SUNDAY

Let the word of Christ dwell in you richly...

—COLOSSIANS 3:16

There are puppy tooth marks at the bottom of the scuffed leather cover. The pages, yellowed and brittled by time and use, are beginning to fall away from the binding. It is one of my most treasured possessions—my mother's personal Bible. The inscription inside the cover reads: "From Mama and Papa, April 4, 1920." The occasion of the gift was Mother's twentieth birthday. Now it is a gift to me, a celebration of the dreams and fears, prayers and tears, loves and triumphs of my mother's life—a living record of one woman's journey of faith.

In the margin by Song of Songs 2:10 is written, "I will follow you, my love—June 17, 1923," my parents' wedding day. By Psalm 46:1 is written, "Tornado destroyed our house," followed by the verse: "God is our refuge and strength, a very present help in trouble." I searched for my birth date and found it beside Mark 9:37. The date beside Isaiah 25:8 is February 10, 1968, the day my father died. Mother's words there warm me like a hug: "We will be together again."

As I sit here holding this tattered book in my hands, I am moved to tears by its precious link with eternity. Will your Bible be a treasured legacy to someone else because of its meaningful and heartfelt notations?

Thank You, Lord, for Your Word that spans the generations.

—MARILYN MORGAN HELLEBERG

22 MONDAY

In the day when I cried thou answeredst me, and strengthenedst me with strength in my soul.

—PSALM 138:3

When I first became a Christian, I thought that my most serious problems would be over. What a shock it was almost immediately to run headlong into several painful crises in my life. *Why is God punishing me?* I wondered. *Maybe I'm not His child after all.*

Then I met a friend who was having to undergo daily therapy following surgery.

"The exercises really hurt," she told me, "but my sons, who are into weight lifting, keep reminding me of the bodybuilders' slogan: 'No pain, no gain.'"

So that was it! I thought to myself. I should have known that God would call upon me to strengthen my spiritual muscles. After all, doesn't being a Christian mean that we must continuously grow in grace?

Now whenever I face a difficult situation, I try to remember those words: "No pain, no gain." Why don't you say them to yourself right now?

I'm exercising, Father. No pain, no gain. Thank You for Your wisdom and support. —MADGE HARRAH

23 TUESDAY

...For with God all things are possible. —MARK 10:27

Recently our local newspaper carried an unusual picture story that showed an oriole trying to drink from a hummingbird feeder.

First the bird fluttered its wings wildly and tried to hover in the air, but its wings couldn't move fast enough to keep it aloft. Then the little bird sat on the spout and tried to drink from above, but it couldn't reach into the opening. At last, refusing to give up, it gripped the spout from underneath and, hanging upside down, was able to enjoy the drink.

Have you ever attempted something that seemed impossible? Just last year as I was going through my files, I came across an article that had been rejected by several publishers—and finally even by myself. Curious, I read it over and, like the oriole, decided to try once again. After asking God's blessing on the rewritten version, I resubmitted it to a publisher. The article was accepted.

Many times a project seems to be impossible only because we give up. But when we ask for God's help and keep on trying, we can usually find a "perch that works."

I can't, Lord, but I know that we can. —DORIS HAASE

---

24 WEDNESDAY
...Nation shall not lift up sword against nation, neither shall they learn war any more. —ISAIAH 2:4

The United Nations delegates who were spending a day in Nashville, Tennessee, were greeted by protesters carrying large signs that read "GO HOME, U.N.!"

Seventeen-year-old Jan Mosley, a native of Nashville who was acting as a summer tour guide, was bothered. She hurried home, where she and her sisters—Melody, sixteen, and Lenora, thirteen—rapidly began to make signs of their own. With gaily colored marking pens they drew huge hearts with the words "NASHVILLE LOVES THE WHOLE WORLD!" printed in tall letters.

Then they raced to the airport, where they held the signs high in the air as the delegates went to their waiting plane. As the Secretary General of the United Nations, Kurt Waldheim, walked by, his eye caught sight of the posters and young sisters.

"I'd like to say a few words to those girls," he told his sponsor. The plane's departure was momentarily delayed as he greeted the young-sters warmly. "When I saw those big hearts," he said, "I knew you cared—and that means more than I can say!"

The three girls blushed happily and giggled. As they watched the plane lift off, they knew that the message that counts most in the welding of nations— and in the meeting of human hearts—is the message of love.

Lord, keep me mindful that even my one small voice can make a big difference. —ZONA B. DAVIS

---

25 THURSDAY
The day is thine, the night also is thine... —PSALM 74:16

Since early childhood, I have been afraid of the dark. As a youngster, I always sent my little sister before me to turn on the light—and as an adult, I prefer bedrooms where streetlights are shining in the window. Whenever I am in total darkness, I encour-age myself by repeating a line from George MacDonald: "But the dark is still God." I hold on to those words until I find the light.

Maybe you don't fear actual darkness as I do. But life has many kinds of darkness—times of uncertainty, times of grief, times of pain and despair. To all of us, these kinds of darkness are bound to bring fear.

Isn't it comforting, then, when we find ourselves in the dark, to know that God created the dark as well as the light—and that He lovingly resides in both?

Dear God, with your Presence leading me through the darkness, I am not afraid. —PATRICIA HOUCK SPRINKLE

26 FRIDAY
...Be thou an example of the believers... —TIMOTHY 4:12

The salesgirl talked on and on. Her voice was smooth and pleasing, she radiated health, and her complexion had the quality of fine porcelain.

"You can't beat the price anywhere," she called. *True.* "The basic ingredient is aloe vera, taken from the plant that worked wonders for the women of the Nile." *Sounds good.* "And, applied properly, this cream can give you a new skin—even," she paused to smile, "go so far as to change your whole life!" *That should clinch it!* But the shoppers merely looked blank and moved on.

Then a sweet-faced old lady stepped up to the counter. "Miss," she said timidly, "do you use this cream yourself?"

"Yes, of course I do," the girl smiled.

"Then say so!" the old lady said. "People need to see an example."

Right on target! Are you a salesperson for Christ? How often have you told others of the wonders that faith has wrought? Have you explained the price and listed the basic ingredients (hope, faith and charity) that promise miracles that can change their lives? *So far, so good.* But have you come right out and said, "I use it myself. See what it has done for me!"

Lord, let me set an example to inspire those who have not yet come to You. —JUNE MASTERS BACHER

27 SATURDAY
I have blotted out, as a thick cloud, thy transgressions, and, as a cloud, thy sins: return unto me; for I have redeemed thee. —ISAIAH 44:22

For most of you who read the sports pages of a certain Sunday in October of 1982, the headline, "Northwestern, Thirty-one—Northern Illinois, Six," probably generated little reaction. But it was a great cause for celebration for an alumnus like me, who had seen Northwestern win only five games during the entire four years I spent at the university.

A thirty-four-game losing streak had set a national collegiate football record. But our new coach, Dennis Green had said, "I can't worry about what happened in the past. I can't shoulder that responsibility. My shoulders aren't big enough."

I suppose that a football game isn't ordinarily the source of a meaningful experience, but I learned a lesson from Coach Green's words that I'll always remember: My shoulders *aren't* big enough— and I can't go back and undo the record. At this point in my life I must leave past mistakes and failures to God. He knows the times of my remorse, He has seen the depths of my repentance—and He has taken them unto Himself, as promised.

It's as Coach Green added: "I think that the team will do much better if we think about the upcoming games we *can* win, not about our past losses."

And so will I—and so will you!

Thank you, Father, for removing the burdens of the past and for strengthening us with faith in the future.　　　　—JEFF JAPINGA

---

28 SUNDAY
Pray without ceasing.　　　　—I THESSALONIANS 5:17

How do you pray when words just won't come?

I rely on imagination.

Scripture gives us many pictures of God, and I find that when I cannot pray with *words*, I can pray through *pictures*.

When a friend is critically ill and I do not know whether to ask for healing or release from pain, I picture myself simply lifting my friend to the throne of grace and into the presence of God (Hebrews 4:16).

When I am baffled by my own circumstances or feelings, I picture myself sitting on God's footstool absorbing peace and waiting for God to speak. Sometimes I even picture myself creeping into my heavenly Father's lap, gratefully aware that "the eternal God is your dwelling place and underneath are the everlasting arms" (Deuteronomy 33:27).

When I am tempted, I recall that "we are surrounded by a cloud of witnesses" (Hebrews 12:1) and picture beloved friends who are now with God bending down from heaven to encourage me.

When I worship (or have trouble worshiping), I picture us all in one corner of God's vast throne room where our praises rise until God Himself is enthroned on our praises (Psalm 22:3).

Language of course, is important as one way to communicate with God. But if words won't come, don't let that stop your prayers. God's gift of imagination can also be a doorway to prayer.

Hear all our prayers, oh Lord—especially those of our imagination.
—PATRICIA HOUCK SPRINKLE

---

29 MONDAY

Come to me, all ye that labour and are heavy laden, and I will give you rest. —MATTHEW 11:28

A long-ago legend has it that, there once lived a man of towering strength, a giant of a man. He was a pagan whose strength perhaps led him to believe that he needed no higher power.

He made his living by carrying travelers across a broad river. One day a beautiful child came to the bank of the river. As the man bent down to allow the child to climb upon his back, the young lad said, "Are you sure you can bear my weight?"

The man laughed. "Why, I've carried full-grown men across this river. You, my little one, will be lighter than a pebble."

"Very well," said the boy. "But I must warn you. I am heavier than I look."

With a grin, the man raised the child upon his massive shoulders and stepped out into the swirling water. But the weight on his back grew strangely heavy. Soon the brawny giant was struggling not to sink. With superhuman effort he crawled up onto the opposite bank and let the child down.

"How can you be so heavy?" the perplexed man asked. "Who *are* you?"

"I am Jesus of Nazareth," replied the boy. "And I carry the burdens of the world on my shoulders. Let me carry yours, too."

And so it was that Christopher, today known as St. Christopher, was converted to Christianity. This story reminds me — I don't need to struggle across each day on my own. There is One stronger than I. He is the Great Burden-bearer. He even carries St. Christopher, yet on his shoulders there is always room for one more.

Jesus, carry me through this day.   —SUE MONK KIDD

---

30   TUESDAY
...Give diligence to make your calling and election sure: for if ye do these things, ye shall never fall...
—II PETER 1:10

One day my fifth-grade teacher handed out a "Test in Following Directions." She told us to read through the entire instructions before beginning. The first instruction read, "Spell your name as loudly as you can." The second said to "Stand on your chair and jump up and down."

Well, you can imagine what happened. The classroom was in chaos in no time flat, as we kids gleefully began carrying out the orders. Not wanting to be left out, I also stopped reading, jumped up and began acting out the commands.

Then, amidst a roar of silly chants and laughter, an odd silence fell on the room as each student neared the end of the instructions. The final item read, "Now disregard all of the above instructions, sit quietly, and you will receive an A. Those of you who have been behaving otherwise will receive an F." Need I tell you more?

Today I have an important career decision to make. Others in my field seem to be doing better than I am. But if my decision is based on what others are doing, I'm certain to make a foolish choice. I must first examine *my own* possibilities—and then await God's final "instructions."

For if I sit quietly—neither bustling about in haste nor wasting my days in blind alleys—He will surely show me the way!

Heavenly Father, help me to wait for Your directions before I act.

—MARILYN MORGAN HELLEBERG

---

31 WEDNESDAY
Train up a child in the way he should go...

—PROVERBS 22:6

Little ghosts decked out as skeletons, witches, brides and clowns trooped boisterously into our house, their high voices shrilling "Trick or treat!" It was Halloween night and the wee goblins arrived in droves, proffering open paper bags, grinning pumpkins and small buckets for their treats.

One little cowboy kept repeating, "John-three-sixteen. John-three-sixteen." When asked why, he replied, "So I won't forget. When we go to Mrs. Hanna's house later, we have to say a Scripture verse before she'll give us a treat."

When I called my friend Ollie Hanna to share the youngsters' excitement with her, I asked her about the Bible-verse project. She told me that she and her husband, both in their eighties, love the children dearly and they had wished they could do more for them than merely drop a treat into a bag. Then she had remembered that while the Druids believed that ghosts, spirits and witches came only to do harm, the Christians made the evening before Holy Day hallowed—hence the name "Halloween." But how could the

Hannas make the evening holy? As a child, Ollie said, she had memorized many Bible verses, which she had treasured ever since. Why not have each child say a Bible verse before she handed out a treat? Should a child not know a verse, she would teach him one.

"We've helped so many children memorize Bible verses in this way," she told me. "It's the best thing we thought we could give them. A treat is gone overnight, but they'll use the verses for the rest of their lives."

Dear Father, as Your children, may we be sensitive to our children.

—ZONA B. DAVIS

Praise Diary for October

1

2

3

4

5

6

7

8

9

10

11

12

13

14

15

16

17

18

19

20

21

22

23

24

25

26

27

28

29

30

31

November

S	M	T	W	T	F	S
				1	2	3
4	5	6	7	8	9	10
11	12	13	14	15	16	17
18	19	20	21	22	23	24
25	26	27	28	29	30	

Although I cannot feel the wind
From where I stand below
The towering reaches of this once great oak,
It seems to—though dead a year now—
And gives a sepulchral groan.
Now it leans into where I've
Notched its trunk, and
Now it's falling, falling,
Creaking like an ancient door
On the slender axis of curing wood
That my bucksaw left.
I wonder that so big a thing comes
Down so softly until it whumps
To the ground neatly between two lesser trees.
The old fellow fell as true as once it grew.
One hundred Springs ago,
A single leaf on threadlike stem;
Two weeks from now, a full cord
Stacked neatly by the barn.
I'm old now, too, Lord,
In my late Autumn, close to Your harvest.
I guess that's why I spend my time
Out here in the woods, close to You,
Where You cause the trees to grow.

James McDermott

GUIDEPEOPLE: A Living Parable for November

1

THURSDAY

A merry heart maketh a cheerful countenance.

—*PROVERBS 15:13*

We've never had a section in *Guideposts* devoted to humor, but we've carried stories by some of the world's funniest people, everybody from Joe E. Brown to Bob Hope. And I still remember a story that the late Harry Hershfield, one of America's most brilliant wits, told us. It was about a man who had become so discouraged with life that he bought a loaf of bread at a store, then went to a railroad crossing and stretched himself out across the tracks.

A policeman saw this bewildering sight and rushed up to him asking, "What do you think you're doing?"

"Waiting for the train to run over me," the man replied.

"But why the loaf of bread?"

"The way the trains run here," the man answered, "you could starve to death while waiting for one."

Harry Hershfield didn't tell that story just to amuse us. He was making a strong point: That there is irony in our lives and even in the darkest situation we can take ourselves too seriously. The greatest therapy in the world is the ability to get out of our own way long enough to observe ourselves—and sometimes even laugh at ourselves.

No, we've never had a humor section in *Guideposts*, but we've made this point often enough: "A merry heart doeth good like a medicine" (Proverbs 17:22).

Lord, teach me ways to mend my spirit—and my neighbor's—with laughter.　　　　　　　　　　　　　　—VAN VARNER

2 FRIDAY

Yet have I made myself servant unto all, that I might gain the more. —I CORINTHIANS 9:19

Martha was never one of my favorite people in the Bible. How could she have allowed herself to get stuck in the kitchen while Jesus was in the next room? I much preferred her sister Mary. She knew when to leave the dishes in the sink.

But recently I changed my mind about Martha.

I had invited our Library Committee to meet in my house because we planned to address a touchy question where the feelings on each side were strong. I thought the meeting might be less stormy were it to be held in a homey environment.

Fine. Except that I didn't get to take part in the discussion at all! I spent most of the evening either in the kitchen, pouring coffee or piling snacks on plates. I was frustrated and angry at myself. *Look at me!* I thought. *I'm not a Mary, I'm a Martha!*

As the committee members left, the chairwoman took my hand and pressed it. "Thank you so much," she said warmly. "We had such a good meeting, and we owe it all to your lovely hospitality."

Well, that gave me something to think about. Apparently pouring coffee hadn't been a complete waste of time. And maybe I wasn't *all* Martha. Maybe I had *some* Mary within me too. And, you know, there's a need for both of them in this world.

When I can't be right out front, Father, let me be a gracious helper in the back. —PHYLLIS HOBE

3 SATURDAY

If it be possible, as much as lieth in you, live peaceably with all men. —ROMANS 12:18

We were sitting in the lounge of the Atlanta airport, my two-year-old son and I, waiting for our flight to depart. The young man beside me looked at the candy in my child's hand and said softly, "That's more sugar than he needs in a week."

How dare he? *Do I look like an irresponsible mother?* I wondered. "He *is* my child, you know," I said curtly, and turned away.

Then a billboard advertisement caught my eye. "It all depends on you," one of the sentences said. I remembered my husband's sermon of the previous Sunday. "Anger and resentment boomerang to hurt *us* far more than the one who offends us," he had said. "We can't always live in peace with everyone, but we can try to make peace when it depends on us."

I turned back to the young man and swallowed hard. "I'm sorry I snapped at you," I said.

He visibly relaxed. "And I'm sorry I spoke as I did. It's just that I run day-care centers for children and I'm so very concerned about their nutrition."

The next half hour became a pleasant time of conversation and play with my little son. We'd made a new friend. And to think—it all depended on me!

Soften my heart, Lord. Let me listen when the stranger speaks. Help me to seek peace when it depends on me.

—PATRICIA HOUCK SPRINKLE

---

4 SUNDAY
...At evening time it shall be light. —ZECHARIAH 14:7

While traveling through Europe with a friend last summer, I was awed by the stupendous height of the mountains in Switzerland, especially since I knew that we were going to have to cross them. One in particular, the White Virgin, stretches so far into the clouds that the snow on the peak never melts. Forever white, huge green-cloaked mountains hover around it.

Shortly after sunset an incredibly beautiful glow blanketed the landscape. My friend told me that it is known as *alpenglow*—the last light of day reflected from the snow-capped mountain after the valleys have grown dark.

"Doesn't it remind you," my friend continued, "that whenever the darkness of disappointment falls, we can still bask in a glow—however faint—of other and brighter hours. I always remember, though, that to see this kind of light, we must look up."

If you are tempted to sink into a dark valley, recall those words. *Look up!* Let the gentle glow of His love enfold you.

Dear Father, thank You for Your light when all else is in shadow.
—ZONA B. DAVIS

---

5 MONDAY
Blessed is the man whose strength is in thee...
—PSALM 84:5

"What a disagreeable job!" I fretted as I began the long-postponed cleaning of the medicine cabinet. The wastebasket clanged as I threw out things.

"Just look at all these old pills and prescriptions." I held up a half-empty bottle for my teen-age daughter to observe. "Most of them only partly used, some not even opened. Why in the world do doctors prescribe more medicine than you're going to need? What a waste!"

"Why, Mother, I should think you'd be glad," she said. "Glad because, first, whoever needed those prescriptions got well without having to take the whole amount. And second, right now nobody's sick!"

"Honey, you're right!" I exclaimed. *Why hadn't I seen it that way too?*

And suddenly what had seemed such a disagreeable undertaking became an opportunity to thank God. I thanked Him for blessing us with splendid doctors and for all these good medications—enough—and more—to meet our needs.

Thank You, Father, for Your love that heals us and makes us strong in spirit as well as body. —MARJORIE HOLMES

---

6 TUESDAY

Unto whomsoever much is given, of him shall be much required... —LUKE 12:48

ELECTION DAY 1984

Today, Lord,
I will stand up to be counted
Among those millions of Americans
Who have learned that
Liberty is responsibility.

Today, Lord,
Neither state of weather
Nor frame of mind
Will keep me from my polling place,
For I have seen too often
How bad officials are placed in charge
By good men and women
Who do not vote.

Today, Lord,
I will stand up to be counted,
Intelligence at work,
Passion at rest.
And when this day is done, Lord,
Let me show respect for the losers
As I pray the winners
Into Your care. —RUTH STAFFORD PEALE

7

WEDNESDAY

I am in my Father, and ye in me, and I in you.

—*JOHN 14:20*

Her name was Donna and she had built walls around herself to keep people away. She felt unworthy.

Then one day, at a friend's encouraging, she attended a prayer meeting. The love, the warmth and the openness of those present touched her deeply and something seemed to break loose within her heart. All the long-buried hurts and pent-up emotions of her life came pouring out in a torrent of tears. Then, suddenly, she stopped crying, appalled to realize that she had given herself away and broken down before others. What would they think of her? She wanted only to run off and hide.

At that moment a young woman walked over, put her arms around Donna and said, "If Jesus is within me, His arms are around you at this moment." It was the turning point in Donna's life.

Do you know anyone who needs to be wrapped in the arms of Jesus today? Would you let Him use your arms?

Blessed Lord Jesus, love through me.

—MARILYN MORGAN HELLEBERG

8

THURSDAY

For none of us liveth to himself…   —*ROMANS 14:7*

I was sitting in a lecture hall waiting to hear a scientist speak on the subject of genetic research. Everyone else in the room seemed to be friendly—waving, chatting. The auditorium buzzed with voices. But not me. I was scrunched low in my chair, hoping I wouldn't be noticed.

Now I'm a friendly person too, but I have had a lifelong battle with shyness. No matter how foolish I tell myself it is, there are times when unaccountably shyness just seems to settle in around me like a fog. And I have to wait—miserable, and angry at myself—until it evaporates.

When the lecturer began to speak something he said dispelled my shyness. "You know," he said, "it's already been proven that we are all related to one another. If you could go back century upon century, you would be able to trace the genetic connections."

During the trip back home that night, I pondered: *We are all closely related in another way too—through one God, our Father.* At that moment I vowed to remember that scientist's statement whenever I feel a spell of shyness coming on. After all, there's no need to be shy around family, is there?

Dear Heavenly Father, please help me to always remember my earthly as well as my spiritual bonds to my brothers and sisters.

—SAMANTHA McGARRITY

---

9 FRIDAY
And of his fulness have all we received, and grace for grace. —JOHN 1:16

One day while on a retreat, I told the director: "It's been one of those years. A close friend died, lightning struck our home, our taxes went up and...."

"You remember *those* things very well," the director said with a sympathetic smile. "Now I dare you to write down ten special graces that God has given you in the last year."

"Graces?"

"You know, an undeserved gift from God, some act or sign of His love," he answered.

Well, I never could resist a good dare. So I sat on a bench under a tree and stared at the blank paper. *Ten?* I thought. *That many?* I jotted down a few obvious things. Then slowly I began to remember. All the nice people who had casually wandered in and out of my life.

Coincidences. A moment of hope. A shared joy. Tender words when I needed them most. A touch. So many wonderful things! I began to write faster and faster.

Finally I stopped and looked at the pages in amazement. *You did all this, Lord?* I thought. I saw then that the graces of God are often so close to us that we don't see them. We become unaware and take them for granted.

Perhaps God has done more in *your* life too than you know. Go on, get some paper. I dare you....

Keep me sensitive to the exquisite blessings You give us every day, Father.   —SUE MONK KIDD

---

10   SATURDAY
Let us run with patience the race that is set before us.
—HEBREWS 12:1

Joe Paterno, whose high character has distinguished both him and the football teams he has coached at Penn State University, once told me that he learned many valuable lessons from his mentor and predecessor, the late Rip Engle. In one big game, Paterno recalls, he discovered that the opposing team, in an all-out effort to win, was using radio communications from the bench to the players on the field, despite rules to the contrary.

Taking the information to Coach Engle, Paterno suggested that they intercept the messages and use them to Penn State's advantage. But Engle did not believe that two wrongs make a right, and he nixed the idea.

"I don't want to win that much," Paterno remembers Engle answering.

And his team didn't. They lost in the final seconds.

Sometimes when the stakes are high—or when we think they are—it is good to stand back and take a hard look at the situation before making a decision. More often than not, the life-or-death

325

dramas of the moment are neither. Momentary victories are never worth the cost of compromised principles. When temptation rears its snakelike head and tries to seduce us into believing that some small indiscretion will not matter, some little lie won't hurt, we need to remember the rhetorical question Jesus once asked: What does it profit us to gain the whole world and lose our souls? (Matthew 16:26)

Lord, the only lasting profit in life is the eternal one—with You.

—FRED BAUER

---

11 SUNDAY
Now therefore ye are no more strangers and foreigners, but fellow-citizens...and of the household of God... —EPHESIANS 2:19

She was young, I'd say in her mid-twenties. Always alone. Over the past month I had seen her at services several times, and finally one day I sat next to her, and introduced myself.

"Maybe you'd like to join a Bible-study class just for singles?" I suggested.

She gave me a tiny smile and shook her head.

"We also have a class in contemporary discipleship—especially designed for singles," I offered.

Again she smiled faintly and shook her head. Finally she said, gently but firmly, "Look, even though I'm single, I'm like anyone else. I want to belong to a church family—not to be set apart."

All through the ensuing service I thought about her words... and wondered. Were we wrong to attempt a ministry to singles? We meant well, of course, but maybe we were setting singles apart from the rest of the congregation.

When the service ended, I turned to her again and held out my hand. "I think you've taught me something, and I want to thank you," I said. "And will you think about joining a Bible-study class—just a plain, ordinary one that anybody can join?"

This time she really smiled. "I'd love to!" she exclaimed. "I thought you'd never ask!"

Teach us not to separate our paths one from another, Father.
—PHYLLIS HOBE

---

12 MONDAY
...Judge me, O Lord, according to my righteousness, and according to mine integrity... —PSALM 7:8

In the first grade, you're introduced to it on the monkey bars in the playground and in those horrendous things you take home called report cards. What do I mean? I mean the competition that tells us we have to be *better* than anyone else.

"I can do it better than you can!" Johnny shouts.

"I got an A. You only got a B," Susie says proudly.

Later you apply for college and interview for jobs and work overtime for promotions. And all the while you're wondering about the adjectives being used to describe your efforts. Better? Smarter? Quicker? And after that, richer? Shrewder? Why, I wonder, must we always be better than someone else? Must we be better workers, better mothers with better children in better houses to be a success? What ever happened to just plain "good"?

Society told Terry Meuwseen when she was chosen to be Miss America that she was better—better than every other young woman in the country. And this is what Terry told society: "Someone advised me before the competition, 'Don't compare yourself with anyone else. If you focus on other people's achievements, you will become either overly proud or unduly resentful. And you will lose—not because other people have defeated you. You will have defeated *yourself.*'"

Perhaps life in this ever-comparing and competitive sense is inescapable as a part of the human condition. I know, though, that if

327

I must be *better*, then let me be better than *I* was yesterday, and no more.

Help me, Lord, in all my strivings, in all my achievements, in all my aspirations —to be the best I can be.   —JEFF JAPINGA

---

13 TUESDAY
I thank my God upon every remembrance of you.
—PHILIPPIANS 1:3

Since the pumpkin pie tested "not done," I sat down and opened the mail while I waited. A letter from Bev Webb? Who was she? She said all sorts of kind things! About me? Bev Webb? The envelope was postmarked in Peoria, Illinois. Finally I put it all together.

"She's the daughter of my cousin Mary Hastings," I told my family. "But why did she send this beautiful letter?"

Later I mentioned the pleasant surprise to Mary. "Oh, Bev likes to write letters during the Thanksgiving season," she explained. "She says she has more time then than later and that the recipients have more time to read her letters than they would in the midst of Christmas greetings. She writes to people she feels deserve special attention, to old friends, to relatives seldom heard from or to newcomers to her church and neighborhood."

I can say for sure that the letter made my day. And it also gave me a splendid idea—I'd like to do the very same thing for someone else! Now—what's the name of that new family down the street?

Thank You, Father, for the gift of kind and loving words from others. Today, let me pass it on.   —ZONA B. DAVIS

14

WEDNESDAY

To every thing there is a season, and a time to every purpose under the heaven... —ECCLESIASTES 3:1

It is an absolutely glorious day. Although the calendar says mid-November, the air is warm and the sky clear and blue. What a perfect day for raking up the last leaves, turning up next spring's flowerbeds and digging unwanted roots from the damp earth. But I hesitate. There are other things I have planned to do. Is it wise to put them off just because the day is ripe for gardening? A breeze tugs at my shirt and with a note of acquiesence I head for the rake and shovel. This is the day for gardening—one like it may not come again this year.

There are days of the Spirit that are like that too. Days when the wind of the Spirit of God tugs at us and says: "This is the perfect time to make that call, write that letter, do that one small deed that will make a difference." We hesitate, torn between the impulse of our heart and the plans we had for the day. Still, the Spirit tugs.

What will we answer? Remember—if this is indeed the day, it may not come again!

Father, when I feel the tug of Your gentle Spirit, I will follow wherever it leads me. —PATRICIA HOUCK SPRINKLE

JESUS, THE MASTER STORYTELLER
Parable of the Prodigal Son
—LUKE 15:11-32

15
THURSDAY

Sometimes I wonder if Jesus had a favorite story. I suppose you could say that, in a way, stories are the storyteller's children, and that therefore he shouldn't have favorites. But the truth is, storytellers *do* have favorites. They come closest to conveying the *heart* of a message, the *essence* of the idea that the storyteller is trying to convey.

If Jesus did have a favorite—and I'm just guessing, of course—I think it might well have been the one we call *The Prodigal Son.* I don't know why we call it that, really. The Bible doesn't mention the word "prodigal," and one might claim the erring son isn't the central character in the story at all; it's the forgiving father.

I think this story would be one of Jesus' favorites because it expresses so beautifully and tenderly a concept that must have seemed very strange to any who believed in a Jehovah who was a fierce and implacable God of wrath. Here is Jesus saying God is a loving Father Who not only forgives sins, but actually runs eagerly toward the sinner and showers him with blessings.

There is a loose end in the story, though: What happened to the older son? Did he continue to refuse to go to the feast? Did he go and then sit there sulking and muttering to himself, "Not fair!"? Or did he somehow put aside his jealousy and his hurt feelings and go up to his wayward kid brother with a smile and say, "Oh, it's so good to see you! I'm so glad you're home!"?

Perhaps Jesus left that loose end dangling because He wanted each of us to put ourselves in the older brother's shoes. I wonder how I would have acted. I wonder, and I wish I were sure of the answer.

How about you?

Lord, help us to see that forgiveness is more important than anything. Even fairness.
                                                            —ARTHUR GORDON

---

16 FRIDAY
Now ye are clean through the word which I have spoken unto you.
                                                            —JOHN 15:3

A dear friend of mine had waged a lifelong battle with

weight. Diets weren't successful. Medication didn't work. Nor did psychotherapy.

In desperation Marjorie consulted her family physician about the advisability of bypass surgery. After putting her through all the necessary tests, he referred her to a specialist—and the operation was performed.

My friend did beautifully. Both of the doctors praised her highly, as did her family and friends. But although she was slim now and had bought a whole new wardrobe of lovely clothes, she still thought of herself as unattractive. She would not be completely healed, inwardly or outwardly, the family doctor said, until she could bring herself to *look*. For to *look* meant to see the new woman—and to accept her wholeheartedly.

There came the day that Marjorie saw herself quite by accident. "I was out browsing" she recounted happily, "and I glanced into a shop window. My eye caught the reflection of a rather nice-looking individual—and it was me!" Her burden of flesh and shame was gone.

Marjorie's story has a special message for me. All my life I seem to have waged battle with various temptations. And every time God has come to my aid and helped me to victory. But, as with Marjorie, I have found that a truly new person emerges only when we stop to *look* at our new self—and joyously accept God's miracle of rebirth.

Thank You, Lord, for removing my shame and creating me anew.
—JUNE MASTERS BACHER

---

17 SATURDAY

And let the peace of God rule in your hearts, to that which also ye are called in one body; and be ye thankful. —COLOSSIANS 3:15

All of our out-of-town relatives were coming to our house for Thanksgiving. I was so excited, I could hardly wait! Then on Wednesday afternoon it started to snow and by four o'clock we were in the throes of a vicious blizzard. Now no one was coming. My heart broke.

Thanksgiving Day stormed in, gray and raging. The driveway was drifted high with snow and we were virtual shut-ins. I put the turkey in the freezer and Rex and John and I had meat loaf for dinner. All afternoon I swallowed tears. Then about five o'clock the phone rang—and there was the happy voice of Jeri, my dearest friend during high-school years. We hadn't been in touch for more than twenty years.

"I'm just calling to tell you that I'm thankful for you," she said.

I was delighted to hear from her and after we had talked a bit, I felt so lightened that I wondered aloud how I could return her favor. Jeri told me: "The only way you can repay me is by calling someone who has been a blessing in *your* life and passing on the spirit of Thanksgiving."

Since then on every Thanksgiving Day, I've made it a point to call an old friend. And, like Jeri, I've suggested to each one that she pass on to someone else the thankfulness of the season.

How about sending the spirit of Thanksgiving to someone special in your life, even if it means calling clear across the continent? It will make the whole world sparkle anew—for your friend, and for you.

Thank You, Lord for the beautiful network of thankfulness that binds us together on this day.   —MARILYN MORGAN HELLEBERG

Celebrating National Bible Week:
ADVENTURES WITH THE GOOD BOOK

18 **DAY ONE**—NATIONAL BIBLE SUNDAY
The grass witherith, the flower fadeth; but the word of our God shall stand forever.   —ISAIAH 40:8

Today marks the first day of National Bible Week, sponsored by the Laymen's National Bible Committee each year to

NOVEMBER 1984

correspond with Thanksgiving week. In a way it is an arbitrary period that—unlike Christmas and Easter, or Chanukah and Passover—it is not rooted in historic spiritual events. Nonetheless it can provide a week of especially profound meaning for Christians everywhere.

Usually my wife Ruth and I formally acknowledge the week by attending a Laymen's National Bible Committee luncheon, but we also work out our own personal plan to deepen our ties to the Bible. When Ruth and I talked over this year's plan, it occurred to us that you might like to join us.

Therefore, together let us diligently make it a practice for one week to refer to the Bible as our "answer book." Whenever a problem arises or an important decision must be made, turn to the Bible *first*—not as a last resort. You will find that an answer is always there when you approach the Bible thoughtfully, carefully and—most important of all—prayerfully.

To give you some hints on how you might use the Bible as an "answer book," in the pages that follow, each day of National Bible Week is honored by a different writer as he or she shares illuminating personal experiences of the eternal truths of the Bible.

In this very special week all of us at *Guideposts* wish you Godspeed in your own living adventures with that great Good Book.

Father God, thank You for lighting our pathways with the eternal truths of the Bible. —NORMAN VINCENT PEALE

---

19 DAY TWO—MONDAY
Faith cometh by hearing, and hearing by the word of God. —ROMANS 10:17

One day last summer my husband and I wandered into a used-books store in Colorado Springs. As usual, I found myself caught up in the Inspiration section, where I gathered an armload of books at bargain prices.

333

Then, on the way to the cash register, something caught my eye. There in the Adventure section, between an Old West novel and a James Bond story, was a King James Bible. I made a mental note to tell the proprietor about the misplaced volume, but as I walked past the History section, I noticed another Bible, sandwiched between two textbooks. And further on there was more: a *Good News for Modern Man* in the Self-Improvement section, a *Living Bible* in the Travel section, a *Jerusalem Bible* in the Health section, and so on throughout the entire store.

When I mentioned my discoveries to the owner, he said, "Well, why not? The Bible is the best book in every one of those categories!"

It's true. I have a whole bookstore between these soft leather covers—plus the opportunity for a wonderful personal relationship with the Author!

Thank You, Lord, for Your Word—let it illuminate every facet of my life.
—MARILYN MORGAN HELLEBERG

---

20 DAY THREE—TUESDAY

I will delight myself in thy statutes: I will not forget thy word.
—PSALM 119:16

I came of age in the early sixties, when psychologists were bandying about phrases such as "primal scream" and advising that it was healthy to vent one's anger. But when I tried that "health plan" at home, I met a stern foe in my mother.

"Any old fool can get angry," she told me. Then she cautioned me: "It was not your father's and my plan to add a barbarian to the general populace when we hatched you. I hope you won't disappoint us." Somehow those words effectively wilted the psychologists' claims and since then I have gone along more or less equably.

Yet I often wondered. Is it really unhealthy to have to discipline one's self against noisy outbursts and screaming tantrums? Do nice guys finish last in the arena of good health? Then recently I stumbled upon psychologist Carol Tavris' book, *Anger: The Misun-derstood Emotion*. I learned that today she and many other therapists feel that letting anger run rampant actually increases hostility, creates more problems for the individual and often reduces one's sense of well-being.

Her thesis intrigued me, and curious, I went to my Bible. Sure enough. I found it in the seventh chapter of Ecclesiastes: "Be not hasty in thy spirit to be angry: for anger resteth in the bosom of fools." It made me chuckle because I instantly recalled my mother's words of so many years earlier.

Now there it was, clearly and elegantly stated in the Bible—the answer to the questions that had nagged at me for over twenty years!

Help me, dear Lord, to be a gentle seeker of Your truths.
—JAMES McDERMOTT

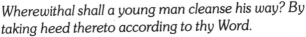

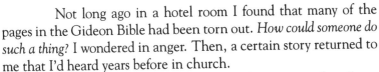

21 **DAY FOUR**—WEDNESDAY
Wherewithal shall a young man cleanse his way? By taking heed thereto according to thy Word.
—PSALM 119:9

Not long ago in a hotel room I found that many of the pages in the Gideon Bible had been torn out. *How could someone do such a thing?* I wondered in anger. Then, a certain story returned to me that I'd heard years before in church.

An unhappy and lonely young man, who was very hostile to Christianity, was staying in a motel when he came upon a Bible on the bedside table. The sight of it raised such anger and disgust in him that he tossed it into his duffel bag, determined to drop it in some trash pile when he left. But he didn't get around to it right away and it remained in the bottom of his bag. Meanwhile, he wandered about growing more depressed.

Finally one night, so desolate he wanted to die, he drove to the ocean where he thought he would drown himself. At the edge of the water, he hesitated, thinking if only he could discover some hope in life he wouldn't go through with it. Suddenly he thought of the stolen Bible in his bag. Before he ended his life shouldn't he at least explore that one last straw?

So the young man walked back to his car and dug out the Bible. He read all night by a flashlight. The next morning he drove away with hope burning inside him and a desire to follow this God who had reached out to him through the pages of the Bible.

As the memory of that story faded I looked down at the Bible with half its pages missing and felt my anger drain away. Of course it was wrong to steal. But I was remembering another important truth. Whenever God's Word is read, there is always the potential for a life-changing moment. A moment of light when someone discovers the God who reaches out for us from the pages, or the answer He sends for a particular problem or the strength needed to face a certain situation.

Such a moment could happen to the person who had torn the pages from this Bible. And, we must never ever forget, such a moment can happen to us.

Speak to me through Your Word today, Lord.

—SUE MONK KIDD

---

22 **DAY FIVE**—THURSDAY

Now therefore ye...are built upon the foundation of the apostles and prophets, Jesus Christ himself being the chief corner stone... —EPHESIANS 2:19, 20

One day recently Lynn and I visited with friends who own a lovely old farmhouse. Probably it was constructed at about the time George Washington was learning to take his first steps, well over two hundred years ago. Our friends have fixed up the place, to be sure, but they were wise enough to leave most of it in its original state. Its stone walls are a foot thick. Nine enormous fireplaces— once the sole source of heat and light—offer cozy places to curl up before on a cold winter's night. An artesian well (the water still clear and drinkable), beautiful wood-plank floors, heavy-timbered ceiling beams—yes, it is truly a delightful place.

The old house, standing on the crest of a little knoll, has weathered long years of scorching sun, the worst of raging storms, the encroaching threats of time—and yet today it stands there as sturdy as ever.

"And that's because," our friend told us, affectionately thumping one of the stone walls, "if you build a place right, it lasts."

Perhaps that thought, as much as any, expresses the message of National Bible Week. If we lay a firm foundation for our lives with the guidance of our daily Bible reading—for only in God's Word do we find the solid rocks of faith upon which to build—our lives will be as strong and sturdy as that beloved and enduring old farmhouse.

Your Word, O God, is the foundation of my life.

—JEFF JAPINGA

23

DAY SIX—FRIDAY

Thy word is a lamp unto my feet, and a light unto my path. —PSALM 119:105

A couple of summers ago our family spent an idyllic month houseboating on the Mississippi River. We covered nearly six hundred miles of water between Minneapolis and St. Louis, enjoying the beautiful scenic vistas that we had no idea existed.

The "Father of Waters" is also a busy commercial river. Because it serves as passageway for thousands of product-laden barges, it is important that pleasure-boaters know and observe the "rules of the road" in order to stay out of trouble. We had radios, lights, a horn, a compass and a depth meter to assist us, but the most important item we had was a navigational chart book. It helped us to locate buoys, shallows, wing dams, bridges, gas and supply facilities, safe beaches, locks and other landmarks.

Most significantly, the chart book helped us to stay in the channel. There one's depth is assured; outside of it there are rocks, tree stumps and impediments that can sink even the biggest of boats. I was reminded of all this the other day while rereading the story of Jesus calming the sea. The disciples were frightened lest their ship sink, but Jesus awoke and rebuked the sea with three words: "Peace, be still" (Mark 4:39).

When our lives become stormy, when we are blown off course and we lose our bearings, it is good to remember that we have an incomparable "navigational guide" in the Bible, and an incomparable Pilot who knows the way.

You know how often we stray from the channel of Your love, Lord. Help us to find our way back.   —FRED BAUER

---

24 DAY SEVEN—SATURDAY
In the beginning was the Word...   —JOHN 1:1

A colleague of mine, who is a great reader as well as a fine writer, tells me that she has a special way of putting herself to sleep when insomnia threatens. Other people may count sheep or visualize peaceful scenes or try deep-breathing exercises, but she repeats certain phrases to herself, phrases remembered from her reading, tiny gems of personal treasure. "Fair stood the wind for France."... "The little rain of China will be falling on my heart...." Phrases like that.

The Bible is filled with passages of great music and majesty too: "Remember now thy Creator in the days of thy youth."... "If I take the wings of the morning and dwell in the uttermost parts of the sea; Even there shall thy hand lead me."... "And the glory of the Lord shone round about them...."

Why not choose some of your own favorite phrases and commit them to memory—and then repeat them to yourself whenever you're feeling tense or can't sleep? I've heard it said that the last words we're aware of as we fall off to sleep sink deep into our sub-conscious and affect our emotional balance and outlook the next day.

So today reread some of your most-loved Bible passages. Then say them to yourself tonight after you're in bed. You should surely sleep soundly, snug and secure in the assurance of His Word.

Thanks, Lord, for Your gift of beautiful words that refresh my soul.
—ARTHUR GORDON

---

25 **DAY EIGHT**—SUNDAY
For the word of God is quick, and powerful, and sharper than any twoedged sword... —HEBREWS 4:12

To me one of the greatest tragedies of the past two thou-sand years lies in the fact that so many people have come to view the Word of God as "only" a book.

Yes, it's gratifying to know that printing presses all over the world have made the Bible available to so many... and in such a wealth of beautiful editions. But a book can be picked up and put down. It leads us to expect a beginning, a middle and an end. And when we reach the end, we've finished the book, we say.

But the Word of God is never finished. It has no end. It is renewed in every moment of our lives, guiding us as we go about our daily chores. There in the Bible we find songs to be sung, sorrows to be mourned, joys to be celebrated, letters to be answered, wisdom to be pondered. There are heroes to follow and love poems to whisper. Truly the very fabric of life itself is woven throughout its pages... lovingly carried down through the generations for us to weave into the fabric of our own lives.

Therefore as we close National Bible Week, let us open with reverence and awe that book we call the Bible... for it is not "only" a book at all. It is the living Voice of our Heavenly Father speaking to us today... sometimes loud and stern as He exhorts us to do bet-ter, sometimes a gentle whisper as He assures us of His eternal love.

As we *read* His Book today, let us remember...above all...to *live* His Word.

Dear Father, today and every day—I will make Your Word the heartbeat of my life. —PATRICIA HOUCK SPRINKLE

---

26 MONDAY
Come ye yourselves apart...and rest a while...
—MARK 6:31

"Hurry! Run!" I urge myself, out of breath from rushing. I board the plane just seconds before it takes off and collapse into my seat, my thoughts beset with *what ifs.*

What if my baggage wasn't put on the plane? *What if* the approaching snowstorm catches up with us and delays our arrival? *What if* it rained? I couldn't remember whether I had closed the basement window. A tooth began to throb —*what if* I had to find a dentist in an unfamiliar city and on a weekend?

Then the plane broke through the gray clouds and into clear, bright sunshine. Looking out the window, I saw that all was closed in below; I couldn't see a thing. But right outside lay the most beautiful serenity...a placid blue sky, wisps of cottony cloudlets off in the distance, a boundless horizon. I stopped worrying. For the first time in days I relaxed, let go, and felt the comforting arms of God around me. By the time we landed, I was refreshed. Even my tooth had stopped throbbing.

I think it helps to be reminded that no matter how many *what ifs* clutter up our life, there is that one special place—bright and clear—where we can be close to God and find refreshment.

And we don't need a trip in a plane to get there. All we need is a moment of quiet, a heartfelt stillness...and *prayer.*

In the busyness of my days, Father, I can take time out to be with you. Even now. —PHYLLIS HOBE

27 TUESDAY
Bless the Lord...who crowneth thee with
lovingkindness... —*PSALM 103:2,4*

I would rather come home to an empty refrigerator than to an empty mailbox. Nothing depresses me more than to turn the key in my box, open the door and realize that nobody's been thinking of me—not even the electric or telephone companies.

It was this way one evening recently when I was feeling particularly down. It was a Friday—the end of the week when I was facing an accumulation of weekend chores. And now I faced an empty mailbox too. Well, probably nothing could have raised me out of the doldrums that night anyway.

The next morning I left my apartment to begin my round of errands. The air was damp, thick gray clouds blanketed the sky, and my spirits hadn't changed much from the way they were the evening before.

Then I saw it! As I opened the car door, I saw a huge heart that had been drawn in the dust clinging to the windshield. It was a very matter-of-fact heart that went right to the point with the printed words "I Love You!"

It was a message just for me—probably left there by one of the children on my block—a message that lifted my heart right out of its gloom. And I made it a point to find a way to pass that message on throughout the day. Find a dusty soul today, one that needs to be shined by your message of love.

Thank You, Dear God, for reminding me countless times...and in countless ways...that I am loved.

—SAMANTHA McGARRITY

28 WEDNESDAY

I have fought a good fight, I have finished my course,
I have kept the faith... —II TIMOTHY 4:7

Last year I watched the New York marathon on television. When the starting gun cracked, thousands of thundering feet surged forward on the twenty-six-mile run ahead.

But long after the winners received their awards and the festivities were over, a cerebral-palsied girl was still inching along the course —agonizing mile after agonizing mile. Deep darkness had settled over the deserted streets by the time she finally crossed the finish line. There were no cheering throngs, no sirens, no blaring bands.

Only one lone television reporter and a few well-wishers recorded her exhausted comment, "I feel good that I finished."

I took heart in reading the story of this girl who would not give up. What struck me the most was her determination to complete the race no matter what. It was not winning, not the notoriety, not the applause of others that mattered. That she finished eight or ten hours after everyone else, that the park was dark, the grandstands empty, the winner's line erased was of no importance. What *was* important was that she had set herself a goal—and met it!

It is truly a lesson in faith and courage for all of us when we have a heavy task ahead of us. As we are told in II Timothy 1:7, "God hath not given us the spirit of fear; but of power, and of love..."

Yes, with God on our side, no handicap—physical or spiritual— can keep us from crossing the finish line!

Keep me pressing forward, Father, toward the goals You have set for me. —ISABEL CHAMP

29 THURSDAY

Behold, God exalteth by his power: who teacheth like him? —JOB 36:22

Because Albert Einstein once lived in Princeton, New Jersey—the place that I've called home for the last twenty years—there are many stories told about him by the natives of the town. One came to mind the other day as I drove past the small frame house that was his homestead.

One day Einstein was asked to give his telephone number. As it's told, he looked puzzled for a minute, then went over to the nearest phone book and looked it up. Forgetful? No, according to his associates, just another piece of evidence that he refused to clutter up his mind with inconsequential information.

I never cease to be amazed by some of the trivia that I remember—and by some of the really important information that I would like to retain but forget. Some of my friends tell me they are plagued with the same problem.

However, one thing for which I am eternally grateful is the Sunday-school teachers I had as a child who had me memorize key Bible verses. Although I didn't especially appreciate it at the time, today I am always thankful to them in times of trial and testing. It is then, for instance, that a verse from Psalms is particularly meaningful to me—the one that says, "Thy word have I hid in my heart, that I might not sin against thee" (Psalm 119:11). In the hectic lives that most of us lead today, it's like finding an oasis—these words of soothing strength and comfort.

Are there any young people you know to whom you might pass along this remarkable gift of Bible-verse memory? If so—and if you do—they will thank you for the rest of their lives!

Father, I thank you for those who teach us Your ways. Help me to share their loving wisdom with others. —FRED BAUER

30 FRIDAY
Greater is he that is in you, than he that is in the world.
—*I JOHN 4:4*

On my desk there are two clippings. One tells of a woman whom my husband knew in college. She's younger than I, but by now she's a famous opera singer, traveling around the world to bring pleasure to millions of people.

Wistfully I look toward my filing cabinet, where ideas for several books gather dust while I keep a house, answer the phone, take children to the playground and bandage skinned knees, help with homework and, occasionally, write something short. How trivial my accomplishments seem compared to those of the famous opera singer.

But then I look at the second clipping. It tells of how the mother of Dwight D. Eisenhower and six other sons was once asked, "Aren't you proud of your son?" She immediately replied, "Which one?"

The world measures "importance" in terms of accomplishment. But do we have to answer to the world for the importance of our accomplishments? No, we don't—because we have a higher Judge, our Heavenly Father, Who loves each one of us and values each of us. My concern as I go through life is not to be "important" in the sense of the world. It is to do those things my Father has set before me in such a way that He will be proud of me.

That's important!

Dear Father, I offer this day to You. I will strive to do all I can to make it one we can both be proud of. Amen.

—PATRICIA HOUCK SPRINKLE

Praise Diary for November

1

2

3

4

5

6

7

8

9

10

11

12

13

14

15

16

17

18

19

20

21

22

23

24

25

26

27

28

29

30

December

S	M	T	W	T	F	S
						1
2	3	4	5	6	7	8
9	10	11	12	13	14	15
16	17	18	19	20	21	22
23	24	25	26	27	28	29
30	31					

It is our little boy who finds me
On this gray December afternoon
Stealing a delicious nap on
The old swaybacked couch.
Wordlessly he grasps my hand
In both of his and tugs,
Then shrieks with joy
At my opened eye.
His warm touch pulses mine
So urgently that it takes me back
To the touch of my father's hand
Showing me how
To throw a ball and bait a hook and…
Oh God, thank You for the magic
Of touch, of human hands that link
Our generations back
And forward
In a bond of human warmth
Unending.
Touch has a confidence
Words can never know—
Yours is a world without end,
Forever,
Amen.   *James McDermott*

CELEBRATING ADVENT:
Prepare Ye The Way

At this time of the year in anticipation of the Christmas season, we will again welcome the Christ Child into our hearts and our homes. Marilyn Morgan Helleberg invites you to join her on the Saturday before the first Sunday of Advent—and follow the steps through each of the four Sundays of Advent, Christmas Eve and Christmas Day—as she lights the candles that herald the coming of our Lord.

Marilyn has chosen as guide the famed prophet from the banks of the River Jordan—he who urged the peoples of Judea to "Prepare ye the way of the Lord"—John the Baptist. He will reveal to us the things we are called upon to do to ready ourselves to receive the Christ Child.

As you light your Advent candles, we at Guideposts *wish you a most joyous and blessed Christmas!* —THE EDITORS

1

SATURDAY BEFORE THE FIRST SUNDAY IN ADVENT
PREPARE YE THE WAY

The people that walked in darkness have seen a great light... —ISAIAH 9:2

I lie awake, gazing out the bedroom window into blackness, the words I've just read echoing against the night. "The people that walked in darkness have seen a great light...seen a great light ...seen a great light." I close my eyes, and for a softly folded moment glimpse a trail of starlight, fine as a silken thread, spanning all the buried years of Israel's hope.

Then suddenly I feel the link! The light that Isaiah glimpsed is the same Light that summoned shepherds to a stable in Bethlehem centuries later...and the Light that now summons me out of my own darkness as I reach, once again, toward celebration of that Bethlehem birth.

Will the light of Christ's Presence grow brighter for me as the weeks unfold? Tomorrow is the beginning of Advent. Every year I promise myself that I'll really take time, during this special season, to prepare my heart to fully receive the Christ Child. But somehow the shopping, baking, decorating, and other holiday activities always seem to intervene, and Christmas often finds me tense, preoccupied, and only partially focused on my Saviour's coming.

This year I want to break out of that old pattern. Would you like to do the same? Then join with me in making a commitment to "Prepare ye the way of the Lord." Just knowing that thousands of us will be sharing in this spiritual adventure can surely help us to refresh our faith.

We'll use the Advent Wreath as a tangible reminder of our goal. This cherished custom of the wreath originated several centuries ago among Lutherans in Germany and quickly spread to all the churches. The wreath's circular shape symbolizes eternity and provides a link between the birth of Jesus 2,000 years ago, His rebirth in our hearts this Holy Season and His coming again.

The evergreens around the wreath stand for life and growth, and its four candles represent the hearts of the children of God, glowing with desire for the coming of the Messiah. The large white candle in the center of the wreath is the Christ candle, which we will light on Christmas Day.

Come. Together let us make this Advent season more than just a lovely tradition. Let's make it a true spiritual pilgrimage. Our guide will be "the voice of one crying in the wilderness," John the Baptist.

Heavenly Father, kindle in us today a glow of holy anticipation as we prepare for Your Son's arrival.

—MARILYN MORGAN HELLEBERG

2

FIRST SUNDAY IN ADVENT

PREPARE YE THE WAY

Prepare ye the way of the Lord, make his paths straight. —MATTHEW 3:3

As we gather to light the first candle on our Advent Wreath, we enter into another time. Turning, we see a swarthy, bearded man in camel's hair clothing step into our living room. As he speaks, we realize that he is John the Baptist, come to counsel us.

"I am the fulfillment of Isaiah's prophecy that God would send a messenger to prepare the way of the Lord. But did you know that *you* are also the fulfillment of Isaiah's prophecy? Even at this very moment God is calling to you to prepare the way for the coming of His Son. If you accept that commission, you will have to begin where I did—in the wilderness.

"Oh, don't worry. You won't be asked to wander about in the Judean Desert as I did. Your wilderness is life itself, overgrown as it may be with your work, your family commitments, meetings, social activities, and, yes—even the press of holiday plans. To make straight His path, you will have to clear a space in your wilderness... and you can do this by spending time alone with God *every day*. You say that this is a busy time of the year, but think of it in these terms:

"What if you knew that in less than four weeks Jesus would step into the world again... right here into the midst of your own town? Wouldn't you want to find some time in which to be with God while you awaited the coming of His Son? Which activities would you forego or postpone in order to make this time? Think carefully. Then start pruning. Resolve now to schedule at least one half-hour of alone-with-God time every day until Christmas. Use that time to speak to Him, to sing to Him, to read His Word, to listen for His voice... or to just sit quietly with Him, sharing the silence in love."

With that, our visitor picks up his sturdy walking stick and goes back into the night.

Loving Father, as I light this first candle on the Advent Wreath,

I promise to make a straight path in my heart for Your Son—by spending time alone with You every day.

—MARILYN MORGAN HELLEBERG

GUIDEPEOPLE: A Living Parable for December

3 MONDAY

Whatsoever ye shall ask in prayer, believing, ye shall receive. —MATTHEW 21:22

I believe in prayer.

That forthright statement was the title of the first story ever to appear in *Guideposts*. In fact, that was the *only* article in the little publication that went out to a handful of readers in March, 1945.

And its writer? Captain Eddie Rickenbacker, a flying hero of World War I and later a distinguished businessman, Chairman of the Board of Eastern Airlines.

Eddie Rickenbacker had a lifetime of reasons for believing in the power of prayer, but none was more dramatic than the one that presented itself in the forlorn wastes of the South Pacific during World War II. Rickenbacker was on an Army mission when his plane crashed. He and seven other men scrambled aboard a life raft, and there huddled day after searing day, night after shivering night. What rations they had, gave out, and by the seventh day it was obvious that without food and water they would all soon die.

Now, Rickenbacker alway carried a pocket Bible, and he took it out and read aloud from Matthew 6:

Therefore, take no thought, saying, What shall we eat? or, What shall we drink? or Wherewithal shall we be clothed?...for your heavenly Father knoweth that ye have need of all these things....

Then Rickenbacker led the men in prayer—a prayer in which they placed their trust in God and in His life-sustaining Word. No more than an hour later a lone seagull flew out of the vast reaches of nowhere, circled overhead curiously, then came down for a landing on the life raft. The men grabbed it. *Food.*

351

The next day the wind rose, the ocean swelled, and the clouds opened up and drenched the men in the raft with rain. *Water.*

On the twenty-first day, the men were rescued.

So that was the first *Guideposts* article, and to this day it remains the typical one. For the Truth hasn't changed. Men and women continue discovering how man's extremity becomes God's opportunity. These are people who have reason to say, as Eddie Rickenbacker:

I believe in prayer.

For all my days, make prayer my lifeline too, Lord.

—VAN VARNER

---

4 TUESDAY
They helped every one his neighbour... —ISAIAH 41:6

It was the day of the East's big blizzard of '83. Three cars that were parked in front of our house were totally obliterated even before the city's municipal plows came along and tossed high banks of snow over them.

Across the street my new neighbor had a similar situation— three buried cars and a drift-laden driveway. As my grown son, a visiting friend and I assessed the situation, my neighbor and his son appeared.

After some deliberation we decided to pool our forces, consisting of five bodies to man four shovels and a broom. We tackled the huge piles of snow...huffing and puffing, muscles straining and backs aching...all the while surreptitiously observing another neighbor operating a fancy snowblower, work silently, finish in half the time and then hurry inside. We just looked at each other—envy on our faces—and doggedly kept going.

By that time our wives had stepped into the act, showing up with pots of steaming coffee, hot chocolate and platters of warm doughnuts. In three hours we cleared seven cars, two driveways, two walks and consumed three pots of coffee and hot chocolate and countless doughnuts. And we had thoroughly relished the camaraderie with our new neighbors...so much so that we agreed to get together later for a wok dinner to mark the occasion.

The hidden blessings of shared adversity wrought a spirit of friendship and cooperation that blossomed with every shovelful. And I wonder—will our neighbor with the snowplow ever know what he missed? If he does, he's welcome to join us next time.

Thank You, Father, for the warm spirit of neighborliness that unfolds in times of adversity. —SAM JUSTICE

---

5 WEDNESDAY
And that from a child thou hast known the holy scriptures... —II TIMOTHY 3:15

I have a friend named Hillary who is eleven years old, bright and incredibly sensitive. Last year she gave me a lesson in love that I will never forget.

I was visiting at Hillary's house one Sunday afternoon in December, helping her family make Christmas decorations. Sitting there in the warm circle of friends, I suddenly felt overcome by some pressing worries and Hillary's mother noticed the sadness on my face.

"Are you okay, Sam?" she asked kindly, and with that, my tears came flooding through.

Everyone murmured sympathetic words but it seemed that nothing would stem the flow. Hillary suddenly disappeared and quickly returned, holding a tiny package of wrapped-up tissue paper. "This is for you," she said gently, handing me the little bundle. I opened it to find nestled there a tiny rhinestone pin, shaped like a delicate flower.

"I found this at a yard sale," Hillary whispered in my ear. "It's your Christmas gift but I'm giving it to you a little early this year." Then she put her arms around me and gave me a big hug.

Hillary's special caring renewed my spirits that day and taught me

353

how important it is that we reach out openly to others in love. And because of its lesson, I consider that little rhinestone pin to be the most valuable treasure in my jewelry box.

Dear Heavenly Father, never let us lose the ability to love one another openly, with innocence and trust.

—SAMANTHA McGARRITY

---

6 THURSDAY

What doth it profit, my brethren, though a man say he hath faith, and have not works? —JAMES 2:14

Christmas shopping was proving to be exhausting. I had only one more gift to buy—but it was the most difficult of all to find. A very special boy, a friend's son confined to a wheelchair by multiple sclerosis, wanted a cowboy hat. The only way Kevin would ever ride a horse would be in his imagination, and the hat would help him do it.

I had gone to many stores but hadn't found just the right hat. My last resort was a shop that specialized in Western clothing. When I entered, I saw hundreds of hats—every one of them handsome— displayed on the walls from floor to ceiling. But I became discouraged when some of the price tickets revealed that they cost more than I could afford.

Then a young saleswoman approached me. "I'm new here," she said. "I don't know the stock well, but let's see if we can find what you're looking for."

Dragging a ladder from the back room, she searched up and down the walls, carefully examining each hat for size and price. I was about ready to give up but she wouldn't hear of it. "It never hurts to try," she said. Finally she called to me excitedly and held out a dandy hat, a young cowboy's dream. And the price was exactly right!

Going home, carrying my gift in a great big box tied with a dashing red ribbon, I wasn't tired any more. I was singing with joy and energy. Kevin was going to be a cowboy! Because someone had believed that "it never hurts to try."

Trying and hoping, Father. Together they make faith, don't they?
—PHYLLIS HOBE

7
The Lord is my shepherd...   —PSALM 23:1

The other day I found on an old program on which I'd scribbled some good lines I wanted to remember...
· Only fools never doubt.
· When you lock the world out, you lock yourself in.
· Violence is not strength; compassion is not weakness.
Do you recognize the words? King Arthur said all of that in "Camelot," the bittersweet musical about a land of unparalleled goodness. But there was another phrase on the program: "Even in Camelot you can't protect yourself from pain." That wasn't Arthur's line. It was mine.

And I know why I wrote it. When Lynn and I saw the musical, there was much uncertainty in our lives, especially about jobs and school and the future. No matter how much I wanted to straighten it out, I couldn't seem to find the answers.

Pain, tough times, uncertainties—I know now that they are always a part of life. While the land of Camelot may be a fancy, our here-and-now lives rest upon a wonderful bedrock of reality that can never be paralleled—not even in Camelot. It was given to us with His words: "Call unto me, and I will answer thee.." (Jeremiah 33:3). It is God's eternal promise of reassurance.

How far I have come since my Camelot days—to learn the blessed truth that the real land of goodness lies in our own humble faith!

Because You are my shepherd, Father, I will not fear.
—JEFF JAPINGA

8

SATURDAY

Arise, shine; for thy light is come, and the glory of the Lord is risen upon thee.　　　　　　　　　—ISAIAH 60:1

One of the Christmas objects that has long occupied our family's fireplace mantle every December is a small, candle-propelled windmill. It has three platforms and on each platform stand hand-carved characters from the story of the Nativity. On one level there is a crêche, with Mary, Joseph and the infant Jesus. On another level you can see tiny shepherds as they tend their sheep. And on the last level, Wise Men come bearing gifts. At the very top a brilliant star gleams over all.

The scene is stationary until one lights the candles that heat the air beneath the windmill blades. As the temperature rises, the little figures begin to move, changing the inanimate scene into a lovely, living tableau.

Each year, as I regard the windmill and then light the candles, I am once again imbued with the Holy Spirit of Christmas. The shepherds, the Wise Men, the little family with the baby Jesus— what a miracle of love it all expresses! And as the characters slowly begin to turn in response to the warmth of the candlelight, I see a parallel in our turning to Jesus as He brought light into a world that lay in darkness.

And I reflect, watching the little figures move about, that we must first light the candle in our hearts to bring the awesome wonder of Christmas to life.

In this holiest of seasons, O Lord, return us to the hallowed origins of our celebration.　　　　　　　　　—FRED BAUER

9

SECOND SUNDAY IN ADVENT
PREPARE YE THE WAY

Repent ye: for the kingdom of heaven is at hand.

—MATTHEW 3:2

In relighting the first candle on our Advent Wreath, we renew our commitment to spend time alone with the Lord every day. Now John the Baptist joins us again and his penetrating eyes grasp our attention.

"Repent, for the kingdom of heaven is at hand.

"I know these are not comfortable words, but *Jesus is coming!* Think of it! In just two weeks and a day the Christ Child will be born. I pray that He will also be born in your heart...but this will not happen unless you have prepared a worthy place for Him.

"Examine your soul. Confess your sins to God.

"Ask your Heavenly Father to wash away your guilt, cleanse your thoughts and purify your motives. Then perform some tangible act as evidence of your repentance. In the River Jordan I baptized those who repented. You may want to take a cleansing bath as an outward symbol of inward purification...or reaffirm your Baptismal vows... or write out your intentions to turn away from your sinfulness... or find some person whom you've wronged and make things right with him.

"Purify your heart. Ready it to receive God's most precious gift. The time is drawing near!"

With these words our visitor leaves...and we are alone with our thoughts.

As I light the second candle on my wreath, Father, I promise to purify my heart this week. I will perform at least one tangible act as evidence of my repentance. —MARILYN MORGAN HELLEBERG

10 MONDAY

Rejoice with them that do rejoice, and weep with them that weep. —ROMANS 12:15

The small girl was very late in coming home from school. When she finally arrived, her worried mother asked her where she had been.

"I was at Mary's house," she replied. "Her favorite doll got broken."

"But what could *you* do about it?" her mother questioned.

The child raised a tear-stained face. "I helped her cry," she said.

How often have I failed to go to someone who has experienced a sorrow, a loss or a big disappointment? I failed not through uncaring or lack of concern but simply because I thought I didn't know what I could do or say. Our world is so full of quick advice, so dedicated to action for the sake of action, that sometimes our words of consolation seem trivial. Yet when Scripture tells us how to respond to others in their times of trouble, it gives us precisely the wisdom of that small girl: *Weep with those who weep. Help them to cry.*

After all, isn't that not the least, but the *most* we can do?

Dear Jesus, so tune my heart to the hearts of others that I can genuinely share their joys. . . and their sorrows.

—PATRICIA HOUCK SPRINKLE

11 TUESDAY

Yea; have ye never read, Out of the mouths of babes . . . thou hast perfected praise? —MATTHEW 21:16

My wife and I were preparing for Christmas. The tree was bought but we were still buying and wrapping presents, sending out late card responses, going over guest lists and invitations. . . .

On one especially hectic evening we were down on our knees decorating the tree when the pressure mounted—and peaked. I wound up saying to Ginny, "If you know so much about decorating, finish it yourself!" I stuffed an ornament back into the box.

Then Danielle, our two-year-old granddaughter who was spending the holidays with us, sidled over to my wife, put her arms around her neck and said softly, "I love you, Grandma." Then she came over to me. "Grandpa, you love Grandma too, don't you?" she asked, her great brown eyes saucer-wide.

By then my eyes were brimming and I pulled her to me and engulfed her in a heart-grateful embrace. I took the tree ornament back out of the box and handed it to Ginny. "Yes, of course I love Grandma too," I replied, my voice not quite even.

We finished the tree trimming that night—and the entire Christmas season—with hearts overflowing in joy and love.

Thank You, Lord, for little children who come unto us with Your simple truths. —SAM JUSTICE

---

12 WEDNESDAY
They that wait upon the Lord shall renew their strength... —ISAIAH 40:31

I was increasingly annoyed with Uncle Charlie's new nurse in the hospital. She was bossy—always telling him to sit up straight, to walk more than he did, to move around. Obviously Uncle Charlie didn't feel up to it. He was arthritic and motion caused him pain. Didn't Mrs. Brigham realize that?

"Come now," she would say, "the good Lord didn't give you legs for nothing. Use them!"

One afternoon I found Uncle Charlie walking down the corridor all by himself. Although he was smiling bravely, I knew that he must be exhausted.

"Here, let me help you," I said, starting to put my shoulder under his.

"Don't you dare!" Uncle Charlie protested. "If you keep putting me back in bed, you'll make an invalid of me!"

I bit my lip and held back my tears. *Of course, of course,* I thought. Uncle Charlie was right. So was Mrs. Brigham. I was wrong. I wanted Uncle Charlie to *save* his strength...and Mrs. Brigham wanted him to *use* it. Three days later—with the aid of a cane—he went home on his own two feet. What's more, he has been doing very well ever since. It seems that the more he uses the strength God gave him, the more strength he has.

Is there some God-given strength you need to draw upon today? Whatever your situation, it is there, in abundance, just waiting for you.

Should I droop and tarry, Father, challenge me!

—PHYLLIS HOBE

---

13 THURSDAY

Inasmuch as ye did it not to one of the least of these, ye did it not to me. —MATTHEW 25:45

A cold wind ripped across the prairie that mid-December evening as the driver of a rusting pickup traveled west on Interstate 70 in Illinois. He struggled to keep going. With his three motherless children, none older than seven, he had driven all night, trying to reach grandma's house in Oklahoma. But now he realized that his diabetic condition was overcoming him, and pulling to the shoulder of the road, he collapsed.

A state trooper shortly discovered the vehicle and rushed the father to the hospital. Then the trooper and his wife Mary Ellen volunteered to care for the children, even though they had twelve of their own at home.

"What a time we had!" Mary Ellen told me later. "We fed them, bathed them and loved them. We included them in all of our Christmas activities. The little girl helped bake cookies and the boys played with our boys. By phone they received daily assurance from their daddy that he loved them. But the smallest lad was too young to understand, and each evening he'd wait at the door, sobbing, for his daddy to come for him. Wil would rock him and croon to him until they both fell asleep.

"They finally reached their grandma's home on Christmas Eve. But our family will never forget how Jesus came to our house, not as a plastic baby in the creche but as three real, live children who needed a home and comfort."

I've wondered...would I have taken the children in? Or would I have said it wasn't my problem and kept my manger spotless and orderly? What would you have done?

Lord, may I serve You in the needs of others—at Christmas and all year 'round.   —ZONA B. DAVIS

---

14 FRIDAY
God is love...   *--I JOHN 4:16*

Recently I read a news article about a series of tornadoes and floods in California where not only had many homes been splintered and washed away, but lives had been lost as well. Photographs accompanying the story illustrated the havoc these storms had brought to the lives of hundreds.

One picture showed a Los Angeles street strewn with litter and debris, and in the background stood a storm-damaged building with a large sign proclaiming: "Jesus Loves You." Everything else around the sign seemed to have given way to the storm—but the sign stood firm.

Could anyone really believe those words while watching his home float away? I wondered. Then I recalled stormy situations in my own life, when I'd watched whole portions of my life being swept away, when disappointments had almost overwhelmed me. At those times the love of Jesus was the only thing holding me fast, keeping me from being washed away into total despair.

As Christians, our lives are in His care...every day. No matter what raging elements we may have to face in life or how grave the loss or damage, our most valuable possession—the only one that will forever withstand life's ravages and vicissitudes—is our life in Christ. And that we can never lose.

Dear God, thank You for Your love that stands firm through the floods and storms of living. —SAMANTHA McGARRITY

JESUS, THE MASTER STORYTELLER
Parable of the House Built on a Rock —MATTHEW 7:24-27

---

15 SATURDAY

At the very end of the Sermon on the Mount, as recorded by Matthew, Jesus draws an important distinction between people who *talk* about doing God's will and people who *do* it. "By their fruits ye shall know them," He says. Or in the words of a city streetworker friend of mine, "Christians must walk their talk."

In fact, Jesus informs his listeners, posturers, posers, pretenders, that Pharisees don't qualify. Then to help his audience remember He gives them a new parable:

"There once was a wise man who built his house on a rock," Jesus began, "and when the rains fell and the floods came and the wind blew, the house didn't give way because it had a solid foundation.

"But there was another man, a foolish fellow who built his house on sand, and when it was hit by rains and floods and wind, it could not withstand them…and great was the fall of it."

Of course, Jesus wasn't talking about houses or foundations or storms. Rather he was cautioning all of us that God isn't fooled by appearances. The litmus test at the end of our lives will be whether or not we walked our talk. The Truth will be written on our hearts.

Keep me building my life on Your truth, Lord—steadfast and eternal. —FRED BAUER

16

THIRD SUNDAY IN ADVENT
PREPARE YE THE WAY

He that hath two coats, let him impart to him that hath none; and he that hath meat, let him do likewise.

—LUKE 3:11

Today we re-light the first two candles of our Advent Wreath and renew the promises we have made to pray daily and to repent sincerely. Now John, our guide from the River Jordan, appears in our midst.

"When people came to me to be baptized, I told them about the One, mightier than I, Who was coming soon. They asked me what they should do in preparation. My answer to them is for you too:

"If you have two coats, give one to someone who has none. If you have even a little food, share it with those who are hungry. In just a week our Lord Christ will be born again.

"Look through your home and your possessions. What can you share? What will you share? You could pick out things you hold in little value. But if you *really* want to prepare for Him, share those things which are of special meaning and importance to you.

"Be sure to include the children in this giving and sharing. Help them choose their own special gifts to share with another child. Then you must decide where to take the things you have collected to give away. Which favorite charity shall you choose? If you personally know a family in need, your giving will mean more to you if you give anonymously. Just think of the joy of going to place your bundle on a doorstep in the dark of the night."

This will be a busy week, Lord, but above all else I must prepare a place in my heart for the Christ Child's birth. As I light the third candle of my wreath, I vow that I will not let this week pass without the sharing of a portion of my possessions with those less fortunate. —MARILYN MORGAN HELLEBERG

17 MONDAY

I bow my knees unto the Father of our Lord Jesus Christ, of whom the whole family in heaven and earth is named... —EPHESIANS 3:14,15

I grew up in the forties, an only child—just my mother and myself. My father died when I was two years old. I never knew him, but I missed not having a daddy. Often I felt different—after all, we weren't a *real* family, not like other families.

Then just before Christmas one year I was going through the stream of Christmas cards that had started arriving—most of them addressed to my mother "and Marion" or "and daughter." But I came across one card that was addressed to "Mrs. Jewette Bond and Family."

Family! I said the word over and over, out loud. I don't think I ever read the card—I just stared at the envelope. We were a family after all—a *real* family, even though there were only the two of us! The word "family" never bothered me after that.

Later, when I was born into the family of God, I came to love the word all over again. I became a part of that special family that's made up of believers in Jesus. We are members of the *family of God.*

If you believe in the Lord Jesus Christ, you too are a part of the same marvelous family...and I love you even though we may never meet, for we're truly kinfolk in the best way of all!

Thank You, Father, for the beautiful "family" of believers!

—MARION BOND WEST

18 TUESDAY

Fear thou not, for I am with thee: be not dismayed; for I am thy God: I will strengthen thee: yea, I will help thee... —ISAIAH 41:10

There's an old fable about two little boys, one of them a hunchback, who were best friends. "I know what you've got in that

364

box on your back," said one to the other. "It's a pair of wings!"

When I first heard the story, I thought, *What a delightful expression of love!* But the more I dwelt on it, the deeper the meaning seemed to become and I began to wonder, *Do we all carry wings in our burdens?*

John Bunyan was held in prison for thirteen years, but while there, he wrote *Pilgrim's Progress.* Milton wrote the great epic, *Paradise Lost,* after losing his sight. Beethoven wrote some of his most magnificent works after becoming totally deaf.

Yes, it's true. Burdens *do* have wings, hidden reservoirs of power that can raise us to greater heights of love, understanding and strength if we will only unfold them—and lift off to God!

Father, whatever my circumstances, I will fly straight to You.
—ZONA B. DAVIS

---

19 WEDNESDAY
I the Lord search the heart, I try the reins, even to give every man according to his ways... —JEREMIAH 17:10

My favorite Hanukkah story appeared in *Guideposts* many years ago. It's the story of a traveler who was driving across the western plains on a December night in the midst of a blizzard. His car broke down and, having no idea of where he was, he got out and began to walk. Soon he was utterly lost. Between the freezing cold, the biting wind and the mounting snowdrifts, the man quickly became exhausted, fearing he would die alone out there in the storm. He prayed to Jesus for the strength to keep going.

Suddenly, far off in the distance, he glimpsed a faint light. As he approached, he saw that it came from a window in a small house. With his last ounce of strength, he knocked on the door and was taken in, his life saved.

It so happened that his hosts were Jews, and the light in the window was from their Hanukkah candles. In Hebrew, "hanukkah" means dedication, and the Feast of Hanukkah is held each year in re-dedication of the temple in Jerusalem after invaders from the north were driven out. For seven consecutive nights an additional candle is lit in the Menorah, and the Feast of Hanukkah is a joyful one.

Yes, each of us holds something of a saving light for all others ...every day of the year.

Father, enlighten us with loving understanding so that our prayers draw together and reach up to You as one voice.

—GLENN KITTLER

---

20 THURSDAY
In quietness and in confidence shall be your strength...
—ISAIAH 30:15

One year as the Christmas season neared, a new approach to gift-giving dawned upon our family.

My son-in-law has a talent for putting together those unassembled kits we order each year. Unhappily his temperament does not always match his talent, and howls of frustration and anger were somewhat dimming the Yule spirit.

Then our daughter read of a man who had ordered a motorcycle from Japan. On the instruction sheet were the words: "Before assembling, obtain peace of mind." Relying on her husband's sense of humor, she had large labels printed bearing this message and then pasted them on the packages scheduled for his workshop. With the first there was a roar of wrath—and then sudden laughter.

"Okay," he said sheepishly. "So I'll say a prayer before I begin." And he did—and it worked wonders!

Later, when his wife was in a frenzy of preparation for her Cub Scouts, he told her with a twinkle in his eye, "Before Scouts assemble, obtain peace of mind"—and together they said a short prayer. It worked! And later yet, my granddaughter hand-lettered a label for my typewriter: "Before assembling words...." Of course I had to obey, and of course it worked!

Today we find it as much a part of our lives to say a prayer before beginning a project as to say grace before beginning a meal.

Prepare me, Father... with peace of mind... for the work before me.
—ELAINE ST. JOHNS

---

21 FRIDAY
Withhold not good from them to whom it is due, when it is in the power of thine hand to do it. —PROVERBS 4:27

One Christmas morning my clock radio awoke me to the strains of a lovely carol. Then as the music faded, the announcer's voice came through.

"Many children will awaken this morning," he said, "to the joy of new toys. But some of the children are going to be disappointed because you parents failed to notice three little words—'Batteries not included'. If that's the case at your house this morning, bring the toys here to the radio station and we'll outfit them with whatever batteries are needed. We've stocked up with all kinds and sizes of batteries and they are yours... free of charge. Let's not allow any child to be unhappy today."

Why, I thought, *how wonderful!* As I prepared for the joyous day ahead, my thoughts dwelled on that announcer, there at work at the radio station even on Christmas morning. Instead of complaining, he was using his job to bring happiness into the life of others.

That's a good lesson for *any* day and *any* job, don't you agree?

Whatever work you give me to do today, Father, help me to find and share the good in it. —DRUE DUKE

22 SATURDAY

But when thou doest alms, let not thy left hand know what thy right hand doeth... —MATTHEW 6:3

"Mama, was there really a Saint Nick?" my young son asked on Christmas.

"Sure there was," I answered, and together we read the enchanting story about this kind-hearted Christian bishop who was born into aristocracy in the third century....

One night when Nicholas was still a youth, he stole into the house of a poor family. The father had three daughters without dowries or hope of marriage and was distraught over how to continue supporting them. Nicholas, thinking himself unnoticed, deposited a mysterious bag on the table; but the father caught sight of him and gave chase.

As he cornered Nicholas, one the of the daughters raced up with the bag, which was filled with gold coins. "What is this about?" demanded the father. Nicholas stammered that he was simply using his inheritance to help the poor, as Jesus asked. But the man was perplexed. "Then why did you sneak in at night?"

"I came secretly because Jesus commanded that when you give to the poor, you should not let your right hand know what your left hand does." Then Nicholas made the man promise that he would not let anyone know where the dowries came from.

And that was the end of the story for my little son and me. Except...on Christmas morning a little white envelope lay under the tree. The inscription read: "To Mama. From a secret person." Inside was a dollar bill—no doubt the "secret person's" allowance. And I could tell by Bob's face that it was moment of unique joy for him...just as it must have been for young Nicholas so long ago.

In fact, it made me wonder if maybe this Christmas you and I shouldn't become "secret persons" too.

Father, today help me give a gift with my right hand that my left hand knows nothing about. —SUE MONK KIDD

23

FOURTH SUNDAY IN ADVENT
PREPARE YE THE WAY

And he shall turn the heart of the fathers to the children, and the heart of the children to their fathers...
—MALACHI 4:6

There's a breathless anticipation in the air as we light the first three candles of our Advent Wreath, renewing our commitment to daily prayer, repentance and sharing. As the candles flare, our guide from the Judean wilderness appears before us.

"I have come to you this night with a very special mission," he tells us. "I stand here before you and ask you to search your hearts.

"Are there any unspoken resentments, any threads of bitterness, any remnants of unforgiveness between you and another member of your family?

"Pause now. Think about your relationship with each of your kin. Ask yourself if there are any invisible walls that might stand in the way of loving closeness.

...TWO-MINUTE PAUSE...

"If I am to fulfill my mission, you must make a sincere effort to heal any and all wounded relationships in your family. Take specific action. Ask forgiveness—or give it. Hug someone whom you haven't hugged for a long time. Do something nice for a family member whom you feel has wronged you. There is probably a member of your family who is aching, right now, to hear you say, 'I love you.' Who is that person? Go ahead. Express your love.

"Turn your hearts to one another in love and you will truly be 'a people prepared for the Lord.'"

The candle glow swells... our visitor vanishes.

God of love, as I light this fourth candle on the Advent Wreath, I promise to express my love in some specific way... this very night ... to every member of my family.

—MARILYN MORGAN HELLEBERG

369

24 CHRISTMAS EVE
PREPARE YE THE WAY

This is my beloved Son... —MATTHEW 3:17

A sacred silence falls over the room as we relight the four Advent candles. We stand, at this moment, poised on the rim of unspeakable mystery. He who has led us to this moment enters our living room. His words rise up like frail white wings of prayer.

"Outside these walls, the unforgetting winds whisper of another time, of music sifting down, of choiring seraphim. A moment caught from all the flow of ages, an angel light, the pulse of sudden joy...'for unto you is born this day in the city of David a Saviour, which is Christ the Lord'.

"Listen to the Voice I heard as I stood in the River Jordan:
'THIS IS MY BELOVED SON...'"

Our Father's holy words arch across the shores of time...

one thousand...

nine hundred...

eighty-four...

and John the Baptist speaks again to us.

"In the stillness of this starlit night, by the grace of our loving God, the Prince of Peace now enters a wounded world. He comes as an infant—gentle, trusting, risking all for you, for me, for this fragile earth, our finite home. He seeks a roof and warmth and some small certainty of peace.

"Take Him in. He seeks His own. There is no place more holy than a gladly offered heart. There is no purer blessing than Christ alive within that heart. He comes to you this night...and for the rest of your life...that you may hereafter mirror His presence in the world.

"Will you allow Him to be reborn in your life now?"

Father, we have earnestly tried to prepare the way, to make a Holy Place within. With swift new gladness rising, we now invite the baby in. As we light the center candle, we join our hearts and pray, "Welcome, gentle Child. Be born in us this day."

—MARILYN MORGAN HELLEBERG

370

25
CHRISTMAS DAY
PREPARE YE THE WAY

He must increase, but I must decrease. — *JOHN 3:30*

This is the hour! It is now! Across the skies, beyond the golden hills, our world is waking to the gift of the Christ Child's grace. The touch, the sound, the flow of His Presence are all about us.

Joy brims and flows over, spilling from the flood of His grace. Five candles glow upon our Advent Wreath as John the Baptist speaks his final words to us.

"Now is the moment the prophets of old awaited. In a thousand dreams I have lived this day and learned the feel of it. This is the hour that holds the shape and plan of Him, Who, dying, lives for you and me. A new Voice will be heard in the temples of Israel. A new Voice will whisper within the chapel of your heart. From this time hence, He must increase, but I must decrease. The Glory Light is His, and I would seek only reflected glow.

"Today are there some who ask your help? Are there those who look to you? Raise His lantern over them; pass His candle quietly; point their eyes away from yourself, to Him; robe yourself in soft humility, and you will count among your gifts this day...

> A spaceless grace, His soundless hymn,
> the dearness of this infant King,
> the form and face and touch of Him;
> this soaring Light that's rising up
> to sing away the misted dark,
> yielding up a richer gift
> than human heart has ever known."

Gentle Child, loving Lord, Your Light already moves among the hills. Your splendor rises on the land. May every human heart reflect Your Glory Light and every nation under God repeat the angel's song: 'Glory to God in the highest, and on earth peace, good will among men.' —MARILYN MORGAN HELLEBERG

26 WEDNESDAY

Surely goodness and mercy shall follow me all the
days of my life… —PSALM 23:6

Christmas is finally past. We've been to church, had our dinner and unwrapped our gifts. As I sit here gazing into the fire now, I remember the manner in which we opened our presents. The baby was frightened by the crinkly paper. How he cried and backed away when we tried to hand him his presents! Our older son clutched his new tin soldiers and retreated into a corner to enjoy them in solitary bliss.

And we adults. We were somewhat ambivalent. Did we really like our gifts? Could we use them? Sometimes I found myself casting a glance at someone else's gift, rather wishing I had been given that one instead of mine. Yet I know that all I received had been carefully chosen just for me, with much love and forethought.

Now I contemplate the biggest gift of all—the year ahead. One by one our Heavenly Parent will drop the gift of days into our lives. How graciously will I receive mine? With what expressions of gratitude? Some days will be dark and somber, others bright and sunny—but either way, I will feel no ambivalence, only an eager openness to His gift of loving kindness, day by day.

Thank You, Father, for all 365 gifts!

—PATRICIA HOUCK SPRINKLE

27 THURSDAY

As the door turneth upon his hinges, so doth the
slothful upon his bed. —PROVERBS 26:14

The other day some of us were trying to remember the Seven Deadly Sins, that catalogue of transgressions handed down to us from the Middle Ages. Since none of us could remember all of them, we looked them up, and here they are: Pride, Covetousness, Lust, Envy, Gluttony, Anger and Sloth.

I found myself thinking about that last one. I had always believed that sloth was laziness, or plain physical inertia. If I avoided exertion, dodged exercise, wriggled my way out of hard work, I was a slothful person.

But good grief, if the great medieval poet Dante included it in the *deadly* category, sloth must be a whole lot more than that! I searched further and found that Dorothy Sayers once wrote: "It is the sin which believes in nothing, cares for nothing, enjoys nothing, loves nothing, hates nothing, finds purpose in nothing, and only remains alive because there is nothing it would die for."

And now I know—it's *indifference* that is the slothful sin. I am going to try to be more alert to it from now on. To avoid sloth means to stay alive in spirit, sensitive to others, committed to our Christian values and living by His Word. That means that we *care*—the exact opposite of indifference!

Sloth—truly a deadly sin, especially when we practice it among those whom we love and those who need us.

Father, I care.   —ARTHUR GORDON

---

28 FRIDAY
For what is a man advantaged, if he gain the whole world, and lose himself...   —LUKE 9:25

The news report said that he was one of the richest men in the United States. He was worth hundreds of millions of dollars. But as the shadows of his life lengthened, he said that it was not the size of his fortune that occupied his mind, but his legacy.

"In the evenings I often go up into the mountains and look out across the valley and ponder this question: *How will I be remembered? Will it be only for having been rich, for having been acquisitive, for having been financially successful?*"

I began to ask myself the same question: *How will I be remembered?* Certainly not as one of the richest men in the United States. But would my family and friends remember me as one who put too much emphasis on material things and the acquisition of them? If so, I will have little to leave behind.

But if the center of my life is focused on other people, on serving, giving, helping, loving, caring, and sharing, then my gifts to those who follow will truly be a living legacy. I can leave a powerful testimony to my love of Christ, to the value of the timeless over the transient, to the lasting over the passing and to the wheat over the chaff.

Today why not take time to look back over your life as you have spent it so far? How do you think you will be remembered?

Lord, give me the wisdom to discern between life's jewels and life's jetsam. —FRED BAUER

---

29 SATURDAY
Blessed is the people that know the joyful sound: they shall walk, O Lord, in the light of thy countenance.
—*PSALM 89:15*

I will always remember the first time I heard our symphony perform. I had arrived early, taken my seat, settled back and then couldn't believe the dreadful sounds that reached my ears. The orchestra members were tuning up, each in a different way, each playing a special kind of scale, and all at the same time. Such discordance!

Then the concert master came on stage, lifted his violin to his shoulder and sounded one single pure note. Again there was a dire cacophony, but obviously all of the musicians were striving toward a similar goal—a replication of that one perfect note. As their tones gradually came to blend, the accumulated sound emerged clear and sweet.

Finally the maestro appeared. Striding to the center of the stage, he raised his baton, held it poised in mid-air for a moment and then lowered it in a downbeat. Instantly the entire assemble responded as one... and the sound was rapturous.

Which reminds me that no matter how talented and able we are, we may strike a lot of sour notes as we try to find our way. It's only when each of us strives to emulate that one perfect example set before us—Jesus Christ—that we can hope to achieve the harmony we seek and rise together as one body in songs of praise to our Father.

Dear Father, teach me how to tune my life to Your one perfect note. —PHYLLIS HOBE

---

30 SUNDAY
And again, I will put my trust in him. And again...
—HEBREWS 2:13

"Okay, the directions say to turn left at this corner," Lynn said.

"Left?" I asked. "It can't be. I thought we wanted to go south. If we turn left, we'll be headed north."

"Well, I don't know about that. I only know that the directions on this map say to turn left."

I surveyed the situation for a while longer and was just about to turn right—I just knew it had to be correct!—when suddenly, for no reason I can account for, I turned left. And after a bend in the road, we were headed south!

Trust. Of course the mapmaker knew more about the area than I did, and yet I couldn't bring myself to trust his knowledge. I guess I just don't trust easily. And I know that this trait sometimes spreads to other areas of my life too—like when I question God. In moments of grief and sorrow, I demand answers from Him and when they aren't the ones I expect, I'm upset and angry with Him.

Instead I must trust the Mapmaker who stands with me at each

375

crossroad of my life, pointing me in the right direction. Today I know that this kind of trust is, very simply, faith—the assurance of things hoped for, the evidence of things not seen.

Father, I believe. You have never let me down. —JEFF JAPINGA

---

31 MONDAY

Therefore are they before the throne of God, and serve him day and night... —REVELATION 7:15

One New Year's Eve, my brother announced that first among his New Year's resolutions was to read the Bible from beginning to end in the coming year. I considered this a formidable effort, and wished him well. Several months later, I asked him about his resolution.

"I had to give it up," he replied. "I found out that I didn't know enough Biblical history and that I had to do too much supplemental reading to really understand the Bible."

"So you broke your New Year's resolution," I said, teasing him.

"No, I didn't break it," he said. "I just stretched it out. I expected to do something within a year that I know now will take me the rest of my life."

We all make New Year's resolutions, and usually we all break them. Not because we're lax, but because we don't anticipate their full meaning and their requirements of us. This year as we make our resolutions, let's first ask God what special things He would like us to do in the coming year. The gift of three hundred and sixty-five days—each one freely given—surely calls upon us to respond with all the love and gratitude our hearts can hold.

RESOLVED: That I, _____, will, in our Lord's year of 1985, _____ for my Father.

From the first day of the year, Father, to the last, use me as You will. —GLENN KITTLER

Praise Diary for December

1

2

3

4

5

6

7

8

9

10

11

12

13

14

15

16

17

18

19

20

21

22

23

24

25

26

27

28

29

30

31

COME... *meet old friends and new ones*

JUNE MASTERS BACHER, former teacher, now full-time writer, contributes to over a dozen religious publications. She is a published poet as well, and her writing interests are expanding into the field of Christian romance novels. June and her husband George, a teacher and the agent for her writing, live in sunny Escondido, California.

FRED BAUER is an author-writer of many books and articles, as well as head of his own publishing company in Princeton, New Jersey. His recent book is *Tailwind*, about a Vietnam veteran's story of redemption. Highlights of the past year have been the arrival of his first granddaughter, Jessica, born in April, and the thirtieth wedding anniversary of Fred and his wife Shirley.

ISABEL CHAMP. Last February 17, Isabel passed her three-score mark. But that doesn't keep this busy writer away from her trusty typewriter. She and her husband-writer are collaborators on various book projects and make their home in Syracuse, New York. A cruise to the Inner Passage of Alaska and a trip to the South Pacific to visit her missionary son in New Guinea were unforgettable adventures of the last year.

ZONA B. DAVIS. For this writer, the past year was marked by the publication of a five-pound, 810-page history book of her hometown, Effingham, Illinois, which she compiled. A trip to Europe with her husband Plaford was a special event of the year as well. "We'll take it again and again in our memory in years to come," she says.

DRUE DUKE is especially encouraged by the response of readers to her past devotionals. "These are pearls to string, and in times of discouragement go back and count!" she says. Last year she and husband Bob celebrated their fortieth wedding anniversary—doing what they love best: dancing. The Dukes make their home in Sheffield, Alabama.

ARTHUR GORDON. This former Editorial Director of *Guideposts* is busier and more active than ever now that he is "retired." The past year has included a trans-Canada train trip, a cruise on the QE II down to the Caribbean and through the Canal, to Mobile for Mardi Gras and back again later in the year to judge the Junior Miss Pageant, and a Christmas trip to wife Pam's homeland, England. Back in Savannah, Georgia he's working on a number of exciting writing projects.

DORIS HAASE works by day and writes by night. She was recently promoted to Senior Secretary in the Office of the Superintendent of Schools for Los Angeles. In the past year, she moved to Sherman Oaks, California and feels blessed with her new home and surroundings. Reflecting back over the year, Doris says, "I have many things to thank Him for!"

MADGE HARRAH was the first place winner in an international radio writing contest. Her play, *The Prize*, which won the contest was nationally broadcast on NBC radio as a special Easter program last year. Now that her two grown children have "flown the nest," Madge is enjoying rediscovering the joys of marriage with her husband Larry. The Harrahs make their home in Albuquerque, New Mexico.

MARILYN MORGAN HELLEBERG gave up her college teaching position to become a full-time inspirational writer and speaker. Nearly 300 of her articles, poems and stories have appeared in national publications. Besides the birth of her first granddaughter, Dawn Joy, her year has been especially blessed by "the hundreds of letters and phone calls from readers of my books and devotionals." She and her husband, Rex, an architect, and their 15-year-old son, John, reside in Kearney, Nebraska.

PHYLLIS LAURA HOBE is author of some of *Guideposts'* most popular books on prayer and Christian living. This year she is experiencing the joys and comforts of settling into her new home and surroundings in Flourtown, Pennsylvania. "Little by little the tiny, fibrous roots of my daily life are reaching out, taking hold of the community around me and drawing nourishment from its soil," she says. She misses her 14-year-old terrier, Trooper, who died during the year, but is finding joy in her new young puppy, Kate.

MARJORIE HOLMES is one of America's favorite inspirational writers. Among her best-seller books are *I've Got to Talk to Somebody, God* (now in its 25th printing) *Two From Galilee*, and, most recently, *To Help You Through the Hurting*. She and her doctor-husband, George, reside in McMurray, Pennsylvania.

JEFF JAPINGA, an assistant editor at *Guideposts*, is also the magazine's number one sportswriter. An accomplished and avid athlete himself, Jeff enjoys baseball, tennis, and golf among other sports. This past year was marked by his first sub-100 on his golf scorecard and a proud second wedding anniversary ("Which will no doubt be topped by the third and fourth and..."). This year his wife, Lynn, graduates from Princeton Theological Seminary.

SAM JUSTICE was born in Buenos Aries, Argentina, the son of missionaries. He has been a newspaperman, a television newswriter and teacher of journalism and communication. Besides the thrill of becoming a new writer for *Daily Guideposts*, the past year was highlighted by a trip to Israel and gaining "a better feel for my spiritual roots." Sam is a health nut, gardener, bicyclist and golfer. He and his wife, Ginny, live in Yonkers, New York.

SUE MONK KIDD continues to spend her mornings at the typewriter doing what she loves best, writing. Last year she and her husband Bob, a campus minister, chaperoned eight students to Bermuda to conduct vacation Bible schools on the island. Sue loves to swim, jog and white water canoe. Her past year was filled with small, simple, but cherished moments with son Bob, 10 and daughter Ann, 7.

GLENN KITTLER began as a Roving Reporter for *Guideposts* over thirty years ago. He is a prolific writer of many books and magazine articles and has just completed a mystery-crime novel. When not enjoying the affections of his alley cat Louie, Glenn's interest turns to attending the lively arts in New York City, and enjoying good food. He is a fine chef with tastes that are ethnic—Japanese, German and Italian.

JAMES McDERMOTT, whose lovely poems open each month of *Daily Guideposts*, is a Senior Editor of *Guideposts* magazine. His love of poetry was inspired from childhood by his journalist father who also taught poetry to college students. A memorable moment last year, was when, as a proud father, he heard his two-year-old son David form his first sentences. He and his wife Judy live in a brownstone in Brooklyn and both share an affection for the outdoors and sailing.

SAMANTHA McGARRITY—we call her "Sam"—came to Guideposts in 1982. She spent her first year on the road collecting 20,000 miles worth of stories. Sam was born in Peru, grew up in Georgia, and now lives in a Polish neighborhood in Brooklyn, New York. Her free time is spent at an old cottage in the Hudson Valley where she gardens and swims in the summer and cross-country skis in the winter. Hikes along the Appalachian Trail with her brother John are treasured moments.

NORMAN VINCENT PEALE is founder, co-publisher and co-editor-in chief of *Guideposts* with his wife, Ruth. He is the author of 29 inspirational books and Minister of Marble Collegiate Church in New York City.

RUTH STAFFORD PEALE. Being General Secretary and Editor-in-chief of the Foundation for Christian Living is a priority activity for Ruth Peale. She is a nationally syndicated columnist and lecturer who still manages to have time to travel enthusiastically with Dr. Peale. The Peales have three grown children and eight grandchildren.

ELAINE ST. JOHNS, *Guideposts* West Coast contributing editor, makes her home in beautiful Arroyo Grande, California. She has been a newspaper feature writer, an author of books, biographies, autobiographies, novels and of course magazine articles. She is a popular inspirational speaker as well, and her valuable "scouting" alerts our New York staff to potential magazine stories from her part of the U.S.

ELIZABETH SHERRILL began her career as a travel writer in Europe. She started writing for *Guideposts* in 1951, joining the staff in 1963. In collaboration with her husband, John, she has written inspirational books selling in the millions. The Sherrills have three children (all married now) and two granddaughters. In addition to writing and editing, Elizabeth teaches Christian-writing workshops on five continents.

PATRICIA HOUCK SPRINKLE, her husband and two young sons live in Chicago, Illinois. Patti, an avid reader and writer, has just completed her first in a series of mystery novels. "This has been a life-long dream of mine and to see it realized is exciting beyond description!" Last fall, Patti made a pilgrimage back to her roots in the South, including a visit with her parents and longtime friends from the Carolinas. "I feel as though my past has been brought up to date with my present," she says.

VAN VARNER. Nineteen eighty-three was a full and significant year for Van. It marked the completion of his first and successful year as Editor of *Guideposts*, a position he assumed in January, 1982, after twenty-five years as a staff editor. Last year was also the year *Guideposts* reached its four-millionth subscriber. "To be part of this great and ever growing family," Van says beaming, *"now that's meaningful!"* The year also marked the arrival of Van's 60th year. On a sad note, his old dog Clay, the pointer he used to write about, died. "I miss him," Van says. "And I have yet to figure out how to stop this ache, but I am learning to see life and death as a logical and beautiful completeness."

MARION BOND WEST is one of *Guideposts* best-read writers. We've followed the West's family life through broken dishwashers, twins Jon and Jeremy losing and winning ballgames, the death of Mollie the family collie, and the marriage of daughter Julie. In 1982 Marion's remarkable faith was challenged when her husband Jerry battled cancer and died in July of 1983. In September, Marion shares in this year's *Daily Guideposts*, "My Lessons in Faith," some intimate moments of faith-building surrounding this experience.

A NOTE FROM THE EDITORS

This devotional book was prepared by the same editorial staff that creates *Guideposts*, a monthly magazine filled with true stories of people's adventures in faith.

If you have found enjoyment in *Daily Guideposts*, we think you'll find monthly enjoyment—and inspiration—in the exciting and faith-filling stories that appear in our magazine.

Guideposts is not sold on the newstand. It's available by subscription only. And subscribing is easy. All you have to do is write Guideposts Associates, Inc.; Carmel, New York 10512. A year's subscription costs only $5.95 in the United States, $7.95 in Canada and overseas.

When you subscribe, each month you can count on receiving exciting new evidence of God's presence, His guidance and His limitless love for all of us.